James Allen
On F1 – 2012
The Year of Living Dangerously

James Allen
On F1 – 2012
The Year of Living Dangerously

Photography by Darren Heath

SPEED MERCHANTS LIMITED

First published in 2012
by Speed Merchants Ltd

Cataloguing in Publication Data is available from the British Library

ISBN: 978-0-9564187-3-9

Cover and picture section designed by John Brown Media Ltd., London

www.jamesallenonf1.com

Printed and bound by CPI Group (UK) Ltd, Croydon, CR0 4YY

Contents

Foreword
By Jake Humphrey
BBC TV Formula One presenter

Before coming into this job I sat down with Steve Rider, who was the presenter before me, and he said, "You'll never have a season as good as the one we've just had," which was Lewis Hamilton snatching the title at the end of 2008.

But then we had the phoenix from the flames act by Brawn in 2009, which made that year special, then 2010 was Sebastian Vettel's remarkable comeback and then the Vettel domination year. I remember thinking at the start of this season, "What will 2012 give us that we haven't seen before?"

My abiding memory of this season is standing in the pit lane in Monaco after the race in May with Eddie Jordan and David Coulthard. We'd had a different winner at every race so far and Eddie, who's seen it all in F1, was agog at what was happening. David's a classic motor racing driver in that he's emotionally detached, but even he couldn't eulogise enough about how special this season had been. I really hope that the fans at home realise that they've just seen something really quite remarkable.

But this year was a record breaker not just in terms of seven different winners at the start of the season: we also saw a big move for Lewis Hamilton, the return to winning ways of Williams and Sebastian Vettel doing what he does best and winning title number three. He's the youngest-ever triple world champion and only the third man to make it three in a row, following in the footsteps of Fangio and Schumacher.

Different winners in the first seven races was the standout story of the first half of the season, punctuated by some amazing moments, like the win for Pastor Maldonado in Spain. I was in the Williams motorhome the night before the race. It was a special evening with Sir Frank Williams celebrating his 70th birthday and then Pastor hearing that he had inherited pole position. To cap it all, of course, he went on to win the race. It was great for British F1 fans to see Williams back on top.

The second half of the season saw the amazing rise of Red Bull once again. In India the standout quote was Fernando Alonso saying, "I'm no longer racing Vettel, I'm racing Adrian Newey." Red Bull showed once again that when they need to they can find the speed and the form and Vettel has also shown that once he has a car capable of winning a race he can do just that.

Then we had speculation about the driver market: what would the future hold for Michael Schumacher? It was a shame to see him limp towards the end of his comeback. We also had the Lewis Hamilton story: one that Eddie Jordan first revealed to the world and no one believed him. But it happened.

It's been a wild season.

I have loved the opportunity to work in this sport for the last four years as BBC presenter. I feel as though I've opened the lid on a mad world, a completely strange world. I had no idea of the jockeying for position and the politics and the deal making that goes on in the F1 paddock.

I've loved it mainly because of something that I think is remarkable about F1 – and that is how far ahead it is of all the other top sports in realising the importance of the media. I love the access you get in F1. I still can't really believe that with ten minutes to go before the start of a race we can stand on the grid and speak to a driver – who is about to risk his life, fighting for a world championship at 200 miles an hour – and he'll give us a few minutes of his time! I think this is where the fans really benefit.

Despite it being a hard-nosed and ruthless sport, I feel really privileged to have done the job and I've made some great friends along the way. Working on a Formula 1 season is like being in a bubble, or part of a travelling circus, and it's been great to travel the world for the last four years with some familiar faces.

I think everyone that buys this book is going to benefit massively: it's a really special thing each year to be able to look back at the key stories of the season. I must confess that over the last few years one of the things I've done on a Grand Prix Friday is log on to James's website and make sure I hoover up any stories that I may have missed. So if I'm presenting the BBC coverage and I'm using James's amazing knowledge of F1 and his ability to write beautifully, then so should you by buying this book.

Introduction

This is the story of a genuinely exciting season of Formula 1 racing, with so many twists and turns in a plot that ran to the final episode in Brazil. It was F1's longest ever season, with 20 Grands Prix, and we had some brilliant races this year, involving a wider range of drivers than normal, the momentum switching from team to team throughout the year. The first seven races of the season were won by seven different drivers as the teams struggled to adjust to new aerodynamic rules and new Pirelli tyres.

No one could have foreseen in February that the Ferrari, so slow and awkward-looking in winter testing, would lead the drivers' championship for much of the season. Fernando Alonso was in the form of his life as he took the championship battle right down to the wire in Brazil, but he missed out by just three points.

His main rival was not Lewis Hamilton, despite the fact that the McLaren was the fastest car at the beginning, middle and end of the season. Hamilton was back on song in 2012 after a difficult 2011 season, driving beautifully, but let down by team operational errors and reliability issues. His flourish at the end of the season with a win in Austin and pole at São Paulo served only to remind everyone of what might have been in 2012. His decision to leave the McLaren team, which had nurtured him from a boy to a household name, was the leading story of the year.

It seems odd to say that Sebastian Vettel came of age this year, given that he was a two-time world champion already. But this was a season where Vettel became one of the all-time greats, with a third world title. He did not have a dominant car, especially early on, nor a particularly reliable one. He did what he could with it in the first half of the season, but when the team locked into the right development path, he put together a sequence of unbeatable performances in September and October to wrestle control of the points' table from Alonso.

At 25 years of age, with only 101 Grand Prix starts on the board, he is only the third driver after Juan Manuel Fangio and Michael Schumacher to win three consecutive titles. He is a phenomenon and there is every reason to expect that his duel with Alonso will carry on through 2013.

We called this book, "The Year of Living Dangerously" because there were many aspects of the season which were right on the edge: the last race of the season where the title hung in the balance in a chaotic rain-hit race, Hamilton's decision to leave McLaren for the underperforming Mercedes team, the incidents and accidents triggered by Romain Grosjean and Pastor Maldonado in particular, which had an effect on the outcome of the championship, the strange behaviour of the Pirelli tyres at the start of the season, which led to the established order being turned on its head, the behind-the-scenes machinations and tough negotiations over the future of the sport and the conviction in Germany of F1's former chairman, Gerhard Gribkowsky, for receiving payments from Bernie Ecclestone, which the German prosecutors declared to be bribes.

As the season drew to a close the atmosphere in the paddock was uneasy: the Spanish HRT team appeared to have reached the end of the road, sending out redundancy notices to its staff and failing to place an entry for 2013. The visit of James Murdoch to the paddock in Abu Dhabi and his tour of the Formula One Management Broadcast Centre, triggered rumours that the commercial side of the sport, controlled by Ecclestone and CVC Capital Partners, was about to be taken over by News Corp or another interested party. Change was in the air.

It was the best year to date for the *JA on F1* website. With the worldwide base of readers growing to 1.5 million, we expanded the site and its reach with innovative ideas and strong partnerships with some of the sport's leading brands. Together with our new partner Tata Communications, we added a new section to the website on innovation and technology, highlighting one of the sport's greatest assets. The Race Strategy Briefings and Reports, produced for every Grand Prix in association with UBS, also enjoyed tremendous growth this year. As well as being a hit on the *JA on F1* website, they now appear in ten different languages on some of the leading F1 sites around the world, reaching almost 10 million fans.

And through our competitions and other initiatives, we sent many fans to races who would not otherwise have had the chance. In September we organised "The Ultimate F1 Road Trip" with Shell, sending eight fans on an unforgettable three-day trip to the Shell Belgian Grand Prix at Spa, with behind-the-scenes access to the Ferrari team. And we sent several lucky fans to enjoy the exclusive F1 Paddock Club experience in Spain, Germany and Abu Dhabi.

Helping to bring the readers closer to the sport has always been the main objective of *JA on F1*. We are all about producing content that people all over the world want to read and providing a platform for readers to interact with that content and with each other; the 70,000 comments we receive annually from readers are testament to that.

This is the fourth year we have published the *JA on F1* yearbook, a limited edition collectable, telling the stories behind the season. Once again, with the stunning images of F1's leading photographer, Darren Heath, this book is to be enjoyed now and also to be pulled down from the shelf in years to come to rekindle memories of a very special year in F1.

For help in producing this book and support throughout the year on *JA on F1* I'd like to thank Pip Calvert. Thanks are also due to Bill Allen, Chris Parker and Andrew Hirsch at John Brown Group, Geoff Fisher at CPI, Catherine Ryan, Julian Flanders, Sara Linney and Jon Lloyd at Grand Prix Legends, James Galloway, Mandy Scott-Johnson, Darren Heath, Russell Batchelor at XPB.cc, Alex Salter, Neil Campbell, Darren Odam, Pete Young, Simon Ryley, Jake Humphrey for the Foreword, Mark Newman and Matt Meadows.

Thanks to our sponsors: Jean Christophe Babin, Rob Diver and Francoise Bezzola at TAG Heuer; Bjorn Waspe, Jonas Karpf, Sven Schaefer and Preethi Nair at UBS; Vinod Kumar, Mehul Kapadia and Bijaya Basu at Tata Communications; Richard Bracewell and Katy Barber at Shell and Alessandro Cattaneo at Pirelli.

Thanks finally to the readers of *JA on F1* for making 2012 so enjoyable.

James Allen
London, November 2012

To Andrew Marriott
Everyone needs a first break in their career
and he gave me mine

Chapter One
January 2012

*As the New Year dawned there were still some empty seats on the F1
grid, at Williams and HRT. One of the candidates for a place was
Adrian Sutil, but his options were cut down early in the New Year
when he was found guilty of inflicting grievous bodily harm on Lotus
F1 team co-owner Eric Lux in a Shanghai nightclub the previous
Easter. It led to him being blackballed within F1, despite having
shown his capabilities alongside the highly rated Paul di Resta during
2011. Sometimes a moment of madness can have a lasting effect.*

Who will fill the final seats on the F1 grid?
2 January 2012

With a month to go before the start of the new car testing season and two
months to the first race there are still two race seats available. Most of the seats
were filled in the weeks leading up to Christmas with Lotus Renault, Toro
Rosso and Force India filling in their entry cards. But what of Williams and
HRT?

The contenders for Williams seem quite straightforward: Rubens Barrichello
is the choice of the Williams engineers, who rate the Brazilian highly and were
pleased with his performances in the closing stages of last season. Meanwhile,
Adrian Sutil has experience, is fast and brings some sponsorship budget. He
had some strong performances in the closing races of the season.

However, *Auto Motor und Sport* in Germany is reporting that Sutil only wants
a one-year contract in order to keep open his chances of taking Felipe Massa's
seat at Ferrari in 2013. Whether those chances are realistic only time will tell,
but it does seem as though there will be a seat available alongside Fernando
Alonso in 2013. Ferrari are likely to want someone who is fast and consistent,
but who would be prepared to keep the seat warm in anticipation of a bid for
Sebastian Vettel at the end of 2014, when his Red Bull contract expires.

According to the magazine, Sutil's position makes Barrichello's Williams candidacy pretty strong, even though the Brazilian has not always seen eye-to-eye with team boss Adam Parr. Meanwhile, veteran technical boss and team co-founder Patrick Head has stepped down from the board and will henceforth focus his attentions on Williams' hybrid power business.

HRT has a space to fill alongside Pedro de la Rosa. The team, which is becoming increasingly Spanish, appointed Luis Perez Sala as team principal just before Christmas, cutting ties with Colin Kolles. Sala is a former Minardi driver, who has been acting as a consultant since the summer.

It's clear that the team will need a driver who brings a budget in the seat. Jaime Alguersuari's father is a powerful figure in Spanish motorsport circles, but whether that would lead to a budget big enough to trump any others remains to be seen. Bruno Senna had an unhappy time at HRT when Kolles was in charge and it's not clear whether he would see a return to the team, even under different management, as a worthwhile step in his career. His name has also been linked with Williams, but not so much in recent weeks. Narain Karthikeyan stands by as another contender.

One of the stranger moves of the winter was the decision by Red Bull's Helmut Marko to replace both the Toro Rosso drivers. The decision came so late that it left no opportunity for Jaime Alguersuari and Sebastien Buemi to find alternative drives. Buemi eventually settled for a rather forlorn role as Red Bull Racing test driver.

Alguersuari had offers from two other teams going into the final race of the 2011 season, but had turned them down as he had been told that he would be with Toro Rosso again in 2012. It was a painful lesson for the 21-year-old, who had certainly impressed in the second half of the season. I put him in my top five drivers of 2011 for his ability to extend stints on the Pirelli tyres, getting a number of strong points finishes as a result. It showed Alguersuari's intelligence and his feel for a racing car. Ironically, being sacked by Marko led to Alguersuari and I working very closely together with BBC Radio Five Live. He was looking for a way of staying close to F1 in 2012 and this, combined with the role of Pirelli test driver, gave him exactly that platform.

I thoroughly enjoyed my season with Jaime, who was not only articulate in a second language, but also very perceptive. We learned a lot from each other this year: he learned more about F1 and how it works in a few months than he had in two and half years as a driver, while I learned a lot about the inner workings of how a modern F1 driver engages with his team.

Alguersuari and Buemi "not winners" says Red Bull's Helmut Marko
8 January 2012

Helmut Marko, whose influence on Red Bull in F1 is significant, has explained why the company decided to drop Jaime Alguersuari and Sebastien Buemi from the Toro Rosso team. "Toro Rosso was created to give young drivers a chance," he told *Gazzetta dello Sport* yesterday. "Alguersuari and Buemi had that chance for three years and after that period it's possible to evaluate a driver's development ... We didn't see in them any possibility of growth. Both are Grand Prix drivers, but for us that's not enough. We want Grand Prix winners."

Although it's a tough decision, you can see what Marko's getting at. Both drivers showed some signs of doing well, Alguersuari in particular seemed to be getting stronger in the second half of the season and put in some very strong drives using the clever strategies devised by Giorgio Ascanelli. But the company has unlimited tools for measuring performance and progress and these indicated that the pair might not have what it takes to become winners in the highly competitive environment of F1.

Buemi has always had problems with inconsistency, but Alguersuari is a different matter. Fans have made much of the incident in Korea when Marko was furious with the young Brazilian for holding up Sebastian Vettel during practice, but I don't think that is the reason for his demise. He was thrown into the fray at the age of 19, without the experience or the knowledge to capitalize on the opportunity. I hope that Red Bull and Marko have realized that throwing a driver in too young is a mistake – one for which Alguersuari is now paying the price. It would be interesting to talk to Jenson Button about this as he had a similar experience with Williams and Benetton/Renault when he started at just 20 years of age.

Although something of a shock at the time, Marko's announcement last December to drop both his drivers in favour of Jean-Eric Vergne and Daniel Ricciardo does make sense for Toro Rosso. His job is to keep the team competitive and both his new drivers have promise, experience and are ready to make the next move. They will now have two years to prove that they have the consistency, the intelligence and, above all, the speed to make it as Grand Prix winners.

Whatever the rights and wrongs of this particular decision, it is important to remember what Red Bull are doing with Toro Rosso. Although the drivers are not paid top dollar, the scheme still costs Red Bull around €4 million per driver to get them to F1 with the Toro Rosso budget costing another €70–€80 million a year. By funding young drivers on this first rung up the F1 ladder they are giving them the chance to develop their driving skills and prove themselves at the highest level. Without the Red Bull investment most of them wouldn't get that chance.

One of the more compelling storylines of the year was the return to F1 of Kimi Raikkonen after two seasons in rallying. I must confess I hadn't realized until I started JA on F1 just how popular Raikkonen is with fans all over the world. He doesn't say much, but they don't care about that. They just love watching him drive and he showed in 2012 that he had lost none of his ability.

Raikkonen was a revelation: he scored six podiums in the first 12 races and had a couple of good chances of a win. If there was a weakness it was that he was 0.2 seconds down on his old qualifying pace, but that started to come back in the second half of the season. It was a good year for a number of drivers, but Raikkonen was right up there with Alonso and Hamilton as one of the very best performers of the year.

Kimi Raikkonen: "There's nothing better than an F1 car"
27 January 2012

Kimi Raikkonen completed his F1 comeback test this week and has spoken about his feelings at driving an F1 car after two years away.

Raikkonen, the 2007 F1 world champion now aged 32, drove for two days at

Valencia's Ricardo Tormo circuit, which has been used for F1 testing for many years. Testing restrictions meant that he was in a two-year-old Renault on Pirelli demonstration tyres, but the Finn said it was enough to give him back the old feelings and to show that he's still got it. "I was a little concerned about finding the sport had really moved on. But frankly, on Monday and Tuesday I wasn't surprised. I didn't feel any difference," he told *L'Equipe* today.

"The memories came back, all those times I spent driving various F1 cars, on this track. The old reflexes and feelings came back really fast. Of course, it took me a while to find the limit. But after a first day of acclimatization, on Tuesday it went much better, even if there's still room for improvement."

Raikkonen also explained that the main motivation for turning his back on rally driving and returning to the F1 fold was the desire to go wheel-to-wheel against other drivers. "Last year I did a test in NASCAR and I loved rediscovering competition. I really had a good time. In rally you are alone, racing against the clock. In NASCAR you're in a peloton, battling with forty cars," he said.

"It was the first time in two years that I raced against others and I just wanted to relive that feeling of real combat. And on a racetrack there's nothing better than an F1 car. We had some discussions with Williams, but then very quickly Lotus approached me and everything went together to get an agreement."

Raikkonen becomes the sixth F1 champion on the grid this season, the first time in the sport's history that this has happened. He is famous for not enjoying the obligations that come with being an F1 champion, such as dealing with promotions and media, but he says he has his eyes open about this for his comeback, "In this sport there are loads of things I don't like and which weigh you down. But when you're racing, everything's OK. I love racing other people. It's what I do best and what gives me the most pleasure."

When F1 drivers move on to other roles in life they all say that nothing matches the feeling of driving the most incredible cars in the world. Rubens Barrichello clung on to his F1 dream for longer than any other driver in history: he came in as a fresh-faced boy in 1993 and stayed for almost two decades, notching up over 300 Grands

Prix starts. He had a great career, albeit one that will always be defined by his role as number two in the all-conquering Schumacher/Ferrari era. One day he will tell the story of that extraordinary period. But for now he is still driving.

Not in F1 any longer, however. His services were no longer required when Bruno Senna came along to claim his Williams seat, armed with some sponsorship money, it has to be said. The irony of the situation was not lost on anyone who knows their recent F1 history – Senna had been Barrichello's main rival for the Brawn seat in 2009, but Ross Brawn went for Barrichello's experience and it gave him more wins and an Indian Summer. Now Senna was making it stick.

Rubens Barrichello and the promise he once made to his wife
31 January 2012

Rubens Barrichello drove an IndyCar this week in a specially arranged test session at Sebring, Florida. The Brazilian, who lost his seat at Williams for this season to Bruno Senna, completed 94 laps and was on the pace of the KV Racing Team's lead driver Tony Kanaan. "I'm truly happy and I like what I saw," said 39-year-old Barrichello. "I just need to see what comes up. I need to talk to my family and to Jimmy (Vasser – KV team owner).

Barrichello certainly needs to speak to his wife, Silvana, because he made her a promise that he would not race on the oval at Indianapolis. "I'd love to race at Indy," he told *JA on F1* last June, "But it's the one thing my wife asked me not to do, because she thinks it's dangerous." It's a promise that would be impossible to keep if he were to accept a drive in the IndyCar series.

There are echoes of the past everywhere in this story. Barrichello took part in 322 Grands Prix – exactly double the number of starts made by his idol Ayrton Senna – making him by far the most experienced driver in the history of F1. Coincidentally Ayrton Senna also tested an IndyCar, 22 years ago, at the end of a 1992 season in which his McLaren team had been pulverized by the active suspension of Nigel Mansell's Williams. Senna had no intention of moving to IndyCar at the time, but he wanted to send a strong signal to McLaren, to their sponsors Marlboro and to F1 boss Bernie Ecclestone that the technical playing field needed levelling in F1 or he might seek pastures new.

In contrast to Senna, Barrichello's F1 career looks to have run its course, and though his passion for racing is still very strong it seems he must now look for pastures new. With Bruno Senna taking his seat at Williams, Barrichello finds himself without a drive for the first time in his F1 career, stretching back to 1993. Hence the test.

The quote above about promises to his wife comes from a fascinating question and answer session I did with Barrichello in front of a US and Canadian audience in Montreal last year. He gave some great answers looking back over a long F1 career during which he raced against 12 of the 32 drivers who have won the F1 world title without ever being the champion himself (he was runner-up in 2002 and 2004).

On how much of his long career he can remember:

"Sometimes between planes I get to write a bit of my book, I don't know if it will ever come out, but it's a pleasure to write my stories down. I remember most of my races vividly, even kart races from the 1980s.

"The Brawn year (2009) was incredible. I was four months without a job. I was desperate to drive and all Ross Brawn said to me was 'Keep fit, I'll call you when I know.'

"It was one of the best days of my life when I drove the car for the first time and realized it was a good car. The win at Monza was very special, to be in white overalls and all the Ferrari fans were down below me and they clearly hadn't forgotten me."

On the pressure of driving for Ferrari:

"To drive for Ferrari was fantastic. The first day to see my name on the side of the car was just great. When I was a kid I dreamed of it. But when you start driving you have to forget you are in a red car with a horse on it. Mentally you've got to do that because otherwise it could get too much. At Ferrari you learn to live with it and if you want to win in F1 it you have to push on because there is so much pressure from the press, the country and so on.

"You cannot say everything that you would have liked to. So you just have to focus on why you are driving."

You have two sons. To me the question is not, "Will your kids race?" But rather "Do your kids feel a great pressure to race?"

"Eduardo (the older boy) doesn't want the pressure. I don't think he'll be a racing driver. I would love him to race, but he doesn't like pressure. He always asks me why I have to exercise so much and travel or whatever.

"He loves driving. I take him karting and it's fantastic. But it showed me something. One day I said to him, 'Can you take that corner flat, throttle down?' He said, 'Do you want me to, Daddy?' I thought it could be dangerous, but anyway I said, 'Yes'.

"So he went out and he took the corner flat, but then the next lap he lifted. If that had been me at his age I'd have been mad flat, so it showed me there that it was what I wanted, not what he wanted.

"So I just want him to do what he wants.

"The younger one is just nuts. He takes everything flat!"

On his massive Twitter following:

"Twitter is a good thing to interact. For people who love F1 its great because if they cannot be there, it's like they are there."

On his future after F1:

"Racing is in my blood. The months when we are off over the winter eventually you start driving too fast on the road. So I need something to drive. I think eventually I will do stock cars in Brazil. It's a great series. Maybe I'll be at home a bit more and still racing."

On staying fit approaching his 40th birthday:

"I run six days a week, between 6 and 16 kilometres. I also do a training programme where I go fast for a few seconds then slow then fast, simulating the corners on a racetrack. The heartbeat in a racing car is between 140 and 180 beats per minute. It goes down on the straights. My resting heartbeat is 55."

Chapter Two
February 2012

February saw the launch of the new cars and the start of the winter testing season. The McLaren certainly looked right. After a difficult 2011 season, where the team won races with both drivers but saw Lewis Hamilton go through some personal difficulties off-track and lose focus to the extent that he was beaten by a teammate for the first time in his career, the whole team wanted a strong 2012. The car looked fit for purpose and early testing and the start of the racing season confirmed it. However, it was mid-season before the team really hit its stride.

Ferrari, meanwhile, launched a radical new car, which turned out to be a misfit and required a lot of work behind the scenes to make it competitive. Luckily for them Fernando Alonso was in stunning form in 2012 and led the championship at the halfway stage, despite his car's deficiencies.

And Red Bull launched the car we all thought that the rest would have to beat. Having won both the previous two years' world titles, they were expected to pick up were they left off. But the banning of the exhaust blown diffuser technology hurt them more than anyone had realized and they were in catch-up mode for much of the season. Further knockbacks from the FIA on engine mapping didn't help.

Angry Alguersuari has his say on Toro Rosso
7 February 2012

On the day that Toro Rosso began testing its new F1 car, the team's former driver Jaime Alguersuari has told his side of the story of how he was abruptly dropped by the team. The young Spaniard, who looks likely to appear in the F1 paddock this year as reserve driver for Mercedes, thought he had been given verbal confirmation before the end of the season that his seat at Toro Rosso was secure. But two weeks after the last race he was told that he was out.

Speaking on his own website, Alguersuari said, "On 13 December, when Red Bull Racing told me that I was no longer part of the family, I said that I was not going to judge them, that this was not a drama and that I did not feel like a victim.

"But let me say just one thing: they hurt me, and moreover, it was unnecessary.

"I was verbally confirmed during the Brazilian GP. Hence, being confirmed by Red Bull and STR, I rejected a very good offer. Back on 11 December, Toro Rosso sent me to a PR event at the Cepsa headquarters in Madrid. I went to their Christmas dinner as a guest and to help present medals to long-serving employees. I made a speech with a very well prepared script from Faenza in which I talked about Toro Rosso, Cepsa and myself in 2012. Two days later, I received a phone call saying that they were not counting on me. There were two phone calls, no longer than two minutes each.

"Neither I nor anyone else will ever understand why, having largely fulfilled all the team's expectations, having improved my position from 2010 and beaten my teammate, I was dropped on 14 December with no time to have a good option to run in 2012."

The man in charge of Red Bull's driver programme, Helmut Marko, has already explained his reasons for dropping Alguersuari and Sebastien Buemi. In the event, Toro Rosso now have Daniel Ricciardo and Jean-Eric Vergne in the cars for 2012 and they started testing today in Jerez alongside the other contenders. It's a great opportunity for both men, one of whom will aspire to fill a seat at Red Bull alongside Sebastian Vettel at some point in the future, depending on what happens with Mark Webber.

"I am not thinking about 2013 … obviously there is probably a chance for 2013 with Red Bull Racing, but I will not answer these kinds of questions because at the moment I don't want to look too far ahead," said Vergne. Ricciardo, meanwhile, is the more experienced of the pair, having driven half a season with HRT last year. "It's a bit emotional actually, seeing the first F1 car that will be mine to drive from the start of the season," he said.

Ricciardo was one of a few drivers on the grid of Italian extraction, alongside Paul di Resta and Felipe Massa, but the idea that there

*could be an F1 grid without a single Italian driver on it was unthinka-
ble. And yet it happened in 2012. There had been rumours that Jarno
Trulli's position at Caterham was not secure and so it proved when he
was dropped just a few weeks ahead of the new season.*

*Italy has not had a world champion since Alberto Ascari in 1953 and
the wait will now go on. But how has the country that gave the world
Ferrari and some of the greatest ever kart racers managed to get itself
into this position?*

Why are there no Italian drivers in F1?
17 February 2012

The news that Jarno Trulli has lost his drive to Vitaly Petrov means that there
will be no Italian driver in the F1 field for the first time since 1969. For the
country that gave the world Ferrari, Maserati, the Mille Miglia, Ascari and so
many other motorsport legends, it's hard to believe that there will be no
driver on the grid in 2012. France, where the sport was born and which gave
the name "Grand Prix" to the F1 events, went through the same thing
recently. Today they are represented again with Grosjean, Pic and Vergne;
now it is Italy's turn to do some soul searching.

This situation has been coming for some time. When you speak to Italian
drivers they always say that Ferrari is so powerful – such a dominant force in
the country – that they will always be in its shadow. It's very hard for them
to get sponsors especially at the higher end. Far from being a rallying point
for motorsport in the country, creating a culture of excellence, Ferrari *is*
motorsport in the eyes of many Italians and it draws attention away from
up-and-coming talent and other team operators. Toro Rosso is based in
Faenza, but only because that's where Minardi was based. And when that
team couldn't carry on the struggle to survive any longer Red Bull bought it
and decided to keep it there, not because Italy is a centre of excellence, but
because the facilities were in already in place.

To their credit, Ferrari recognized this situation and has made efforts to
address the problem in recent years, for example, by inducting young Italian
drivers into the Ferrari Driver Academy. So far it's not produced any real
talents, but that's not stopped them from continuing to plug away.

"I am very sad that after so long there will not be an Italian driver in the

Formula 1 World Championship field," said Ferrari team principal Stefano Domenicali on the Ferrari website. "It's a difficult moment for our sport, partly for external reasons. For a few years now, Ferrari, through its Driver Academy, which works also in collaboration with the CSAI (the Italian motorsport federation), has established a long-term plan to create a new generation of young drivers, and I am pleased to see that just now, we can announce that two talented youngsters, Raffaele Marciello and Brandon Maisano, will be given a great opportunity to progress in the sport." The pair are being supported to race in F3 this year.

But, of course, this "impoverishment" as Jarno Trulli calls it, of Italian talent is not just about the long-term story of Italian motorsport and business failing to establish a conveyor belt of talent. It is exacerbated by the financial crisis which Italy is suffering at the moment, meaning that even if there were some Italian companies who wanted to sponsor drivers, they would either not be able to afford it or would find it hard to justify. In the past many Italian drivers were backed by Marlboro, but now that tobacco sponsorship is no longer allowed, they've been left without a leg up the ladder.

Trulli described the fate of current Italian drivers as "a problem that hasn't just appeared out of the blue," and blamed some people for "just closing an eye and letting it come about." He explained: "In Italy there isn't a system that helps drivers to emerge at high levels and it's normal for things like this to happen. The talent is there, but if no one supports them, they have no hope whatsoever. I would like to see more involvement, on everyone's part, but at a time of crisis like this in our country, I can't see how a young driver can break through and find help in order to be considered by a team."

He went on, "I personally have no regrets. I was expecting a separation from Caterham, as I knew that the difficult economic situation would have prompted them to seek a driver with substantial sponsorship backing. The smaller teams have certain needs and contracts state this clearly. I hope that with Petrov's contribution everyone who works there can have a more secure future."

It is also a statement about the way that the global financial crisis is finally impacting on F1. It's taken a while to work through, because many of the sponsorships were contracted before the downturn began. Now, looking at the field and at some of the drivers, it's clear that bringing a budget is a priority. But that's a story for another time.

Italian drivers may not be in great supply in F1, but the health of Italy's most illustrious car maker is very robust. Defying the economic crisis that has engulfed Europe and the US, Ferrari posted very healthy sales figures for the year and with the F1 team among the best sponsored and well funded, the financial health of Ferrari has never been better.

Behind the scenes in F1 its position has never been stronger either. Having broken away from the Formula One Teams' Association before Christmas, Ferrari was free to pursue the best deal with Bernie Ecclestone for its continued involvement in the sport. And it certainly leveraged its unique position, which had already been reinforced by the threatened FOTA breakaway in 2009.

As the year went on and the sport moved towards a flotation, sales documents revealed the full extent of Ferrari's position of influence which included: a right of veto over rule changes and over the F1 CEO, as well as a very lucrative deal which gave it extra payments and privileges as the "longest standing team" including a seat on the F1 board.

Ferrari posts strongest sales figures in its history
20 February 2012

Ferrari has posted the strongest sales figures in its history, despite the economic squeeze and the worsening euro crisis. The luxury sports car maker broke through €2 billion in sales for the first time in 2011, reporting a net profit of €209 million. This was on sales of 7,195 cars, the most that Maranello has ever produced and sold in a year and almost 10 per cent up on the 2010 sales figures.

Interestingly, although the USA remains the leading market, sales in China increased 62 per cent and the country has moved straight into second position. And despite the anxiety in Europe, sales in the UK were up 23 per cent and in Germany were up 14 per cent.

"We can only be satisfied with these results," said chairman Luca di Montezemolo. "They were achieved against an economic backdrop that remains challenging, particularly in Europe. They are the fruit of heavy investment and a culture of innovation that covers all areas of the business.

Our international expansion continues and Ferrari today has a network covering 58 nations."

Ferrari's F1 team is also in robust shape with long-term deals recently renewed with major backers Santander, Shell and Philip Morris. This contrasts with the picture across the F1 grid where there are clear signs that a significant number of teams are being obliged to prioritize drivers who bring budget with them.

Ferrari withdrew from the FOTA in late 2011 in a disagreement over how to police cost cutting measures, but says it remains committed to working with the other teams to control costs in the sport. Red Bull Racing has also taken a similar stance. Attempts to resolve this and the engagement of the F1 teams in a new Concorde Agreement with the FIA and FOM will be one of the main talking points of 2012.

It was clear in 2012 that F1 was going through some massive structural changes. A new Concorde Agreement for eight years, with the roles of the FIA and the top teams being reviewed, not to mention the sell-off of a large stake in the F1 stock by CVC Capital Partners and efforts to float the business on the Singapore Stock Exchange highlighted that the sport was undergoing a major refit.

This was also true in terms of infrastructure, as a new communications company entered the sport with the intention of changing it forever. F1's success of the last 30 years had been built on satellite television giving it a global reach that Bernie Ecclestone and the teams were able to monetize. Then along came Tata Communications with a deal to connect the Grands Prix venues to the world in a whole new way – a way that would future proof the sport for new technologies and open up limitless possibilities for global interaction.

The deal that changes F1 forever
23 February 2012

Today in London, F1's commercial boss Bernie Ecclestone unveiled a deal that will transform the way live F1 races are broadcast and all other forms of digital content are consumed. "It's the most significant moment for F1 since the advent of satellites," says Eddie Baker, the man responsible for broadcasting F1 television and data around the world.

Satellite TV revolutionized the sport in the late 1970s, by making it possible for millions of fans to watch races live around the world. This was Ecclestone's first revolution, providing the platform that made F1 a global sport, raising billions in revenues.

This long-term deal with Tata Communications opens the door even wider: including broadcasting F1 on the internet, and enabling interactivity between audience and the broadcasters at the circuits. Tata has the largest network of undersea cables in the world and, using Multiprotocol Label Switching (MPLS) technology, provides very fast and cost effective bi-directional communication. "Formula 1 wants to transform the way it broadcasts the races and we can and will be a big part of it," said Tata CEO Vinod Kumar.

The deal begins with Tata setting up fixed-line connectivity at all the 20 Grands Prix circuits for the FOM to send its data, such as track maps. Capacity will start out at ten times what is currently available. Within a few years it will be up to a hundred times larger, and with no delays it will be the means by which the world feed TV pictures are broadcast. It will also handle video playouts by all the broadcasters on site, and all other communications by the media.

It brings a standardization to the means of delivery of content from F1 races, connecting the sport to the world in a completely new way. It increases the amount of connectivity because, unlike a satellite, it's always on, and as it's bi-directional it also allows the audience to interact with the sport, rather than just sit back and consume. Looking well down the line this means that F1 can have individual relationships with fans, supplying and receiving information instantly from all parts of the globe.

It will also greatly reduce the tonnage of equipment that FOM TV sends around the world during the season as images can be sent back instantly and processed at the FOM broadcast centre in the UK.

I put it to Baker that Ecclestone is renowned for being suspicious of the internet and has been accused of missing opportunities as a result. According to Baker this deal opens the door to endless possibilities, "It gives him the ability to do whatever rights deals he feels are correct, without limitations," said Baker. "That means he can assess every opportunity and react to it appropriately, he can move with the times in perhaps a way that we were not able to do in the past."

At the launch Ecclestone quipped that he'd not done a deal like this previously because, "I'm getting old!" But there's no doubt that this is a complete game changer for the sport and the way fans receive it. Many will fear that it spells the end of F1 on free-to-air TV. But that business is under threat anyway. As traditional broadcasters like ITV and BBC in the UK and TF1 in France struggle with the changing media model and the ability to afford massive rights deals, F1 will have to look in future to new models. Clearly pay TV deals like SKY TV are one way of doing it, but they speak to small audiences. To maintain its mass appeal live paid streaming on the internet is another option, and it already sponsors funded mass market streaming in specific countries. F1, like any business, needs to find revenue and audience growth and this new tool appears to enable the sport to explore all the options.

Whether Ecclestone is still the man doing the deals five years from now when this technology really hits its stride remains to be seen. But it's a deal F1 needed to do now and the sport seems well set for the future.

Of course, this makes F1 more valuable as a business and more attractive to potential bidders should Ecclestone and CVC wish to sell the commercial rights at some point soon.

Chapter Three
March 2012

The signs from this year's pre-season testing, which ran from early February to early March, were that McLaren had built a very good car, Red Bull had lost a lot of performance, while Ferrari looked to be really struggling with a "radical" and "adventurous" car.

In fact, chief designer Nicholas Tombazis would later admit that radical wasn't the word for it – there were some areas on the aerodynamics side on which the team had not "done its home-work" properly. The result was that the Ferrari was over a second off the pace heading into the first race in Australia and a frantic job to rework the car was launched in Maranello.

Williams, however, looked to be in the best shape they had been for some time with a new car from an all-new technical manage-ment group. With the return to Renault engines, after the end of their partnership with Cosworth, the 2012 Williams appeared to be one of the best cars in the field.

Back at base there was further proof of a shift in the management of the team with Patrick Head retired and Sir Frank Williams stepping backwards. Everyone thought that Adam Parr was his chosen successor, but he would soon be unceremoniously dumped and Toto Wolff would increase his influence over the team, essen-tially becoming deputy team principal.

Frank Williams steps down
2 March 2012

Sir Frank Williams, who oversaw the eight constructors' championships for his team between 1980 and 1997, has taken another step back with the announcement today that he is to step down from the board of the team he founded. This highly phased process follows on from his partner Patrick Head withdrawing from the F1 team at the end of last year.

Williams, who will be 70 in April, described it as "the next stage in the gradual, but inevitable process of handing over the reins". He remains team principal for the moment, but that will surely change at some point too. Williams is the last of the "old guard" team principals, like Ron Dennis, Jean Todt and Flavio Briatore, all of whom have moved on from running F1 teams.

At the same time, Sir Frank's daughter Claire has been promoted to the board. Claire has worked her way up through the business, mainly on the communications side, and now takes over the critical responsibility for sponsorship, media and communications. She will also represent the Williams family's interests on the board. Her father is still a 51 per cent shareholder, even though Head sold the majority of his shares via last year's flotation.

Williams chairman Adam Parr said, "Claire will be accountable for acquiring new partners for the Williams F1 team as well as continuing to be responsible for ensuring effective communication about the team and the Group as a whole."

It's a significant responsibility, one that has been handled recently by Dominic Reilly, who's leaving the team to set up his own business, though there are indications that this business will work alongside Williams in some areas.

"This is an opportune moment," said Sir Frank, "for me to consider my own role in the team … It's not as dramatic a move as it may appear: I shall continue to work full-time as team principal and I shall continue to attend all board meetings as an observer."

There was a lot of activity in 2012 relating to the ongoing ownership of the business that owns F1's commercial rights. CVC Capital Partners, which had acquired a 65 per cent stake in the sport in 2005-06, was looking to realize value while there were also some other shareholdings on the market. Over the course of the year CVC reduced its holding to around 35 per cent in a series of disposals to cornerstone investors, which netted the firm $2.1 billion and gave *them the luxury of being able to bide their time on a flotation of the F1 business. A flotation on the Singapore Stock Exchange was prepared for the autumn of 2012, with a prospectus issued, but the move was put on hold due to volatile market conditions and the fallout over the Facebook flotation in May.*

Following the partial collapse of the F1 Teams' Association, several of the leading teams have been negotiating behind the scenes with Bernie Ecclestone over individual commercial deals for the next eight years. As a result they are now truly divided and conquered. Once again Ecclestone had won, this time probably on a bigger and more lucrative scale than ever before. As the year went on the teams found themselves in an increasingly vulnerable position, with several fundamental changes proposed, which will inevitably divide them up into the haves and the have nots.

Could F1 teams take a stake in the sport?
9 March 2012

There are some interesting things going on behind the scenes in F1 at the moment that could have a significant bearing on the ownership of the sport in the future. It has been revealed that 15 per cent of the shares in F1's holding company will soon come up for sale. At the same time the media regulator in the UK has said that it is ramping up its probe into whether News Corp and James Murdoch pass the "fit and proper person" test for controlling BSKYB, which now has the UK F1 TV rights.

According to a report in the *Guardian* from a source close to Bernie Ecclestone, the company holding the assets of bankrupt US bank Lehman Brothers will sell its stake in F1 stake within the next two years. "Lehman is the second-biggest shareholder in Formula One's Jersey-based holding company, Delta Topco, which is majority owned by private equity firm CVC. Lehman owns a 15.3 per cent stake and a senior Formula One source says that Topco is worth "more than $10 billion", said the report.

This is interesting for a number of reasons, not least who might purchase the stake. There are three obvious contenders: the teams, News Corp/Exor and the Abu Dhabi investment vehicle Mubadala.

Clearly the best thing for the sport would be for the teams to have a stake. But could this happen? The teams have often said that it would be good for the sport if they were to hold a stake. It would also be very attractive to any future buyer of CVC's majority stake as it would stabilize the sport for the long term, and investors hate uncertainty. F1 is a unique global business with huge potential for growth, but uncertainty over the behaviour of the teams, for example over breakaways as they threatened in 2009, or demanding too much money, undermines confidence.

In an interview for the *Financial Times* in November 2011, FOTA chairman Martin Whitmarsh told me, "The teams' equity involvement is a stabilizing force. I'm not saying that have to own it. But if you are trying to create partnership in a business then a bit of cross equity is useful ... If teams were equity holders then the inherent continuity would encourage all stakeholders and potential investing partners; going from one Concorde negotiation to the next with standoffs doesn't.

"If I was private equity and I knew the teams were committed through their owning a percentage, then the value I hold if I'm trying to exit has got to be enhanced – because I know the teams are tied into the sport. That's a win-win."

It is obvious and entirely logical. But these are not always qualities one sees in F1's business dealings. A major blow to the concept is that the FOTA has now split as an organization, with Ferrari leading a walkout of Red Bull, Sauber and Toro Rosso, leaving a rump of seven teams. Mercedes boss Ross Brawn describes this as a "tragedy"; the teams in question putting self interest in front of the opportunity to make a better future for the whole sport as a whole. I think he'll be proved right.

Now divided and squabbling, it could be tough for Whitmarsh to cajole the others into looking at buying the Lehman stake, especially at a time when several teams are short of the money needed to race, let alone buy a share in the sport. Valuation is also going to be tricky: $10 billion looks like a high figure, but relative to turnover and its potential as a business, clearly it's going to be a somewhere between that and the $2.8 billion that CVC paid for the shares six years ago.

"It depends how much teams want to be burdened with debt," said Whitmarsh. "But at the moment in expressing my opinions too frankly, it could be considered that I'm opening up negotiations in public and I don't think that's useful. At the moment there is an owner and it's not us. CVC have invested in our sport, it's been a good investment and they have profited well."

They have indeed and this latest piece of news is another step towards their plan of exiting at some point with maximum value. The negotiations for the new Concorde Agreement have started and, although it could be a messy year while deals are agreed, CVC urgently need to see all the teams signed up to participate for five years.

In all other respects the business is very well set up now. With many long-term TV and media rights contracts in place, along with long term-deals with circuits and Tata Communications' new network for fixed-line connectivity at all races, the sport is pretty future proofed and ripe for selling once the teams are all on board. CVC have said that they don't plan to sell, but if they don't sell now, it could be another five to seven years before the timing would be right again.

Another potential buyer of the Lehman stake is News Corp, which is still working on its dossier announced last year with Agnelli family investment vehicle Exor to consider a bid for the sport. Today's *Financial Times* reports that UK media regulator Ofcom is setting up a project team called Project Apple to investigate whether the phone hacking allegations in the newspaper side of the business caused the organization to fail the "fit and proper person" test over its control of the broadcaster BSKYB. News Corp owns 39 per cent of BSKYB and James Murdoch remains its chairman. If Ofcom decide that it does, then they have the power to force News Corp to sell off part of its stake, reducing it to a level at which it no longer controls the broadcaster.

Last summer, under pressure from the UK government, News Corp had to give up on its planned £7.8 billion takeover of the BSKYB shares it does not own over the phone hacking allegations. Its next move after that was to declare its interest in buying the F1 TV rights. With a large cash pot and a desire to control a major global sport, it could be the time for them to revive their move on F1.

Meanwhile, in another business story this week, Bernie Ecclestone has confirmed that the two Spanish Grand Prix venues Barcelona and Valencia will alternate from 2013 onwards. And the French Grand Prix is looking to come back in a shared deal with Belgium.

In early March Marussia paved the way for a female driver to compete in an official Formula 1 test by signing Spaniard Maria de Villota as a test driver. The 32-year-old daughter of former F1 driver Emilio de Villota made her first F1 test appearance for Lotus-Renault at Paul Ricard last year. She also has race experience in Formula Palmer Audi and the football-themed Superleague Series. The original plan was for De Villota to do the young driver test at the end of the season in Abu Dhabi, but that fell victim to the disarray among teams, with the result that Marussia and a few others tested at Silverstone instead, while some teams did a test at Magny Cours in September and the rest did the scheduled Yas Marina test.

De Villota's chance came at a straight line aero test shortly before the British Grand Prix in July at Duxford, but it went tragically wrong when she hit the tailgate of a truck parked near the team's awning, losing an eye and suffering severe facial injuries.

As predicted by pre-season testing, the McLaren was the fastest car at the start of the season; the team duly qualified both cars on the front row and won the race with Jenson Button.

Bragging rights at McLaren go to Button after dramatic season opener
18 March 2012

Jenson Button won a dramatic Australian Grand Prix ahead of Red Bull's Sebastian Vettel, with Lewis Hamilton dropping from pole position to third at the flag. Hamilton was disconsolate afterwards, while Button was delighted, having won the bragging rights within the team at the outset of the season.

It was Button's 13th career victory and his third here in Melbourne and it was all done at the first corner, where he dived down the inside of Hamilton to take the lead. He managed to survive a late safety car, which cut his 10-second lead to nothing, while Vettel and Red Bull took the opportunity to pit for the second stop and rejoin ahead of Hamilton, a position he maintained to the flag.

Vettel was more than satisfied with the result, after a difficult weekend in which the revised version of the Red Bull had proved tricky to handle and vulnerable on the straights. Mercedes' race pace was disappointing, while

Ferrari's was better than expected, at least in the hands of Fernando Alonso, who finished fifth behind Mark Webber, whose fourth is the best ever result for an Australian in his home Grand Prix.

Meanwhile, there was heartbreak for Pastor Maldonado who was running sixth, half a lap from scoring Williams' best result in two years, when he crashed into a wall. This provoked a reshuffle of the cars behind, with Kamui Kobayashi jumping up to sixth place from ninth on the final lap.

Button made a clean start to pass Lewis Hamilton into turn 1 and controlled the race from then on, setting the fastest lap in the process. Both Romain Grosjean, who qualified a brilliant third, and Mark Webber made slow getaways, allowing the Mercedes of Michael Schumacher and a fast-starting Nico Rosberg to fill in behind the McLarens. There was trouble in the midfield as Daniel Ricciardo and Bruno Senna came together, resulting in the Brazilian spinning at the first corner. Nico Hulkenberg was the first retirement of the race, quickly followed by Romain Grosjean who had his suspension broken by the Williams of Pastor Maldonado as the Venezuelan lunged up the inside at turn 13.

As the two McLarens pulled away, Vettel made a great move on Nico Rosberg and set off in pursuit of Schumacher who ran wide at turn 1 and promptly retired at the end of lap 11 with a gearbox problem.

After the first set of pit stops Hamilton dropped back in behind Kimi Raikkonen and Sergio Perez, who was the only driver in the top ten to one-stop today. This slowed Hamilton down, allowing Vettel to close the gap to second. Alonso made a good start and began to pursue the podium places as Ferrari's race pace proved to be much more promising than their qualifying times. However, the same could not be said for Felipe Massa who spent much of the race battling with Kamui Kobayashi and Kimi Raikkonen and the Brazilian's race finally came to an end following a collision with his compatriot Bruno Senna. Senna had a difficult weekend compared to his teammate, with Maldonado qualifying eighth and putting in a very impressive performance, proving a threat to Alonso, Webber and Rosberg before a heavy crash on the final lap robbed him of his highest Formula One finish to date.

Button was able to hold a 10-second lead over Hamilton, despite vibration from his second set of tyres. The race order was looking stable until, during the second pit stop phase, the Caterham of Vitaly Petrov stopped on the inside of the pit straight resulting in a safety car. Fortunately for Vettel he was close to the pits and reacted quickly to make his stop and return to the track ahead of Hamilton, who had come in with Button just before the safety car was deployed.

At the restart Button quickly opened up a three-second gap over Vettel on the first lap and left his pursuers in his wake. Webber had also gained a position over Alonso during the safety car period and the Australian made the battle for second into a three-way race. Alonso spent the remainder of the race holding off Maldonado for fifth position, which ended successfully following the Williams driver's lack of concentration on the final lap. This pushed Kobayashi, Raikkonen and Perez up into sixth, seventh and eighth respectively.

Further back there was a tremendous scrap for the last points as Rosberg dropped back on the final lap, slowing down Jean-Eric Vergne in the process which allowed his Toro Rosso teammate and the Force India of Paul di Resta to grab the final points.

Further back, Marussia's Timo Glock was 14th, the former Virgin team's best result in F1 to date, in a car that had not tested before the race.

Australian Grand Prix
Melbourne 58 laps

1. Button	McLaren-Mercedes	1h34:09.565
2. Vettel	Red Bull-Renault	+2.139
3. Hamilton	McLaren-Mercedes	+4.075
4. Webber	Red Bull-Renault	+4.547
5. Alonso	Ferrari	+21.565
6. Kobayashi	Sauber-Ferrari	+36.766
7. Raikkonen	Lotus-Renault	+38.014
8. Perez	Sauber-Ferrari	+39.458
9. Ricciardo	Toro Rosso-Ferrari	+39.556
10. Di Resta	Force India-Mercedes	+39.737
11. Vergne	Toro Rosso-Ferrari	+39.848
12. Rosberg	Mercedes	+57.642
13. Maldonado	Williams-Renault	+1 lap
14. Glock	Marussia-Cosworth	+1 lap
15. Pic	Marussia-Cosworth	+2 laps
16. Senna	Williams-Renault	+4 laps

Drivers' Championship Standings

1. Button	25 pts
2. Vettel	18
3. Hamilton	15
4. Webber	12
5. Alonso	10
6. Kobayashi	8

Constructors' Championship Standings

1. McLaren-Mercedes	40 pts
2. Red Bull-Renault	30
3. Sauber-Ferrari	12
4. Ferrari	10
5. Lotus-Renault	6
6. Toro Rosso-Ferrari	2

After a disappointing start to the season by Ferrari, with Alonso qualifying 12th, almost a second slower than the McLarens, we wondered how long it might take for Ferrari to turn things round with only one week to go before the next race in Malaysia. Luckily for them the weather intervened to give us one of the most entertaining races of the season and an extraordinary battle between Alonso and Sauber's Sergio Perez.

Alonso turns form book on its head to win rain-hit Malaysian Grand Prix
25 March 2012

Fernando Alonso produced a scintillating performance today, with the Ferrari strategists and pit crew making all the right moves, to win a rain hit Malaysian Grand Prix. The track has always been good to the Spaniard: he took his first pole position and podium here and has won the race twice before.

It was classic Alonso; the weather conditions offered an opportunity to level the playing field and Alonso snatched it gratefully.

But even he had to admit that he was lucky not to lose the victory in the closing stages to 22-year-old Sergio Perez, who was challenging for the lead with seven laps to go but made a mistake, losing four seconds and giving Alonso breathing space to win the race. It was the 28th victory of Alonso's career and moves him ahead of Jackie Stewart in the all-time winners' list. Perez finished second, the first Mexican to stand on an F1 podium for 41 years, with Hamilton again finishing third after starting on pole position as he had done in Australia.

The track was wet at the start and most drivers started on intermediate tyres, but the rain intensified as the cars made their way around the opening lap. An early tangle between Romain Grosjean and Michael Schumacher, dropping them out of third and fourth places, allowed the Red Bulls to take their positions as the rain began to fall harder. Sauber pitted Perez for full wets from 11th place and it proved an inspired call as it took him to third place before everyone else followed suit. Early indications were that the McLarens were going to match their qualifying dominance as they navigated their way through the familiar puddles at Sepang.

The race had to be suspended after nine laps because of a heavy downpour. By the time the red-flag was dropped the whole grid had changed to the full wets apart from Narain Karthikeyan, who began the race on them, and Jean-Eric Vergne who had managed to stay on-track with the intermediates. The rules state that all cars must restart the race on the full wet tyres, this gave Vergne a free set of tyres with no lost time in the pits, and put him in seventh place.

The turning point of the race was the second round of pit stops on lap 14 when the drivers moved from full wet to intermediate tyres. Alonso came in behind Hamilton, but fast pit work by Ferrari got him moving and then McLaren had to hold Hamilton in his pit box as Massa swept into the next-door Ferrari box. This meant Alonso left the pits ahead of Hamilton. Perez had stayed out, but when he stopped a lap later he also emerged ahead of Hamilton. The order stayed that way to the end.

Perez found incredible pace on his ever-degrading intermediates and he began to catch Alonso at around a second a lap, setting continuous fastest laps in the process. The track was looking ready for slicks, a point proved when Daniel Ricciardo took the medium compound slicks on lap 37 and set the timing screens alight, dropping the fastest lap mark by three seconds. Sensing their advantage Sauber made a bold call and put hard compound tyres on Perez's car for the remaining 14 laps, a call that proved to be inspired as they warmed up more quickly than the mediums on Alonso's Ferrari. Perez moved ever closer to the rear of the Ferrari. However, a small mistake saw him touch a wet kerb and run wide at turn 14 on lap 49, undoing the majority of his hard work.

Jenson Button and Sebastian Vettel both made uncharacteristic errors when passing the HRT of Narain Karthikeyan. Button misjudged his braking as he looked to pass the Indian down the inside and slid into him, breaking off one end of his front wing. He could not recover enough to get back into the points. Vettel was running fourth when he sliced his left rear tyre on the HRT's front wing as he moved back on to the racing line after lapping it. The tyre shredded and after it was changed there was some confusion as he was told to pit and retire; then the order was overturned, then reinstated.

Further back there were also tremendous drives from Mark Webber, Kimi Raikkonen and Bruno Senna who completed the top six, with Raikkonen having the final say on fastest lap whilst producing another strong points finish in fifth place for Lotus who once again saw Romain Grosjean exit the race early with a trip into the gravel. Mark Webber showed again that the Red Bull has reasonable race pace, coming home in fourth place.

It was Senna's highest race finish to date, but it could have been even better if he had not come together with teammate Pastor Maldonado on the first lap. Senna was forced to pit for a new nose. Maldonado's poor luck in races continued as an engine problem put him out of tenth place with only one lap remaining.

Force India also had another points scoring Sunday as Paul di Resta in seventh and Nico Hulkenberg in ninth were split by the Toro Rosso of Vergne, claiming his first points in Formula One after narrowly missing out in Melbourne. Michael Schumacher claimed the final point on another very forgettable race day for Mercedes: Schumacher having spun on lap one and Nico Rosberg unable to keep up his early pace as he rapidly dropped down the field from fourth to 13th.

Felipe Massa also had a weekend to forget, finishing 15th, despite battling with Di Resta at one point. It's hard to escape the feeling that today was an audition for Perez to take Massa's seat sooner or later. Ferrari don't like firing drivers mid-season, but Perez is a Ferrari Academy driver and the pressure is building for the team to take some action. The Mugello test on 1 May is the obvious place to give Perez a chance in the Ferrari, so China is a critical race for Massa.

Malaysian Grand Prix
Sepang 56 laps

1. Alonso	Ferrari	2h44:51.812
2. Perez	Sauber-Ferrari	+2.263
3. Hamilton	McLaren-Mercedes	+14.591
4. Webber	Red Bull-Renault	+17.688
5. Raikkonen	Lotus-Renault	+29.456
6. Senna	Williams-Renault	+37.667
7. Di Resta	Force India-Mercedes	+44.412
8. Vergne	Toro Rosso-Ferrari	+46.985
9. Hulkenberg	Force India-Mercedes	+47.892
10. Schumacher	Mercedes	+49.996
11. Vettel	Red Bull-Renault	+1:15.527
12. Ricciardo	Toro Rosso-Ferrari	+1:16.826
13. Rosberg	Mercedes	+1:18.593
14. Button	McLaren-Mercedes	+1:19.719
15. Massa	Ferrari	+1:37.319
16. Petrov	Caterham-Renault	+1 lap
17. Glock	Marussia-Cosworth	+1 lap
18. Kovalainen	Caterham-Renault	+1 lap
19. Maldonado	Williams-Renault	+2 laps
20. Pic	Marussia-Cosworth	+2 laps
21. Karthikeyan	HRT-Cosworth	+2 laps
22. De la Rosa	HRT-Cosworth	+2 laps

Drivers' Championship Standings

1. Alonso	35 pts
2. Hamilton	30
3. Button	25
4. Webber	24
5. Perez	22
6. Vettel	18

Constructors' Championship Standings

1. McLaren-Mercedes	55 pts
2. Red Bull-Renault	42
3. Ferrari	35
4. Sauber-Ferrari	30

5. Lotus-Renault   16
6. Force India-Mercedes   9

At the end of the month I was part of a small group of journalists and other interested parties invited to the RAC Club in London's Pall Mall for a meeting with the Bahrain GP organizers. It was interesting to see who was there and prepared to stand up and be counted alongside the Bahrainis.

There was a lot of anxiety generally about F1 going to Bahrain in the build-up to the new season, with reports of human rights violations from the 2011 uprising and also since then. Human rights groups both in Bahrain and outside were calling for F1 to cancel the event. There was still violence on the streets and most people who work in the sport were deeply uneasy about the idea of going there. It was one of the biggest stories of the year and an extremely uncomfortable one for all those connected with the sport.

In the end the race went ahead amidst a blizzard of publicity, with the protest groups in Bahrain being given ample opportunity to tell the world of their concerns and their problems. F1 came out of it looking morally dubious, while Bahrain was painted as dysfunctional and troubled. It was not F1's finest hour. As media we were obliged to attend out of professional duty. We were not representing F1; rather we were there to cover the race. Some media got completely carried away and acted like trainee war reporters, while others chose to play with a straighter bat.

F1 bosses in show of support for Bahrain Grand Prix
28 March 2012

At a lunch today at the RAC Club in London the organizers of the Bahrain Grand Prix met with Bernie Ecclestone, several leading F1 team principals and journalists to discuss the forthcoming Bahrain Grand Prix. The message from Bahrain and from the F1 teams was clear: the race is on, despite continuing unrest in the country and the rumours of impending cancellation that have surfaced from time to time during the first two races of the season.

Last year's Grand Prix was cancelled after an outbreak of violent protest in

February that led to many deaths and thousands of arrests. A commission of enquiry report issued last November found evidence of human rights abuses and police brutality in dealing with the protests. As a result, many of the people who work in the sport have privately expressed concern about the race taking place.

Among those representing Bahrain were the CEO of the circuit, Shaikh Salman bin Isa Al Khalifa of the ruling family, and Zayed al Zayani, who is responsible for the race. F1 was represented by Ecclestone, Sir Frank Williams, McLaren boss Martin Whitmarsh, Red Bull boss Christian Horner, Mercedes AMG CEO Nick Fry, Pirelli motorsport boss Paul Hembery as well as the FIA's Communications Director Norman Howell.

The Grand Prix is due to take place in three weeks, following the Chinese Grand Prix, and the Bahrainis wanted to get the message across that the security situation is back to normal and that teams, media and fans can be reassured that the event will pass safely and that despite reports of continuing outbreaks of violence, there will be no need for additional security. They believe that the country is on the road to change and that "the Grand Prix has the power and the potential to be a force for good."

In turn, Ecclestone says he is happy for the sport to be used to play a supportive role in that message, "We'd be happy to do whatever. I don't see that we can help much but we're there, we have confidence in Bahrain. The good thing about Bahrain is that it's more democratic than most places. The people there are allowed to say what they want and they can protest if they want to."

"F1 is a sport at the end of the day and we've always enjoyed racing in Bahrain," said Christian Horner. "It's on the calendar and the FIA and promoters deem it right to hold a race in Bahrain … We've had assurances from the FIA that they are happy [about security arrangements]. When you enter the championship, you enter to compete in all the races and we look forward to racing in Bahrain."

Shaikh Salman and Zayed al Zayani both underlined the economic importance of the event to Bahrain. They said that economic analysts put the economic benefit of the race at $220 million annually to the country, and its cancellation last year, they said, had a significant impact on local businesses. For example, 29 largely Shia staff were laid off by the circuit, though 25 of those have since returned to their work, according to Zayed.

"We're very excited," said Shaikh Salman. "The Grand Prix ties us to the world. Bahrain is such a small country and we get a chance to play on a global scale. And our small country really punches above its weight during that time. As Bahrainis that's what makes us proud. The Grand Prix plays a huge part in Bahrain, the economic impact everyone benefits from, the taxi drivers, hotels and so on.

"The Grand Prix is a huge event and security measures are part of that. We've shown them what we've done every year and it hasn't changed that much.

"We have moved on from what happened and the unfortunate incidents of last year. The Grand Prix coming back says that."

Chapter Four
April 2012

Over the last weeks of March the majority of F1 teams reached individual commercial agreements with Bernie Ecclestone to stay in the sport until 2020. This paved the way for the signing of a new Concorde Agreement, but there was still a lot to be done before that happened and it ended up being very delayed. The FIA had their say in the matter, demanding a greater share of the sport's revenues. This issue rumbled on all year with discussions on a proposal that teams pay a higher entry fee plus a "tax" per point scored. The suggestion was that this would push a top team's payment to the Federation up to around €4 million per season.

However, an even more important issue on the agenda recently has been reaching an agreement on the best method of cost control going forward. Ecclestone had been pushing the thorny subject of budget caps. Sauber CEO Monisha Kaltenborn endorsed the idea of budget caps to replace the Resource Restriction Agreement, which was put in place by the teams at the end of 2008 when the economic crisis hit. It was a disagreement over how to police the RRA that ultimately led to the break up of the F1 Teams' Association.

The teams gathered in Shanghai, China, where Mercedes Nico Rosberg won his first Grand Prix, but overshadowing the weekend was the imminent Bahrain Grand Prix. As lobby groups and protestors ramped up their efforts to get the race cancelled, F1 bosses issued a very robust statement during the Shanghai weekend saying that the race was very definitely on.

Rosberg converts first pole to first win in Chinese GP thriller
15 April 2012

Nico Rosberg joined the exclusive club of drivers who have converted their first pole position into their first victory with a dominant performance in Shanghai. It was Mercedes first win as a constructor since 1955. And it meant that team boss Ross Brawn has now won races as a senior manager with four different teams, a unique achievement.

Rosberg produced a faultless drive and it gave him that elusive first win after 111 starts, and the first for the Silver Arrows for 57 years. Rosberg completed the race 20 seconds clear of the McLaren duo of Jenson Button and Lewis Hamilton.

He was helped by a pit stop wheel gun blunder on lap 39 by the McLaren team on Button's car, which cost him five seconds and dropped him into a pack of cars instead of back into second place on Rosberg's heels. If the stop had been normal, McLaren believe he would have been 12 seconds behind Rosberg with 17 laps to go and on tyres that would have been five laps newer. He might have closed the gap, but whether he would have had a genuine chance to win is open to doubt.

The Mercedes had a considerably faster race pace than had been expected and was able to match the McLaren duo on the prime tyres, which were much faster than the softer option tyres even for the cars that opted for a three-stop strategy. Much against expectations, Rosberg made one less stop then the McLarens and would have been under pressure from Button later in the race were it not for the error during his final pit stop.

Rosberg pulled away from the line perfectly and was able to open up a six-second gap before the first round of pit stops. Behind him at this point was teammate Michael Schumacher, who also put in a good first stint before a loose wheel nut forced him to retire from the race. Jenson Button was able to inherit second place and looked as though he was going to make good use of his three-stop strategy and claim his second victory of the year. He failed, but will be happy to have put McLaren a fair distance ahead in the constructors' championship.

The race saw a huge number of overtakes and changes in position as cars constantly found themselves being dropped back into the pack following their pit stops. Hamilton and Mark Webber, in particular, found themselves in this position for much of the race, limiting their progress on fresh tyres, with Webber eventually coming home in fourth after passing Sebastian Vettel on the penultimate lap. Vettel had made a poor start from 11th on the grid and dropped three places, but he was able to make his two-stop strategy work and make his tyres last the distance.

Romain Grosjean also had a strong race to finish his first Grand Prix for Lotus and take sixth place. He managed to make his two-stop strategy work, unlike his teammate Kimi Raikkonen. The Finn drove a very good race and with ten laps remaining he was in second position, albeit with increasing pressure from a seven-strong train of cars behind. However, Vettel put him on the marbles around the outside on turn 7 and he dropped back to 14th by the chequered flag.

There were more good points for Williams with Bruno Senna and Pastor Maldonado in seventh and eighth places respectively. Similarly to the Malaysian Grand Prix they showed very consistent race pace and kept the Ferrari of Fernando Alonso and both Saubers at bay in the latter stages. Alonso opted to use a second set of option tyres after his first pit stop, against the general trend, and this lost him a lot of track time on Webber. Kamui Kobayashi claimed the final point for Sauber, but it could have been very different as his teammate Sergio Perez defended extremely aggressively on the run down to turn 14.

Chinese Grand Prix
Shanghai 56 laps

1. Rosberg	Mercedes	1h36:26.929
2. Button	McLaren-Mercedes	+20.626
3. Hamilton	McLaren-Mercedes	+26.012
4. Webber	Red Bull-Renault	+27.924
5. Vettel	Red Bull-Renault	+30.483
6. Grosjean	Lotus-Renault	+31.491
7. Senna	Williams-Renault	+34.597
8. Maldonado	Williams-Renault	+35.643
9. Alonso	Ferrari	+37.256
10. Kobayashi	Sauber-Ferrari	+38.720
11. Perez	Sauber-Ferrari	+41.066
12. Di Resta	Force India-Mercedes	+42.273
13. Massa	Ferrari	+42.700
14. Raikkonen	Lotus-Renault	+50.500
15. Hulkenberg	Force India-Mercedes	+51.200
16. Vergne	Toro Rosso-Ferrari	+51.700
17. Ricciardo	Toro Rosso-Ferrari	+1:03.100
18. Petrov	Caterham-Renault	+1 lap
19. Glock	Marussia-Cosworth	+1 lap

20. Pic	Marussia-Cosworth	+1 lap
21. De la Rosa	HRT-Cosworth	+1 lap
22. Karthikeyan	HRT-Cosworth	+2 laps
23. Kovalainen	Caterham-Renault	+3 laps

Drivers' Championship Standings

1. Hamilton	45 pts
2. Button	43
3. Alonso	37
4. Webber	36
5. Vettel	28
6. Rosberg	25

Constructors' Championship Standings

1. McLaren-Mercedes	88 pts
2. Red Bull-Renault	64
3. Ferrari	37
4. Sauber-Ferrari	31
5. Mercedes	26
6. Lotus-Renault	24

Nico Rosberg was clearly the readers' choice as driver of the day in Shanghai, with 61 per cent of the votes. It was a breakthrough win for the likeable German, but he wasn't able to follow it up. A second place in Monaco was encouraging, but the Mercedes fell off the pace of the McLaren, Red Bull and Ferrari and Rosberg began to be outperformed by his teammate Michael Schumacher.

Meanwhile, Ferrari's senior technical figure, Pat Fry, admitted after China that there are some deep-rooted problems in the team's technical set-up that need to be resolved if Ferrari is to enjoy sustained long-term success again. Fry took the reins of Ferrari's technical department last year, following the axing of team stalwart Aldo Costa, and promptly instigated a more aggressive design focus. In Shanghai he delivered what was a frank assessment of what he believes are the team's shortcomings. The Briton said that a fundamental overhaul was required in its "methodologies", in other words the fundamentals of the way Maranello designs and develops its F1 cars. His words hinted at a long-term fix aimed at returning the Scuderia to the glory days of the 2000s. "I don't really want to go into what all the problems are – it's not just a case of us trying to build a quicker car, we need to fundamentally change the methodologies that we use to select, design and manufacture so that we are competitive long term," Fry said over the weekend.

"There's work to do on all fronts, not just work going into what we're taking to Barcelona, there's also a huge amount of work in just trying to change the fundamentals of what we do so we can actually take a step forward and be competitive with everyone else."

Hamilton: "Everything's better this year"
17 April 2012

Lewis Hamilton has spoken of his renewed happiness both on and off the racetrack after a start to the season that has taken him back to the top of the world championship standings for the first time in nearly two years. The tumultuous nature of Hamilton's 2011 was well documented, with setbacks in both his racing and his private life contributing to his self-described worst year in Formula 1. But a productive winter allowed him the chance to re-focus and piece back together the ingredients he sees as being key to his personal equilibrium.

Speaking to the British media in China following his third successive third-place finish on Sunday, he said: "I just think everything's better this year. The team is better, the car is better and I'm a lot better. I've got my dad here, you know, and that's not fake. That's real, a good bond we've got now and on the up. Things are great with my mum, things are great with my girlfriend, so things are great and that's reflecting in my performances I think."

The appearance of his dad Anthony in the McLaren garage during track sessions in Shanghai underlined the apparent reconciliation that has taken place between father and son over the winter, the pair having split professionally in 2010 when Lewis opted to take control of his own management decisions.

Although Hamilton has yet to take his first victory of 2012, despite claiming pole position for the first two races, the 27-year-old has been keen to focus on the positives of being the only driver to finish on the podium in every round so far. This is already in stark contrast to last season when he failed to string together back-to-back top-three finishes at any point of the campaign despite having the second-fastest car. McLaren's step ahead of Red Bull also means he is likely to have his best chance of winning the world championship again.

However, with just eight months remaining on his five-year deal with the Woking squad, he is insisting he doesn't plan to rush into agreeing a new deal, even if he "could not be happier" at the team. He had said at the launch of its 2012 car in February that "after the first couple of races it's something we will probably want to get out of the way", but now he appears to be putting a longer time frame on the process. Today he said: "I don't need persuading. When I need to, which can be within any time frame I want so long as it is before next year, then I will decide about my future."

Hamilton may have been happier than in 2011, but he was also looking to move on. Ever since his not-so-private meeting with Red Bull's Christian Horner in Canada the previous year, there had been signs that Hamilton was looking for a change. It was clear that his only real option was taking Michael Schumacher's seat at Mercedes and sure enough, as the season went on, that became increasingly likely and culminated in the announcement at the end of September. Hamilton said then that he was looking for a new challenge; he wanted to emulate what Michael Schumacher had done at Ferrari in 1996, moving to a team that was struggling and working together with them to raise the team up to championship level.

Everyone who boarded the plane to Bahrain did so with some trepidation. There were stories swirling around of riots, protests and firebomb attacks. Most people working in F1 felt that the sport and its participants were putting themselves in an unnecessary position.

When some members of the Force India team were caught up in an incident on the road back to town from the circuit, tensions heightened. When Force India management decided not to send the cars out in Friday practice, the ripples began to get bigger, but nothing else happened beyond that and gradually the situation normalised, so that by race day it was just another Formula 1 Grand Prix.

Nevertheless, over the course of the weekend some people asked to be allowed to go home, others, having refused to go, were sacked by their teams. It was an emotive issue.

Uneasy sense of calm as F1 settles down to business in Bahrain
19 April 2012

The F1 paddock went about its everyday business today: media briefings, team managers' meetings, all gearing up for Sunday's Bahrain Grand Prix. Lewis Hamilton says that he's a better man in 2012 for his difficult years, Sebastian Vettel says that he's going to use the new specification Red Bull exhausts, Michael Schumacher says that Mercedes challenge is to hit the sweet spot on the race tyres like they did in China.

The Grand Prix is moving up into gear. Everywhere there are banners proclaiming that Bahrain is "UniF1ied", while the slogan "back on track" is also evident. It's quite surprising the extent to which the FIA and Bernie Ecclestone have allowed the government to use the F1 brand in its political messaging about the country moving forward. The road to the circuit is lined with chequered flags interlinked with Bahraini flags. A former leader of the opposition Al Wefaq party, Jasim Husain, was paraded around the paddock this morning, giving the event the thumbs up, but outside in the real world, the anti F1 rhetoric from the current opposition and from human rights campaigners is unequivocal.

Inside the paddock there is an edge in the air, a sense of uneasy calm, for the moment. Pre-race uncertainty and anxiety about what kind of situation the hard working professionals of this sport would be walking into this weekend found a focus in a frightening incident involving four Force India technicians and mechanics as they drove along the highway back into town around 8 p.m. on Wednesday night.

A temporary roadblock had been thrown up by activists and in the melee as the traffic slowed, a Molotov cocktail was thrown and exploded a few metres from their car. There was no sense that they were targeted nor that the perpetrators had any idea that there were F1 people in the traffic jam.

But this is the kind of spontaneous and random act of violence that is hard to anticipate or prevent and in which no one wants to get caught. Two members of the team, one of whom was not even in the car, have been allowed to travel back to the UK.

Comparisons are being made with the road out of the circuit in São Paolo, where gun toting gangs occasionally terrorized F1 personnel in their cars until the police cleaned up the slum area for last year's race. Such an incident happened to Jenson Button and his entourage two years ago, as well as to several mechanics. São Paolo is a place where it is easy to get mugged on the street, you have to take care, but this is different, as one doesn't feel targeted in that sense. However, there is a feeling of volatility, a fear of getting caught up in someone else's violent protest. The police, after all, cannot be everywhere all the time.

"My wife happened to be travelling on that road at the same time and she sent me a picture of it," said Zayed al Zayani, the manager of the Bahrain International Circuit. "It was an unfortunate incident and hopefully it won't happen again.

"We are 'back on track' in the sense that the cars are racing on our track. Some people have interpreted that we are saying that the country is back on track. I don't think so and I've made it clear that politically there is a long way to go to get the stability we had before. But that's not our job, that's left to the government; we run a social and sports event."

Former Metropolitan Police chief John Yates, now consulting for the Bahraini police, was not exactly reassuring in his assessment of the situation, "There will be protests over the weekend," he said. "But we want to make this a sporting event not a security event. I judge it more likely there will be protests on the route and protests around the villages. I just hope it's a good event and I hope it goes off without too much trouble."

The security on arrival at the track today was surprisingly sparse, a couple of men in yellow shirts, no military, no guns. That is sure to change as the weekend goes on. There is no sign on the roads or in the city of any problems, but they can spring up from nowhere. Everyone will breathe a sigh of relief on Sunday night if they can get out of here without a major incident.

The drivers aren't keen to get drawn into discussions about the political side of this issue. Some rather naively say that the racing is "more important", others just say that they are "here because it's on" and leave it at that. Others, such as Paul di Resta and Nico Hulkenberg, shared their team's anxiety over the incident on the road last night. Hulkenberg said, "It is obviously not right that that sort of stuff happens," he said. "We are here to race. The F1 business is about entertainment, and these sorts of things should not really be happening to us."

Once the cars start running on Friday a greater sense of normality should descend on the weekend, but it will only take one serious incident for everyone who works in F1 to feel very differently about being here.

The sport is holding its breath.

Faultless Vettel holds off comeback king Raikkonen to win Bahrain GP
22 April 2012

Sebastian Vettel produced a faultless drive from pole position to win the Bahrain Grand Prix ahead of the two Lotus cars of Kimi Raikkonen and Romain Grosjean. This is Red Bull Racing's first victory of 2012 and makes it four different winners in as many races this season. It was Vettel's 22nd F1 career victory and his first of the season.

If Vettel's pace in qualifying was a surprise, it was the performance of Lotus that really caught the eye on race day. Raikkonen, starting in 11th place, had a chance to win the race and was frustrated afterwards not to have done so. It's a sign of how sharp the 2007 champion is after his two-year layoff and how Lotus has produced a very good car. The team brought a raft of updates to this race including a new rear wing, floor and bargeboards and this made an already fast and consistent car into arguably the fastest car of the weekend.

Vettel now leads the drivers' championship table, while Red Bull take over the lead in the constructors' table as McLaren had a very poor day in the office, which saw Jenson Button retire on the penultimate lap and Lewis Hamilton suffer two slow pit stops resulting in an eighth position finish. In total he lost 16 seconds and inevitably ended up with a lot of traffic. But McLaren were struggling anyway with race pace and the rear tyre wear was clear from early on in the race. Red Bull collected 37 points this afternoon to McLaren's three as Mark Webber continued his consistent form, finishing in fourth place, for the fourth time this season.

Vettel led the race from lights-to-flag and a perfect start allowed him to open up a gap of almost six seconds before the first round of pit stops. Behind him, both Lotuses had scythed through the field during the opening stint and found themselves knocking on the door of the podium after their first tyre change. During these stops Raikkonen opted for another set of the soft option tyres, unlike many of the field, and he was soon up into second position after passing Webber and Grosjean before the second phase of pit stops.

Seeing the Lotus's pace on the soft tyres, Red Bull gave Vettel another set of softs during his second stop to try and maintain the gap to Raikkonen. By now the Finn was on a new set of prime tyres. The Lotus once again showed very good pace as the tyres got older and the former world champion closed to within 0.5 seconds of the current one. However, Raikkonen was unable to pass Vettel before the final set of pit stops and barring a couple of fast laps from the second-placed car the gap stayed constant through to the end of the race.

Grosjean had a fairly quiet race after a brilliant first stint, but still claimed France's first podium finish since Jean Alesi in 1998. Webber had a fairly lonely afternoon, finishing the race in the middle of a 45-second chasm between third and fifth positions.

In contrast, Nico Rosberg had a very eventful race, having dropped down to ninth from the start he managed to claw his way back to fifth position, making two very aggressive defensive moves in the process on Hamilton and Fernando Alonso that landed him in trouble with the stewards. However, they ruled that Hamilton was always behind Rosberg when he made the move to block and so awarded no penalty.

Behind Rosberg was Paul di Resta, the Scot making just two stops during the race as he defended very well to keep Alonso and Hamilton at bay until the chequered flag. Alonso was another very fast starter, making his way up to fifth position during the first lap, although the Ferrari driver was unable to match the pace of Rosberg and Webber. Hamilton had a frustrating race, compounded by two slow pit stops.

Felipe Massa was much closer to his teammate than previously and finished the race in ninth place. Michael Schumacher added another point to his solitary point from Malaysia as he made his way from 22nd on the grid to take the final points position.

Sergio Perez's Sauber headed the remainder of the field, ahead of the second Force India of Nico Hulkenberg and the Toro Rosso of Jean-Eric Vergne. Vergne was able to beat teammate Daniel Ricciardo after the Australian made a poor start from sixth on the grid and finished the race in 15th. The Caterhams came home line astern, with Vitaly Petrov beating Heikki Kovalainen to 16th place. Kovalainen received a puncture on the first lap, which ruined any chances of him progressing on from a great qualifying effort.

Bahrain Grand Prix
Sakhir Circuit 57 laps

1. Vettel	Red Bull-Renault	1h35:10.990
2. Raikkonen	Lotus-Renault	+3.333
3. Grosjean	Lotus-Renault	+10.194
4. Webber	Red Bull-Renault	+38.788
5. Rosberg	Mercedes	+55.460
6. Di Resta	Force India-Mercedes	+57.543
7. Alonso	Ferrari	+57.803
8. Hamilton	McLaren-Mercedes	+58.984
9. Massa	Ferrari	+1:04.999
10. Schumacher	Mercedes	+1:11.490
11. Perez	Sauber-Ferrari	+1:12.702
12. Hulkenberg	Force India-Mercedes	+1:16.539
13. Vergne	Toro Rosso-Ferrari	+1:30.334
14. Kobayashi	Sauber-Ferrari	+1:33.723
15. Ricciardo	Toro Rosso-Ferrari	+1 lap
16. Petrov	Caterham-Renault	+1 lap
17. Kovalainen	Caterham-Renault	+1 lap
18. Button	McLaren-Mercedes	+1 lap
19. Glock	Marussia-Cosworth	+2 laps
20. De la Rosa	HRT-Cosworth	+2 laps
21. Karthikeyan	HRT-Cosworth	+2 laps
22. Senna	Williams-Renault	+3 laps

Drivers' Championship Standings

1. Vettel	53 pts
2. Hamilton	49
3. Webber	48
4. Button	43
5. Alonso	43
6. Rosberg	35

Constructors' Championship Standings

1. Red Bull-Renault	101 pts
2. McLaren-Mercedes	92
3. Lotus-Renault	57
4. Ferrari	45
5. Mercedes	37
6. Sauber-Ferrari	31

After the race, Michael Schumacher launched an attack on the Pirelli tyres, claiming that they were too big an influence on the races and that they were forcing drivers to nurse the tyres rather than drive on the limit. Certainly the tyres had played a significant part in the outcome of the early races this year with every race having a different winner and teams and drivers caught out by the way the tyre performance changed from circuit to circuit.

Many fans agreed with him, especially the ones whose favourite drivers were thought to be losing out because of the inconsistency of their cars on the tyres. However, for the neutral it made for a very lively start to the season and kept things mixed up. No one was able to run away with the championship table, in fact it was Fernando Alonso who emerged with the upper hand as the season developed through simple consistency and good race management by Ferrari.

Pirelli surprised by Schumacher attack on short-life tyres
23 April 2012

Pirelli have reacted to Michael Schumacher's attack on their 2012 tyres, saying that other drivers "were getting on with the job and getting their tyres to work". Schumacher suffered a frustrating weekend in Bahrain, with technical problems in qualifying relegating him to the back of the field. He took a tactical gearbox change, which moved him back to 22nd place and although he made a great start and had all new sets of tyres for the race, he only managed to finish tenth.

"The main thing I feel unhappy about is that everyone has to drive well below a driver's, and in particular, the car's limits to maintain the tyres," he said after the race. "I just question whether the tyres should play such an important role, or whether they should last a bit longer, and that you can drive at normal racing car speed and not cruise around as though we have a safety car. I'm not happy about the situation; let's see what happens in future. If it was a one-off car issue, you could say it's up to us to deal with it."

There is some debate among fans about this subject, with fans of hard charging drivers like Lewis Hamilton unhappy that their drivers aren't able to show what they can do while smoother drivers, who can manage the tyres, are profiting.

It's an interesting one: F1 has always been about managing tyres as the races are 300 kilometres in length, so they are about endurance rather than a sprint. However, in the Bridgestone era the tyres would last a whole race if required. The key thing is not the wear – the Pirelli tyres could last a whole race from that point of view – it's the degradation. This means the amount of lap time lost with each lap that passes. The tyres get slower and slower until the lap time is uncompetitive and you have to pit for a new set.

What makes the 2012 situation so interesting is that the tyres have an operating window that is quite hard to hit, which is why we have seen different teams hitting the sweet spot at different times. In Malaysia, for example, Sauber were strong, in China Mercedes flew and in Bahrain Lotus had arguably the best set-up for the tyres and Red Bull also managed the race to perfection. This is because the tyres have opened up different strategies as some car/driver packages can get them to last longer than others and there is also the tactic of saving new sets of tyres by doing less in qualifying, as Raikkonen and Di Resta did to great effect this weekend.

Schumacher's heyday was the era of flat-out sprints on Bridgestone tyres, when Ferrari had a testing budget from the Japanese manufacturer of over $20 million and so did hundreds of thousands of testing miles. Cost cutting measures introduced in 2008 have put paid to that.

"I'm disappointed to hear those comments from someone of Michael's experience," said Pirelli motorsport boss Paul Hembery. "His comments during winter testing were that he was very happy with the tyres, and now he seems to have changed his tune."

While fans are divided, F1 insiders are, on the whole, excited by the 2012 style of racing, believing that the tyres are the same for everyone and that the racing is exciting. At the moment the top teams, who aren't able to test under the current restrictions, are finding less well-funded teams close to them on performance. In the past they would test constantly, develop new parts that would pull them well clear of the midfield with the ideal set-ups for maximizing tyre performance at every event, often making the races processional and predictable. The field has closed up and it's making it much harder for the top teams to make a break and get the results.

F1 should be about excellence, the best of the best. But it's hard for the cream to rise to the top this season. We've had four different winners and three different pole sitters in four races. The top teams will inevitably pull away over the season because of their resources, but the current structure is making for exciting races, with cliffhanger endings. Tyre management has always been as important a skill as having raw pace in F1.

In a poll 46 per cent of readers agreed with Schumacher's view on the tyres, while 32 per cent disagreed and 20 per cent said it wasn't clear-cut. The situation carried on for the first half of the season, with seven different winners in the first seven Grands Prix, a unique statistic. However, the situation normalized as we moved into the second half of the season as most teams got on top of the new generation Pirelli tyres and no one described it as a "lottery" again.

Chapter Five
May 2012

May began with a test at Mugello, the Ferrari-owned track near Florence, Italy. It's a lovely spot, but for many teams this one-off mid-season test was a bit of a waste of time as the track layout doesn't correspond with many of the upcoming circuits. The weather didn't help either; the first day was a total washout.

The one positive was that it gave valuable seat time to some of the younger drivers who are denied the opportunity to test due to the in-season ban. Events throughout the year would show that drivers like Grosjean and Maldonado would benefit from more time in the cars, which in turn would make them less desperate when they are under pressure for results in a race weekend.

Ferrari was clearly looking around at its best options for a driver to partner Fernando Alonso. Adrift in the constructors' championship once again due to the poor form of Felipe Massa, who had not stood on an F1 podium since Korea 2010, the Scuderia was keen to secure either Mark Webber or Jenson Button for 2103. In the end they didn't get either of them.

Mark Webber and Ferrari
2 May 2012

Ferrari knows that it needs more points than it is scoring at the moment from its second car. Last year Felipe Massa scored only 45 per cent of Fernando Alonso's points tally. This season so far, described as make or break for Massa by both team boss Stefano Domenicali and Ferrari president Luca Montezemolo, Massa has 4 per cent. And so rumours have begun to swirl again about the possibility of Ferrari hiring Mark Webber to partner Alonso on a short-term contract.

The story originated in Spain's *El Confidencial*, which claimed that the deal was already done, and has been fanned by the Australian media. Webber, 35, addressed the rumours in a media briefing last night in Mugello. He said that he had not signed anything, but stopped short of denying that there was anything going on. "Sergio [Perez] was flavour of the month last week for the Ferrari drive; now it's me," Webber said. "I'm focusing 100 per cent on this season and doing the best job for myself and Red Bull Racing. I'm not putting any energy into anything else. We have a whole season ahead before we start thinking about our future. One day there is talk that Jenson [Button] will go to Ferrari, then Sergio, now me.

"I have not signed anything. Just think about my team: we have made a good start to the season, we've done only four races and the road is still very, very long before you start talking about the future."

I've written about this before, several times. There has been contact in the past between the two and Webber has been on Ferrari's radar for a number of reasons: he gets on well with Fernando Alonso and is liked by Stefano Domenicali and others, he's uncomplicated and he's fast. He also has a lot of experience and solid engineering understanding, both of which Ferrari prize.

Many people assume that Sergio Perez is the natural choice for the Ferrari team, as they groomed him at their academy in much the same way as Felipe Massa. His berth at Sauber is part of that time-honoured process. However, the Mexican still has a lot to prove. He is only 22 and has only had one season at the top level – it is not Ferrari's way to sign a driver with so little experience. Massa was a bit of an exception, coming to them at 25 after three seasons with Sauber from 2002 to 2005. He also had a stint as Ferrari test driver in the days when that meant covering serious mileage.

It'll be a year or two before Perez is ready for Ferrari. So it is logical, if Ferrari is thinking of dropping Massa, that it should look for a solution for the next two years, making Webber the obvious choice. He is on a rolling one-year contract at Red Bull and is keeping his options open on both sides.

There are two obvious question marks for Webber. Firstly, he is a very competitive individual, so the thought of moving from Red Bull to Ferrari, if it is not a competitive car, would require some reflection. But as a keen student of the sport's history, he may feel that with one or two years of F1 left, a stint at Ferrari would add a prestigious cap to his career.

Secondly, there is the question of "not bad for a number two driver" – Webber's famous line from the British Grand Prix of 2010 where he was disadvantaged by the team when they gave his front wing to teammate Vettel. This aspect of Webber's character is not compatible with the "Fernando is faster than you" school of management at Ferrari, to quote engineer Rob Smedley's line when asking Felipe Massa to move aside for his teammate in Germany in 2010. Alonso is clearly the point man at Ferrari and Webber would have to find a way of dealing with that.

Leaving aside those philosophical issues, let's examine the practicalities. Webber's position at Red Bull is underpinned by the support of two key people in the team: Adrian Newey and the owner Dietrich Mateschitz. Newey uses him as a reference point and trusts his instincts, while Mateschitz has always supported Webber and has a strong personal relationship with the driver. Webber does his deals directly with the boss.

Others within Red Bull are keen to see new drivers come into the team, primarily Helmut Marko, who is responsible for the young driver development programme. For this programme to maintain its credibility it needs to produce another top quality driver from Toro Rosso, ready to drive a Red Bull. By abruptly dropping Jaime Alguersuari and Sebastien Buemi last Christmas they left themselves in the position of having two inexperienced drivers in the team in Daniel Ricciardo and Jean-Eric Vergne. It would be asking a lot of either of them to step up to Red Bull alongside Vettel next year.

Vettel himself took that path, but by the time he moved up he had done 26 races, many of them in a competitive 2008 Toro Rosso. Ricciardo has done 15 Grands Prix to date, mostly at the back of the field, and will have done 31 by the time this season ends, whereas Vergne is in his first season of F1 and has twice failed to get out of Q1. It would be a gamble to go with either man to sit alongside Vettel, who is a two-times world champion at the top of his game in a team built around him.

A move by Webber towards Ferrari might force the issue.

Teams brand Mugello test a waste of time and money
3 May 2012

"It's very beautiful and the food is very good, but we are spending a lot of money and honestly we didn't feel the need to come here," said Red Bull boss Christian Horner when asked about the usefulness of testing at Mugello in Tuscany. Lotus boss Eric Boullier described the test as "money spent needlessly", while one of Mercedes senior engineers told *Gazzetta dello Sport*, "I wonder about the sense of having so few test sessions during the season. Either we do more tests or we forget it."

Some of the teams are complaining, but the drivers on the whole have been having a ball on the 5.25-kilometre track, which is in one of the most beautiful parts of Italy. The circuit has many high-speed corners and is a thrill to drive in a modern F1 car, according to most of them. "Spectacular", "incredibly fast" and "stunning" are just some of the reactions from the F1 drivers at the test. Mugello has an average lap speed of 138mph.

But they will also admit that there has been a limit to the value that the engineers have been able to derive from testing new parts on their cars on this atypical circuit. Mark Webber summed up their feelings neatly when he said, "It would be amazing to hold a Grand Prix here, but it's too fast for a test. In the calendar there isn't another track like it."

The logical thing to do would have been to test at Barcelona this week and then leave the trucks and equipment down there for next week's Grand Prix, which is what the teams used to do in the early 2000s. In reality this made for rather dull Spanish Grands Prix as everyone had such a good set-up for the race that the order was entirely predictable. But at least Barcelona is representative of what the teams will face for most of the season in terms of the variety of corners. Mugello only prepares them for Spa and half of Silverstone.

Today Fernando Alonso got his hands on an updated Ferrari with a new rear wing, rear bodywork and new exhausts, but then crashed it. He went off, damaging the nose section of the car, which came to rest with its left side in the barriers. "At least two hours to repair the damages. It is a shame, but that's testing!" said the official Ferrari tweet.

Vitaly Petrov had said on Wednesday that he felt the track wasn't suited to F1 cars, "I don't think we should have come here," he said. "It is not safe and wide enough. If you lose it, the walls are so close and you will smash into the tyres. It is not for Formula 1 and, if you lost the steering or the tyre pressure dropped or whatever, then it will be a big crash."

Ferrari's full update kit, featuring a new front wing and new diffuser, has not been seen in Mugello this week. It will only break cover in Spain next week, the team saying that it wanted more time in the wind tunnel. Felipe Massa appeared to criticize this decision in the Italian media yesterday, saying, "It would have been better to test everything here, but we are not ready. To close the gap to the top we need to grow faster than them. But I think that in the next few weeks we will find two- or three-tenths."

Meanwhile, Sauber's chief designer Matt Morris has spoken out about the feasibility of copying the Mercedes Double DRS system, which was definitively passed as legal by the FIA last month. It seems that only the richest teams are likely to consider copying it, as the cost to benefit ratio doesn't stack up for most. "We have done some evaluation on it in the factory, but at the moment it's not really working for us in terms of cost versus performance," Morris told autosport.com. "Beyond that, it's difficult to know exactly what the potential benefits are and then it's only really useful in qualifying as well.

"It's definitely a few tenths of a second in qualifying, but to get that [benefit] so many parts in the car would have to be changed. That's the problem."

The three-day test ended with Lotus's Romain Grosjean setting the fastest time on a day when, according to Pirelli, the 11 teams covered 1,134 laps of the Tuscan circuit, equivalent to 43 Grand Prix distances. The teams chomped their way through 207 sets of tyres, despite limited running on day 1 due to rain.

Most of the leading F1 teams had signed up to individual commercial deals with Bernie Ecclestone for 2013–20, but the notable exception was Mercedes. It was clear that the offer on the table to them – less than that offered to Red Bull, Ferrari and McLaren and no seat on the F1 board – did not position them as one of the most important teams, which is where they see themselves. There was quite a bit of posturing around this time as Mercedes tested the water to see what F1 bosses would think if they were to pull out of the sport... and there were plenty of rumours to that effect. This dragged on until September and the Lewis Hamilton capture had to wait until the Mercedes board had made up their minds.

Mercedes keen to establish what it means to Formula 1
8 May 2012

What is Mercedes' place in Formula 1? Is it one of the great names of the sport, given that its cars were winning Grands Prix in the 1920s and 30s, before F1 was even invented? Or is it another one of the flighty car manufacturers, which come and go as the markets dictate, as indicated by its absence from the sport between 1955 and 1993?

This question is at the forefront of people's minds at the moment as the German manufacturer is at odds with commercial rights holders CVC and Bernie Ecclestone over its place in the sport and what rights and benefits should follow. Mercedes believes that it deserves more than is being offered by the commercial rights holder, claiming that its history in F1 is significant and its role as a supplier of engines to three teams is fundamental to the running of the sport. There is also the question of the Brackley-based team that it took over, which was originally Tyrrell, was then bought by British American Racing, which became Honda, then Brawn then Mercedes. Surely, somewhere in all of that there has to be a bit more added value?

F1 is heading for a partial flotation in the autumn on the Singapore Stock Exchange and that is why teams are being signed up for eight years and the issue is focusing minds.

F1 always likes to head for deadlines. Former FIA president Max Mosley used to impose sudden, short deadlines as a way of getting things done. The flotation is important because it's about F1 going public: selling shares to institutions and private investors. It needs all its ducks in a row. It has to look its best when it comes to market and that's why there have been some tidy back room deals done lately with Ferrari, Red Bull and McLaren, tying them into the sport for the long term with all manner of financial "sweeteners" and even a seat on the F1 board for each of them. Meanwhile, the midfield teams have resigned themselves to reality and accepted whatever they could get.

Mercedes is isolated. It's not willing to accept the terms on offer because they do not reflect the team's position among the elite. So what to do about it? One option is to quit the sport, or at least threaten to, in order to put pressure on the other side. Mercedes could survive without F1. It would be tough because it's been such an important part of its marketing plan for 20 years, but life – and business – goes on.

F1 would undoubtedly lose some prestige without Mercedes. But they've only been present as a team since 2010, so how do you quantify it? It would miss its engine supply, that's for sure. It would leave only Ferrari, Cosworth and Renault as engine suppliers. In 2014 everything changes with a new engine formula and it's not yet clear what Cosworth's part in that will be. They are supplying HRT and Marussia, who as I understood it recently, haven't yet got a Concorde Agreement deal on the table for the future. There is PURE, of course, a mysterious engine programme which involves Craig Pollock and Gilles Simon and who knows, perhaps that programme was inspired by the powers in F1 knowing that they may lose Mercedes before 2014?

Mercedes has denied the stories that emanated over the weekend from *The Times* about the team being ready to quit F1. Motorsport boss Norbert Haug has said that the story is untrue. My veteran French colleague Jean Louis Moncet, who has sometimes been ahead of the curve on Mercedes news in the last few years, said in his blog in the last few days that, "the Mercedes board will vote on whether to stop the F1 programme at the end of 2012, and consequently will not sign the agreements offered by Bernie Ecclestone."

However, there are doubts about whether this is actually the case. This looks like a story that did not originate with either Mercedes or Ecclestone, but has been carried by the "Internet echo" where stories are picked up and gain momentum. There are some heavy-duty negotiations going on behind the scenes, but it doesn't feel to me like Mercedes are on their way out of this sport any time soon. For example, they announced today a new sponsorship agreement with deluxe watchmaker IWC Schaffhausen, starting in January 2013.

If Mercedes were to leave it would leave no major manufacturers participating in F1: FIAT is present via Ferrari, but it's to promote Ferrari not FIAT; while Renault is there only to make money as an engine supplier. Toyota,

Honda, BMW are all gone. There remain lots of small volume car makers like Lotus, Caterham and Marussia, but none of the troublesome OEMs who have made life so difficult for Ecclestone and the FIA in the last ten years.

No doubt there will be plenty of discussion about this in Barcelona this weekend.

He's not everyone's idea of a great Grand Prix driver and he's certainly had more than his fair share of visits to the stewards in 2012, but on his day Pastor Maldonado is as fast as anyone out there and in Barcelona it all came together with Maldonado taking pole after Lewis Hamilton was penalised for a fuel irregularity and dropped to the back of the grid. Maldonado soaked up the pressure, held off a spirited challenge from Fernando Alonso and won the race, Williams first victory since 2004.

Maldonado makes Williams winners again with brilliant victory in Spain
13 May 2012

Pastor Maldonado gave Williams its first F1 win since 2004 with a brilliantly judged victory in the Spanish Grand Prix at Barcelona, ahead of Ferrari's Fernando Alonso and the Lotus of Kimi Raikkonen. It was Maldonado's first win in his 24th Grand Prix start and the first ever for a Venezuelan. He is the fifth winner-and-car combination in five Grands Prix, the first time that has happened since 1983. "We are getting better race after race," said Maldonado. "This is a dream for Venezuela and a great moment for our country."

Maldonado started from pole position following Lewis Hamilton's demotion. He lost the lead to Alonso almost immediately, but got it back by undercutting the Ferrari at the second stop and then held on to the flag. On slightly older tyres than Alonso he saw the Spaniard close up on him, but his ability to drive sector 3 of the lap, with the slow chicane leading to the high-speed final corner on to the straight, meant that he was able to measure the gap to the Ferrari and stay out of reach in the DRS zone, in much the same way as Vettel did with Hamilton here last season. It was a brilliantly judged win.

Hamilton managed to come through the field on a two-stop strategy, whereas everyone else did three stops. He finished in eighth place, ahead of teammate Jenson Button, managing his tyres through two long stints of 21 and 31 laps respectively. After the huge disappointment of his grid penalty, it was a very strong drive by Hamilton. Romain Grosjean finished fourth with Kamui Kobayashi making sure the updates to the Sauber yielded a good result in fifth place. Vettel was sixth and Rosberg seventh.

It was an entertaining race with plenty of action throughout the field. Tyre strategies were fairly standard in comparison to last year's race, with three stops the choice of most drivers. The harder tyres seemed to be the better race tyres on the day.

At the start Maldonado was jumped by Alonso, who steamed up the inside into turn 1. Raikkonen also made a good start, moving ahead of teammate Grosjean, who fell behind the Mercedes of Nico Rosberg.

Alonso held a steady gap of three seconds to Maldonado until the second phase of pit stops. At this point Williams opted to pit early, and a combination of very fast in/out laps from Maldonado and Alonso being held up by the Marussia of Charles Pic allowed Maldonado to take the lead. Maldonado was then able to withstand sustained pressure from Alonso in the final 20 laps of the race and conserve his tyres sufficiently, finishing the race three seconds clear of the Spaniard.

Raikkonen, the pre-race favourite for many, followed closely home in third position having had a fairly quiet race, making his way into third at the start and never being troubled from then on. The sister Lotus of Grosjean made a poor start and he found himself behind Nico Rosberg and Sebastian Vettel on the first lap. However, Grosjean was able to re-pass those in front and set the fastest lap on the way to another high points scoring finish.

Kamui Kobayashi drove a great race to fifth position, the Sauber driver starting from tenth and making some characteristically brave moves to make his way through the field towards the end of the Grand Prix. Vettel was sixth, the double world champion having a frustrating day consisting of traffic and a drive-through penalty for not respecting yellow flags. Although he will be quite satisfied to increase his points lead over the

McLarens. Hamilton had run as highly as fourth in the race, following his exclusion from qualifying, and an ambitious two-stop strategy paid off for the Briton as he moved ever closer to the Mercedes of Nico Rosberg in the latter stages, just missing out on seventh place by 0.2 seconds. Mercedes gained only seven points from the Grand Prix after Michael Schumacher collided with Bruno Senna at turn 1, causing both to retire. Button, meanwhile, had another forgettable race, complaining of grip issues on both sets of tyres and finishing in ninth position.

Completing the points was Nico Hulkenberg; the Force India driver was another to absorb sustained pressure as he denied Mark Webber a points-scoring finish. Webber had lost a lot of ground at the start of the race due to a front-wing change.

It was another race that gave a different picture of the state of play in F1 today, the field is so close on performance and the management of the tyres is important, so we see different winners and different teams competitive at every round.

Alonso lapped the Red Bull of Mark Webber here, for example, a strange turnaround given that he finished almost a minute behind the Red Bull of Sebastian Vettel in Bahrain three weeks ago. Ferrari brought six major changes to its car here and they've certainly made some progress. But the picture is still confused as to the pecking order of the cars as it changes from track to track. It is, however, clear that McLaren has had the fastest car at every race and yet is not leading the championship.

"When we are first and second in qualifying and in the race we can say we have the best car," said Alonso, when asked about Ferrari's progress. "This year it's hard to have a pace advantage or to be happy with the car because it's so close. Consistency will be important this year. We have had probably the most difficult start to the championship and we are leading the championship with Vettel so we have to be proud. I'm a bit surprised by the result, we were hoping for some signs of improvement, so we arrived here with optimism, but the pace this weekend has been better than expected. I still don't really know where we are. Maybe we over-performed a little bit with the car we have and some other teams under-performed."

Raikkonen was third for most of the race, pitting later than the leading pair and was on a charge in the closing stages. Another lap and he would have passed Alonso for second place. His start set him up for a good race, but the choice of soft tyres at the first stop was probably a mistake and it cost him second place. Raikkonen knows that he again had the car to win the race. "We've been doing some small things not correctly and there have been some mistakes on my side and it's going to cost you a lot," he said afterwards. "As long as you give yourself the chance to fight at the front I think our car can do it."

The stewards penalized Michael Schumacher after the race for colliding with Bruno Senna, giving him a five-place penalty at the next race in Monaco. There was drama of a different kind an hour after the race when a fire broke out in the Williams pit garage, the fire brigade had to attend as thick, acrid smoke plumed out across the Catalunya paddock. Four members of staff from Williams, four from Caterham and one from Force India were treated for smoke inhalation, and one person was taken to hospital for suspected burns, but team sources said that no one was badly injured.

Spanish Grand Prix
Barcelona 66 laps

1. Maldonado	Williams-Renault	1h39:09.145
2. Alonso	Ferrari	+3.195
3. Raikkonen	Lotus-Renault	+3.884
4. Grosjean	Lotus-Renault	+14.799
5. Kobayashi	Sauber-Ferrari	+1:14.641
6. Vettel	Red Bull-Renault	+1:17.576
7. Rosberg	Mercedes	+1:27.919
8. Hamilton	McLaren-Mercedes	+1:28.100
9. Button	McLaren-Mercedes	+1:25.200
10. Hulkenberg	Force India-Mercedes	+1 lap
11. Webber	Red Bull-Renault	+1 lap
12. Vergne	Toro Rosso-Ferrari	+1 lap
13. Ricciardo	Toro Rosso-Ferrari	+1 lap
14. Di Resta	Force India-Mercedes	+1 lap
15. Massa	Ferrari	+1 lap
16. Kovalainen	Caterham-Renault	+1 lap
17. Petrov	Caterham-Renault	+1 lap
18. Glock	Marussia-Cosworth	+2 laps

Drivers' Championship Standings

1. Vettel	61 pts
2. Alonso	61
3. Hamilton	53
4. Raikkonen	49
5. Webber	48
6. Button	45

Constructors' Championship Standings

1. Red Bull-Renault	109 pts
2. McLaren-Mercedes	98
3. Lotus-Renault	84
4. Ferrari	63
5. Mercedes	43
6. Williams-Renault	43

One of the most impressive figures in the F1 pit lane is Monisha Kaltenborn, the CEO of the Sauber F1 Team. Her profile in the sport had been rising steadily, and in May Peter Sauber underlined just how important she is to his plans by giving her shares in the team. There were suggestions that Ferrari had been looking to try to hire her to work alongside Stefano Domenicali and that the shares were an incentive to get her to stay, but this was denied by people close to the situation.

Sauber look to future with Kaltenborn shares transfer
16 May 2012

Peter Sauber has put the first stage of his succession plan in place by transferring one-third of the shares in his Formula 1 team to CEO Monisha Kaltenborn, citing the desire to retain "continuity" for the Hinwil-based outfit into the long term.

Indian-born Kaltenborn has been with the team for over a decade, having initially joined to head up its legal department. She was given a front-line role by Sauber when the veteran retook control of his eponymous team at the end of 2009 following BMW's sudden pull-out, becoming Formula 1's first female chief executive. Sauber has already said he sees the 41-year-old as his successor as team principal when he retires again and today has underlined the faith and trust he has in her by transferring 33 per cent of the long-established operation into her name. Sauber retains the remaining two-thirds of equity in the Sauber Group.

The 68-year-old was badly stung by the experiences of late 2009 when, four years on from selling the team he founded to BMW in the belief that this would ensure its long-term future, he felt morally obliged to step back into the breach when the German car maker pulled out of F1. Sauber says Kaltenborn played a key role in that process and, given that she shares his vision for the future of the team, he wanted to reflect that in the ownership structure.

"When BMW pulled out of Formula 1 in 2009, Monisha Kaltenborn was instrumental in the team's survival and since then she has been doing outstanding work in her capacity as CEO," said Sauber in a statement. "Transferring one-third of the stake to her represents an important step for me in providing continuity. My desire is to ensure that the company continues to be led as I would want over the long term. Monisha Kaltenborn and my son Alex, who joined the company as marketing director in 2010 and has since also been a member of the board of management, both embrace this aim. It means we can offer our employees a positive outlook for the future."

Given the transfer appears to have been a gift, the gesture is considerable as it is likely to be worth a minimum of £20 million. Kaltenborn herself has said: "For me this step is a mark of the greatest possible trust, which I will do everything in my power to justify."

After overcoming initial financial and on-track struggles on his return as team owner, Sauber has seen his team make steady progress back up the grid and at the Malaysian GP in March Sergio Perez claimed second place – the team's best-ever race finish under his sole control.

This was a very busy year for F1's commercial boss Bernie Eccle-stone: in parallel with the commercial deals being done with the teams, he was also working with CVC on the future ownership of the sport, as the venture capital firm looked to maximize returns on the investment it made in 2005-06. As part of its plan CVC sold off some of its holding in F1, paving the way for a stock market listing in Singapore. The IPO prospectus revealed many fascinating details of the sport's finances and the relationship between F1 and the teams. However, due to a combination of circumstances and market conditions, the flotation was put on hold.

F1 flotation gets the green light in Singapore
21 May 2012

F1 fans could soon be able to buy shares in their favourite sport. The flotation of the Formula 1 business is a step closer after the Singapore Stock Exchange approved the $3 billion flotation of part of the business, according to Reuters and Bloomberg today.

Pre-marketing is set to start on 22 May, according to a Reuters source close to the deal. The marketing coincides with F1 putting on one of its most spectacular shows of the season at the Monaco Grand Prix this weekend.

CVC pre-sold $1.6 billion of stock to three investors including Black Rock in a deal that establishes the value of F1 at $7 billion. This cuts CVC's stake to around 40 per cent and gives the IPO some credibility as major investment houses might come in. F1 bosses have met with investors and fund managers to assess interest in the flotation. Last week in Barcelona groups of interested parties were shown around the paddock and pit buildings by CVC's Nick Clarry and by Fabiana Flossi, Bernie Ecclestone's fiance. They even made a visit to the media centre when it was in full swing.

CVC Capital Partners is looking to float part of its stake in the sale, along with other investors. They would, however, retain a controlling interest in the business. CVC and their partner Bernie Ecclestone had hoped that the flotation would value the whole business at $10 billion, which would represent a six-fold increase on their investment back in 2005. Ecclestone retains around 5 per cent of the business. CVC boss Donald Mackenzie told a court in Germany, which is trying Gerhard Gribkowsky, a former banker involved in the sale of F1 to CVC, that their purchase was "very high risk" at the time because of the threat of a breakaway by manufacturers.

Today, with Ferrari, Red Bull and McLaren all taking a seat on the F1 board, teams set to receive 47 per cent of all commercial revenues going forward and the majority of teams (except Mercedes) signed up to race in F1 for eight years from 2013 onwards, the business is in a very different place.

Singapore's Stock Exchange, known as SGX, is an ambitious exchange, vying with Hong Kong for high-profile listings. Hong Kong had the Prada listing recently, while Manchester United are also said to be considering Singapore. SGX president Magnus Bocker is no stranger to F1: he hosted the Motor Sport Business Forum in September 2010 along with sports marketing agency JMI, which featured Ecclestone as one of the speakers.

The F1 flotation comes soon after the high-profile flotation of Facebook, which raised $18 billion last week. And, co-incidentally, just as Facebook founder Mark Zuckerberg followed that up by marrying his girlfriend at the weekend, Ecclestone and Flossi are set to wed soon.

The Gribkowsky trial was concluded over the summer, with fascinating consequences for F1 as prosecutors in Germany weighed up the possibility of going after the man whom Gribkowsky alleged had bribed him – Bernie Ecclestone.

Meanwhile, F1's powerbrokers were gathering in Monaco for the season's showcase event. The spotlight was very much on Michael Schumacher, who had been handed a grid penalty for his collision with Bruno Senna in Spain. Schumacher was in the third season of his comeback and had not had the results that he or anyone attached to the project had anticipated.

Ironically he and Mercedes were on great form in Monaco, Schumacher taking pole position, but having to give it up due to the penalty. But it was clear that Mercedes were reviewing their options for the future and very clear to me that sooner or later they would get into serious conversations with Lewis Hamilton.

Schumacher, like Mercedes, finds himself at a crossroads
23 May 2012

Michael Schumacher is a five-times Monaco GP winner, but he arrives in the Principality this weekend with a cloud over his head after his third retirement in five races this season. It leaves him with just two points, his worst ever start to an F1 season. In each of those three retirements he has lasted no more than 12 laps.

Schumacher's frustration is evident: he has fired several salvoes at Pirelli and called Bruno Senna an "idiot" for the collision in Spain, which eliminated both cars. The stewards in Barcelona agreed with many commentators in calling it 100 per cent Schumacher's fault and handing him a five-place grid penalty for this weekend's Monaco GP. With overtaking so hard in Monaco (there were only 11 overtakes last season, the lowest of any race) it will be another frustrating weekend for the German.

And it seems that the question of what happens next is beginning to arise. It brings Schumacher to a crossroads in his second career: to continue or to call it a day at the end of the season? Lewis Hamilton is potentially available for next season and this week Mercedes CEO Nick Fry made some comments about Paul di Resta, which caught the attention, "Paul's on our radar," he said. "He has done a fantastic job, he's a nice guy, he's a great team player and he would be one of the drivers undoubtedly that, if Michael were to decide he didn't want to continue, we would look at. We haven't reached that time in our thinking yet, but we have a lot of admiration for Paul."

Ross Brawn missed the Spanish Grand Prix with illness, but will be back in Monaco to oversee the team. He has stepped in and counterbalanced the talk of life beyond Schumacher. He told *Bild* in Germany that the team has let Schumacher down, rather than the other way around. "A lot has been said and written, but we should not forget that we – the team – have let him down in three of the fives races, not delivering the job we should have," he said. "We must do better. We saw Michael's real quality again in the first race, so it's for that reason that I believe we will see him on the podium this year.

"When the time comes, we will sit down together and talk about the future. I'm sure it will become clear very quickly in what direction we will go."

Speaking in the Monaco paddock on Wednesday Schumacher said, "So far we're not focusing on what happens next year or in the future. It's more about what happens right now and the team and myself will get together, so there's no news for you yet, unfortunately."

Of course, Mercedes also has other matters to consider. Despite supplying 25 per cent of engines to the grid, the message from the commercial rights holders during preparations for this summer's IPO is that F1 does not consider the company a "must have". There are crossroads at every turn for the German car maker.

Webber doubles up in Monaco to become sixth winner in first six races
27 May 2012

Mark Webber made history today becoming the sixth different winner in the first six races of the season – something that has never happened before in F1. In an extremely close finish, the Australian pole sitter won by a margin of 0.6 seconds over Nico Rosberg, his fellow front-row starter, with Fernando Alonso moving from fifth on the grid to third at the finish. The Spanish driver takes sole control of the drivers' world championship table from Sebastian Vettel who went from ninth to fourth.

Improved qualifying has been a key to Webber's performance this season and his pole here, while unexpected, was crucial to his victory. He inherited it from Schumacher courtesy of the German driver's five-place penalty, but he had been quick enough to challenge and take the opportunity.

"I'm very happy, it's good to win here fair and square from pole position," he said. "Consistency is nice, but finishing first is what wins championship. If you get a chance, as I did today, you need to grab it with both hands and everything else. This is the weakest car we've had in the last three years here, but it was good enough to win."

It was a race that had a surprising twist, with the new Pirelli tyres holding out longer than expected allowing the drivers to make just one stop. The leading drivers had expected to make another stop further on in the race, however, Sebastian Vettel proved in the first stint that the harder prime tyres could withstand the final 40 laps and he was able to leapfrog Lewis Hamilton during his stop to take fourth position.

The winding circuit meant that overtaking was scarce and, up until the final ten laps, the race was uneventful with the threat of heavy rain never actually arriving. In that final part of the race the top three cars were joined by Vettel,

Lewis Hamilton and Felipe Massa to make for an exciting climax as the cars made their way through traffic, but the cars finished in the same order.

Webber made a perfect start and controlled the race throughout, only losing the lead to his late-stopping teammate. Behind him there was chaos at the first corner as Romain Grosjean was forced into the Mercedes of Michael Schumacher and spun across the track at turn 1. The remainder of the grid managed to take avoiding action, except for Kamui Kobayashi who hit the Lotus and they both retired from the Grand Prix.

Behind Webber and Rosberg, Hamilton initially led the chasers and sat comfortably in third, but a very quick in-lap from Alonso allowed him to exit the pits ahead of the Briton after staying out an extra lap. Hamilton dropped back further when Vettel eventually stopped and the two came very close on the pit-exit, with Vettel coming out on top. Vettel's pace on worn soft tyres was astonishing and, as the leaders struggled to warm up their new soft tyres after the stops, he was able to get himself into the game. Had Alonso been aware of the warm-up issue, he could have won the race by staying out a few laps longer. This would have got him ahead of Webber and Rosberg. But no one had predicted it and so no one gambled on it.

Felipe Massa had his strongest showing of the season, matching the pace of those in front and pressuring his teammate early in the race. He ended the race only six seconds behind Webber, making for one of the closest top six finishes for many years.

The second group was led by Paul di Resta, the Force India driver getting the better of his teammate to collect a decent haul of points for the Silverstone squad, albeit 35 seconds behind Massa.

Bruno Senna, one of the main gainers during the first lap incident, completed the points' scorers, making up for poor form in qualifying. Further back Heikki Kovalainen had a race-long battle with Jenson Button and they came very close on more then one occasion as Button became frustrated and spun trying to overtake the Caterham driver. Button soon retired and will be happy to see the end of a miserable weekend. Kovalainen, however, will have given his team a lot of confidence, showing competitiveness throughout the weekend.

Button was one of many non-finishers, after Grosjean, Pastor Maldonado, Pedro de la Rosa and Kamui Kobayashi retired on the opening lap. Michael

Schumacher also failed to make the finish due to a fuel pump issue. The fastest qualifier yesterday still has only two points this season and has been extremely unfortunate with reliability.

Monaco Grand Prix
Monte Carlo 78 laps

1. Webber	Red Bull-Renault	1h46:06.557
2. Rosberg	Mercedes	+0.643
3. Alonso	Ferrari	+0.947
4. Vettel	Red Bull-Renault	+1.343
5. Hamilton	McLaren-Mercedes	+4.101
6. Massa	Ferrari	+6.195
7. Di Resta	Force India-Mercedes	+41.500
8. Hulkenberg	Force India-Mercedes	+42.500
9. Raikkonen	Lotus-Renault	+44.000
10. Senna	Williams-Renault	+44.500
11. Perez	Sauber-Ferrari	+1 lap
12. Vergne	Toro Rosso-Ferrari	+1 lap
13. Kovalainen	Caterham-Renault	+1 lap
14. Glock	Marussia-Cosworth	+1 lap
15. Karthikeyan	HRT-Cosworth	+2 laps

Drivers' Championship Standings

1. Alonso	76 pts
2. Vettel	73
3. Webber	73
4. Hamilton	63
5. Rosberg	59
6. Raikkonen	51

Constructors' Championship Standings

1. Red Bull-Renault	146 pts
2. McLaren-Mercedes	108
3. Ferrari	86
4. Lotus-Renault	86
5. Mercedes	61
6. Williams-Renault	44

After six races the top four drivers were separated by just 13 points, with a mere three points separating the three leaders. It was very tight and shaping up to be a classic championship. Fernando Alonso sat on top of the drivers' standings after his third-place finish in the Monaco Grand Prix. But it was more than surprising that Alonso was in that position, given how poor the Ferrari car was in pre-season testing and the early season races. So how did it happen? Consistency was certainly the key for Alonso who, along with Hamilton, was the only driver to have scored points in every race up to Monaco. But there was more to it than that. The tyres played their part in this story; inevitably, the misfortunes of others played their part too.

Alonso's lowest scoring race was China, where he finished ninth, but he had also been on the podium three times, one of them a win in Malaysia. Where no better result was possible, he managed to pick up a fifth and a seventh place. In contrast, his rivals had been more erratic: Webber and Vettel had both had a non-points finish, Button had three. Hamilton had scored in every race, with three third-places early on, but then pit stop and operational issues as well as a lack of pace on race day hit him in the last three races.

Key factors in Ferrari's favour at this stage were that they had consistently the best starts and the best pit stops of any team, although McLaren moved to the top of the league on pit stops as the summer came on.

Alonso had made up many places at the start: 13 places in the first five races and another one in Monaco, Massa had made up 23 in total. They had to do this because the Ferrari wasn't qualifying very well; going into the Monaco GP on Sunday Alonso was averaging only eighth on the supergrid – which aggregates all the drivers' qualifying times – behind the Red Bulls, McLarens, Mercedes and Lotus.

This is the key area Ferrari needed to improve in the second half of the season. To consolidate their position Ferrari need to give Alonso a car that will qualify more strongly. They never quite managed to do that, meaning that it was a struggle for the Spaniard all the way through, but he still kept himself ahead of the opposition.

Chapter Six
June 2012

One of the key themes of the 2012 season was the way that teams reacted to the banning of 2011's must-have device: the exhaust blown diffuser. It had been pioneered by Red Bull and played a significant part in their end-of-season dash for the 2010 title and their domination of the 2011 campaign. So it was not surprising that when it was banned for 2012, they were the team with the most to lose.

The gain in rear end downforce from the EBD was huge and all teams had to make up for what was lost with its passing. This closed the field up significantly; teams like Williams and Sauber, who hadn't really got hold of the technology in 2011, found themselves able to compete in 2012.

Red Bull redesigned most of their car apart from the monocoque several times in 2012 and in the second half of the season became the form team. But their modus operandi of always pushing everything to the limits of legality came unstuck a couple of times as they were knocked back by the FIA on a modification to the brake ducts, holes in the floor and then, later in the summer, an engine mapping ruse.

Red Bull keep Bahrain and Monaco wins, but are forced to modify the car
2 June 2012

A controversy that's been doing the rounds for the last few weeks has been resolved today with the announcement by the FIA that the holes in the rear floor of the Red Bull, which appeared at Bahrain in a car that has gone on to win two of the last three races, are illegal.

Rivals raised doubts about the new system after the race at the Sakhir Circuit, but the FIA's initial response was positive and gave Red Bull the green light to continue with its design. The issue was raised again on race day in Monaco, but there were none of the threatened objections despite Mark Webber's victory. The FIA met team representatives after the race for further discussion.

Today they have issued a technical directive, similar to the ones issued last summer banning off-throttle blowing of the diffusers, saying that the new design is illegal as it contravenes other rules by association.

In essence, the FIA had originally accepted the concept from Red Bull. But once it was implemented on the car and having heard representations from other teams about it, they've changed their minds and now say that the fact that there isn't a rule explicitly banning the idea, doesn't make it legal.

Red Bull's idea is to have a hole in the floor ahead of the rear wheels, through which exhaust gases can blow into the channel of the diffuser, gaining downforce at the rear of the car, which has been severely cut by the ban on blown diffusers this year. Red Bull suffered rear end stability issues at the start of the season, which is why they got off to a slow start this year. This "enclosed hole" solution went a long way towards fixing that problem and the team has scored 45 points, including two wins, with it – more than any other team in that period. Now they will have to find another solution.

This process is similar to the one that rival teams launched – unsuccessfully – against Mercedes over the double DRS system at the start of this season. Because the FIA likes teams to run ideas past them first before implementation and then is open to reviewing their decision if other teams have an argument that proves illegality, the team is allowed to keep its results during the period the idea is on the car.

It couldn't continue, surely; this phenomenon of a different winner at every race had to end soon – but not before Lewis Hamilton had taken his first win of the season on a circuit where he has always excelled. The sight of Hamilton on the limit around Montreal is one of F1's most spectacular experiences; he runs so close to the walls on the outside of the chicanes, judges the braking perfectly for the hairpin and carries exactly the right amount of speed through the final chicane, where the Wall of Champions waits for the unwary.

Hamilton keeps his cool to win Canadian Grand Prix
10 June 2012

Lewis Hamilton became the seventh different winner in seven Grands Prix this season with a cool headed drive on a day of strategy gambles. It was his third Canadian Grand Prix win and the 18th of his career. It gave him the lead in the drivers' championship by two points over Alonso and three points over Vettel. It was McLaren's 13th win in Canada.

The victory was built on a two-stop strategy, which proved the right one, although it produced some nervous moments after his second stop when it became clear that main rivals Fernando Alonso and Sebastian Vettel were only stopping once. Getting the tyres switched on in the first lap was also crucial to Hamilton's success. McLaren admitted after the race that they would not have been able to one-stop with the energy they were putting into the tyres.

Ironically in the end, Alonso and Vettel threw away podium finishes with their one-stop strategies, Vettel losing valuable time in an unscheduled second stop. Instead, Romain Grosjean and Sergio Perez drove brilliantly to take second and third places. They too had one-stopped, but with better tyre wear they had better pace at the end of the race. Perez started 15th and finished third. Vettel finished fourth, ahead of Alonso, Rosberg and Webber. Seven seconds covered the top four at the end. It was a thrilling finish to a race, which had a lively first third and then a long period of inactivity.

"I want to dedicate this one to all the fans who are constantly sending messages and being supportive," said Hamilton. "I loved every single minute of it. I never had a doubt that there wasn't a possibility (of winning). I assumed the guys (Alonso and Vettel) were one-stopping as they were falling behind.

"It's been five years since I won for the first time here. But it feels just as good. This feels like one of the best races I've had for a long time."

The temperature rose steadily in the moments running up to the race and was 40 degrees when it started, the highest it had been all weekend. This got team strategists thinking about the various ways the race might unfold depending on tyre degradation with Button, Raikkonen, Perez, Hulkenberg, Maldonado and De la Rosa all going for the softs.

At the start the top five got away in grid order with Vettel leading from pole, while Rosberg attacked Webber, who held him off into the first chicane. Massa passed Rosberg at the end of lap 2 for fifth place and Di Resta took Rosberg for sixth a lap later. Massa undid all the good work by spinning and dropping down to 13th place. Vettel had a 1.4 second lead over Hamilton in the first couple of laps, keeping him clear of the DRS zone. The ease of making DRS passes might have influenced decision making on the pit wall, as a driver on worn tyres would clearly be vulnerable in the closing stages. On lap 16 Hamilton and Alonso both got within the DRS zone of Vettel, Vettel pitted for new softs and Hamilton and Alonso put the hammer down.

Hamilton pitted on the next lap, while Ferrari left Alonso out once again. Hamilton came out ahead of Vettel, despite a slow getaway from the pit box. Meanwhile, Alonso went around again, as Vettel attacked Hamilton on lap 19. Alonso had done enough in his two laps to pass both Hamilton and Vettel and he emerged from his lap 19 pit stop ahead of them. But Hamilton was in the DRS zone at the end of the lap and passed him into the final corner at the end of lap 21. Grosjean led the race at this point, having not stopped, but he pitted on lap 21, giving Hamilton back the lead.

In the second stint, Hamilton looked stronger on the soft tyres relative to his pursuers. He pulled out 2.4 seconds in three laps and by lap 26 the gap was up to 2.6 seconds. He was now where he wanted to be, out front with a clear track ahead, which as we have seen all year, is extremely important to keeping the tyres in good shape.

Raikkonen and Perez were going well on the soft tyres in fourth and fifth, only 5 seconds behind the leader. Hamilton drove away from Alonso and Vettel through the middle part of the race, the gap climbing to 3.7 seconds by lap 33.

Pirelli's Paul Hembery tweeted on lap 34 that the tyre wear was greater than in free practice, the right rear was the limitation and hence two stops were on the cards for the leaders. Raikkonen and Perez, the two cars who were one stopping, made it to lap 40 before coming in, but Rosberg was able to resist both of them and despite Raikkonen getting ahead initially, he re-passed him for seventh.

Schumacher's DRS rear wing got stuck open and he was forced to retire for the fifth time in seven races. After missing his hot qualifying lap by hundredths of a second at the end of Q3, it was another highly frustrating weekend for the German driver.

Hamilton's gap to Alonso started to come down as the Ferrari again performed better at the end of the stint. Hamilton stopped on lap 50 and it was another slow stop for McLaren, costing him at least a second. Hamilton responded by setting the fastest lap of the race to that point, keeping the gap down to below the crucial 15-second margin that Alonso would need to stop and rejoin ahead. On lap 53 Alonso had a poor lap, 1.1 seconds slower than Hamilton, which swung the balance back towards Hamilton. Vettel stayed out with Alonso.

With 15 laps to go, the thought occurred that Alonso and Vettel might be one-stopping. Hamilton had asked his team earlier in the second stint whether they were sure his rivals would be stopping again and they answered in the affirmative. But the fact was that Hamilton was a second a lap faster than Alonso and Vettel, so they missed the moment to make a second stop.

As it became clear that they would not come in again, Hamilton set off in pursuit. He caught Vettel and passed him easily on lap 63, Vettel pitted on the next lap, dropping behind Grosjean and Perez. Hamilton passed Alonso for the race lead on lap 65 on much fresher tyres and with the DRS wing making overtaking very easy.

Both Grosjean and Perez, on fresh supersofts, passed Alonso as Ferrari's strategy looked increasingly problematic. The gentle action of the Lotus and the Sauber on the tyres allowing the pair to drive smoothly and fast to take the podium at the end.

It was another disappointing race for Jenson Button, who finished 16th, a lap down on his teammate, having made three stops. He started the race in tenth place with the same tyres as Perez. With 45 points, he is now well adrift of Hamilton on 88 points.

Canadian Grand Prix
Montreal 70 laps

1. Hamilton	McLaren-Mercedes	1h32:29.586
2. Grosjean	Lotus-Renault	+2.513
3. Perez	Sauber-Ferrari	+5.260
4. Vettel	Red Bull-Renault	+7.295
5. Alonso	Ferrari	+13.411
6. Rosberg	Mercedes	+13.842
7. Webber	Red Bull-Renault	+15.085
8. Raikkonen	Lotus-Ferrari	+15.567
9. Kobayashi	Sauber-Ferrari	+24.432
10. Massa	Ferrari	+25.272
11. Di Resta	Force India-Mercedes	+37.693
12. Hulkenberg	Force India-Mercedes	+46.236
13. Maldonado	Williams-Renault	+47.052
14. Ricciardo	Toro Rosso-Ferrari	+1:04.475
15. Vergne	Toro Rosso-Ferrari	+1 lap
16. Button	McLaren-Mercedes	+1 lap
17. Senna	Williams-Renault	+1 lap
18. Kovalainen	Caterham-Renault	+1 lap
19. Petrov	Caterham-Renault	+1 lap
20. Pic	Marussia-Cosworth	+2 laps

Drivers' Championship Standings

1. Hamilton	88 pts
2. Alonso	86
3. Vettel	85
4. Webber	79
5. Rosberg	67
6. Raikkonen	55

Constructors' Championship Standings

1. Red Bull-Renault	164 pts
2. McLaren-Mercedes	133
3. Lotus-Renault	108
4. Ferrari	97
5. Mercedes	69
6. Sauber-Ferrari	58

A year ago Montreal had been the scene of a meeting between Hamilton and Red Bull Racing boss Christian Horner, which started people asking whether the 2008 champion was looking to move away from McLaren. There was no opening for him there, but it told us that he was indeed looking for a change, a fresh challenge.

In 2012 this story came to a conclusion; his five-year contract with McLaren was due to come to an end and Mercedes was the most likely place for him to find an alternative. He was after a new contract that would pay him the kind of money he had been earning from one signed before the credit crunch, while Mercedes was still a shareholder of McLaren and pouring money into the team.

Now McLaren had a different outlook: dependent on sponsorship to supplement income from prize money, with a space-age factory and a large workforce meaning massive overhead costs, they needed Hamilton to prioritise dependable performance over the lure of lucre and the challenge of making Mercedes into a championship winning team.

Speaking in October after his move to Mercedes had been announced, Hamilton said that he had felt "for a long time" that he needed a change. It seems that, for all the talk of McLaren trying until the last minute to keep him, both sides knew that divorce was on the cards.

The first signs that this was going to get difficult came after the Canadian Grand Prix in June, as Ron Dennis, who had mentored Hamilton for 14 years, effectively told Sky TV that Hamilton would have to take a pay cut.

Ron Dennis sheds light on Hamilton contract talks
11 June 2012

There has been a lot of talk in recent weeks about championship leader Lewis Hamilton's next F1 contract, with his long-term deal with McLaren due to expire at the end of this season. Hamilton is now managed by Simon Fuller's XIX entertainment group and clearly his next contract is an important one, both financially and in terms of his competitiveness.

Yesterday McLaren group chairman Ron Dennis shed some light on how they see it, in an interview on Sky, "It's a complex situation," said Dennis.

"He is on the end of a contract which was signed at a time when the economy was somewhat different. Now there has to be a balance.

"He's obviously going to look at what's available, where he could go. We're going to look at who's available. At the end of the day, hopefully the fact that he's been part of this team from the beginning of his career will play a significant role in whatever decisions both sides make. But it's a little early to be talking about it.

"He's very highly paid," Dennis added, "He's certainly paid more than I am."

Hamilton signed on to race for McLaren in 2007 and, after a stunning debut season, he inked in a longer contract to the end of 2012. The world economy was indeed in a boom at the time and McLaren also had Mercedes Benz as a partner and shareholder. Since then the global financial crisis and the departure of Mercedes as a shareholder in 2009 means that McLaren is in a different place.

Although the team is set to receive a boost to its share of income from the commercial rights of the sport, via the agreement it made with FOM in March, McLaren clearly feel that they are in a reasonable position in this contract negotiation round.

Hamilton's options are Mercedes, who must be looking carefully at him as a replacement for Michael Schumacher and, perhaps less likely, Red Bull, where his presence would electrify things on a marketing level, but would be considered by the racers in the team to be potentially destabilizing for Sebastian Vettel. However, if they feel that there is a realistic chance of losing Vettel to Ferrari in 2014, then they may move for Hamilton.

Dennis and McLaren F1 team boss Martin Whitmarsh have enormous experience of these kinds of negotiations. Anyone who went through several negotiating rounds with Ayrton Senna, in particular, will have been to hell and back in trying to get the best deal for the team.

Not surprisingly, given that much of the world, particularly Europe, was still in the teeth of a protracted recession, money was a hot topic for everyone in 2012, in a variety of ways. For Hamilton it was about ensuring that his earning potential remained high; for smaller teams it was about surviving.

But when Ferrari, F1's most-monied team, calls for urgent action to cut costs, you know it must be serious. It was revealed in the prospectus for the proposed F1 flotation that Ferrari has some extraordinary payments from the commercial rights holder – for being the longest standing team and for its championship successes of the past. It earns significantly more from F1's revenues than any of its rivals. On top of that, the sponsorship income from Banco Santander, which was renewed this year until 2017, Shell and (still) Philip Morris, meant that Ferrari had more than enough cash to compete with Red Bull Racing's big spending ways.

A deadline was approaching to agree cost cutting rules and make entries for 2013. But no agreement was in place and it looked certain that the deadline would be missed. Red Bull was the blockage in the system, unwilling to fall in with the others on restrictions to spending on the chassis side, because it did not want to lose its competitive advantage. Ferrari president Luca di Montezemolo spoke out on the subject as the deadline loomed.

Montezemolo calls for "urgent" action on F1 costs
12 June 2012

Ferrari president Luca di Montezemolo has issued a call for F1 teams, the FIA and the governing body to come together urgently to resolve the issue of costs in the sport. With Europe teetering on the verge of a major financial crisis as the euro is threatened by the Spanish debt situation, Montezemolo argues that the sport can no longer talk around the subject, but must put a plan in place.

The failure to agree an extended Resource Restriction Agreement was the reason why FOTA fell apart last Christmas when Ferrari and Red Bull withdrew taking Toro Rosso and Sauber with them. The RRA served a purpose up to a point, but was fraught with problems as the big teams all found ways around it, particularly in the last 18 months.

It has been a subject on the agenda ever since the break-up, but now with many of the teams feeling the pinch and some target companies holding back on sponsorship deals due to uncertainty over the economy, the situation is acute.

With the 30 June deadline to bring in a new FIA regulated plan in time for the 2013 season looming, the Ferrari boss says that all parties need to act now in the interests of the sport. "The world economic situation and that of Europe, in particular, is very serious and the world of Formula 1 cannot ignore that fact," he said on ferrari.com today.

"We cannot lose any more time: we need to tackle urgently and with determination the question of costs. Ferrari is in agreement with the FIA's position that drastic intervention is required.

"We are absolutely convinced that, as I have always said, the teams and the commercial rights holder must work together with the federation on this front. This is no longer the moment for getting bogged down in sterile discussions or the meanderings of engineers, usually only concerned in defending the interests of someone or other: the question has to be tackled at the highest level, without further delay."

The smaller teams argue that a cost cap is the only effective solution: teams would be given a budget limit, controlled by the FIA, but they could spend the money however they want. Drivers, marketing and engines would probably have to sit outside it.

At the same time, the subject of the cost of the 2014 engines is also on people's minds, with some factions within the sport keen to see the introduction of the new generation engines delayed. As with all new technology there is significant development cost and although the two main engine manufacturers in F1, Renault and Mercedes, want to go with the new engines, there are plenty of people, led by Bernie Ecclestone, who don't.

The fear is that the cost will be passed on to customers and that will be prohibitive for smaller teams. Mercedes' Norbert Haug admitted that there would be up-front costs for teams, "It's a bit premature to give a figure, but we should realize where we are coming from. The engines cost twice as much ten years ago as they do right now and that's due to the hard work of the manufacturers in the first place. But it's absolutely clear that if you introduce a new engine it will cost more in the beginning," he said at the weekend.

"What we should do is consider a five-year period where the target is close to current spending levels and I think that's achievable."

Watch out for quite a bit of behind the scenes action on costs in the next two weeks as that deadline approaches.

Alonso becomes first two-timer; with comeback pair on podium
24 June 2012

Fernando Alonso became the first two-time race winner in 2012 with a stunning victory in the European Grand Prix. It was a very valuable win as both his main title contenders failed to score points: Lewis Hamilton and Sebastian Vettel both fell by the wayside, giving Alonso the chance to open up a relatively big points lead. He has 111 points with Webber on 91, Hamilton on 88 and Vettel on 85.

After a dramatic final dash to the line, the two comeback kings also got great results: Kimi Raikkonen finished second ahead of Michael Schumacher. It was Schumacher's 155th podium and the first of his three-year comeback.

Starting 11th on the grid, but with the advantage of new tyres saved from missing Q3 yesterday, Alonso gained three places off the start line, fought his way through the field in the opening stint and took the opportunity offered to him by another pit stop problem for McLaren to pass Hamilton. He passed Grosjean for second place then took the lead just after halfway through the race.

The race looked to be Sebastian Vettel's for the taking, the only time he had any company all afternoon was at the start and then mid-race, when the safety car was deployed. But Vettel pulled off the track soon after the restart and into retirement.

"It's difficult to express the feeling, winning a home Grand Prix," said Alonso. "It's unique. To win here in Valencia with this special team, I'm feeling very proud to be a Spanish sportsman. It's probably my most special victory.

"Yesterday we had a tough moment, we were sad not being in Q3, but we didn't give up. Anything can happen; today we had an amazing race a good start, six or seven overtakes. We have to enjoy this."

On the grid, Schumacher, Webber, Perez and Vergne went for the medium tyres, a clear indication that they were planning a one-stop strategy. But their decision to pull out of this and switch to two stops late in the race gave Webber and Schumacher great results.

At the start, Vettel got away well, with Hamilton in second, and Grosjean squeezing past Maldonado for third. Vettel put in a very strong opening couple of laps to be well clear of the DRS zone by the end of lap 2 and after seven laps he had an eight-second lead over second-place Hamilton. Grosjean passed Hamilton on lap 11, dropping him by almost two seconds on the first lap in clean air.

Kobayashi had got himself up to fourth place, while Raikkonen passed Maldonado on the outside on lap 13 for fifth place. There were some great passes from the Lotuses and the Ferraris with Alonso, in particular, battling with Webber and Schumacher just after the first pit stop to move into fourth.

The top three cars were very spread out with Vettel over 20 seconds clear of Grosjean, who was almost 10 seconds clear of Hamilton. Approaching half distance Alonso started to reel in Hamilton.

On lap 29 the safety car was deployed for debris on the track from an incident between Vergne and Kovalainen. Grosjean, Alonso, Raikkonen and Hulkenberg pitted immediately. Hamilton had a problem with a front jack and another long stop meant that Alonso passed him, as did Raikkonen. Hamilton dropped to sixth place.

Vettel pitted a lap later and rejoined in the lead. Now all the front-runners were on the same medium tyres of the same age, which threatened to take away from the drama of the final laps.

At the restart Alonso forced his way past Grosjean into second, a move which turned out to be very important as a few moments later Vettel pulled off the track with no drive, leaving Alonso in the lead. An overheating alternator was blamed for the German's retirement.

Mark Webber climbed up to sixth place, but fell back on lap 37 as his tyres deteriorated. He made a late second stop for soft tyres and made great use of them, ending up fourth from 19th on the grid. Although he had planned a one-stop race Schumacher adopted the same tactic as the Australian giving him the chance to attack in the closing stages. On lap 41 Grosjean pulled off the racetrack into retirement, leaving Hamilton in second place and Raikkonen third with Maldonado and Hulkenberg giving chase.

Raikkonen attacked Hamilton with two laps to go and passed him for second place. Maldonado tried to follow the Finn, but Hamilton defended robustly despite rapidly fading rear tyres. Hamilton refused to allow Maldonado through and as he resisted the two of them collided, Maldonado coming back from outside, in a move most commentators saw as the Venezuelan driver's fault – putting Hamilton out of the race. The enmity between the two from last year was clear to see and won't have been improved by this incident.

Maldonado saw it as Hamilton's fault, "He tried to put me off the track," he said. "He didn't leave any room for me to stay on and do the corner side by side. I jumped over the kerb and I couldn't avoid the accident. I don't know why he drove like that. He was struggling too much with the tyres. He was completely lost and at that moment I was getting very good pace. He tried a very aggressive move on me."

This allowed Schumacher to come through to take the first podium of his comeback.

European Grand Prix
Valencia 57 laps

1. Alonso	Ferrari	1h44:16.449
2. Raikkonen	Lotus-Renault	+6.421
3. Schumacher	Mercedes	+12.639
4. Webber	Red Bull-Renault	+13.628
5. Hulkenberg	Force India-Mercedes	+19.993
6. Rosberg	Mercedes	+21.176
7. Di Resta	Force India-Mercedes	+22.886
8. Button	McLaren-Mercedes	+24.653
9. Perez	Sauber-Ferrari	+27.777
10. Maldonado	Williams-Renault	+34.630
11. Senna	Williams-Renault	+ 35.900
12. Ricciardo	Toro Rosso-Ferrari	+37.000
13. Petrov	Caterham-Renault	+1:15.871
14. Kovalainen	Caterham-Renault	+1:34.654
15. Pic	Marussia-Cosworth	+1:36.565
16. Massa	Ferrari	+1 lap
17. De la Rosa	HRT-Cosworth	+1 lap
18. Karthikeyan	HRT-Cosworth	+1 lap
19. Hamilton	McLaren-Mercedes	+2 laps

Drivers' Championship Standings

1. Alonso	111 pts
2. Webber	91
3. Hamilton	88
4. Vettel	85
5. Rosberg	75
6. Raikkonen	73

Constructors' Championship Standings

1. Red Bull-Renault	176 pts
2. McLaren-Mercedes	137
3. Lotus-Renault	126
4. Ferrari	122
5. Mercedes	92
6. Sauber-Ferrari	60

An apparently rather dull, but probably very significant event happened in June; Formula 1 got a new umbrella body to represent the interests of a key group of stakeholders – the circuits. They came together to form the Formula One Promoters Association (FOPA).

The various race venues joined forces to create a company registered in Geneva, Switzerland and chaired by Australian GP chief Ron Walker, a close ally of Bernie Ecclestone. Silverstone, the home of the British GP, is part of the new body and its chairman Neil England told the newspaper that such an organization was not only overdue, but had common interests to air going forward.

"We have historically lacked a coordinated voice and the Formula One Promoters Association gives us the opportunity to have that," he said. "There are a number of matters of common interest and I think it is important that those are voiced."

Although nothing much is expected from FOPA in the short term, while Ecclestone is running the sport, long term the move is likely to prove significant: circuit promoter fees account for 33.6 per cent of F1's total turnover of $1.22 billion, which is 1.6 per cent more than the sport gets from TV and broadcast contracts. It is also seen as one of the key areas of growth for F1 revenues in future. But many *circuits run at a loss and require heavy government backing. The signs are that FOPA will stand up to the commercial rights holder at some point in the future and with F1 so hard to stage safely, the circuits holding a whip-hand is something that the future commercial rights holder will have to be careful with.*

Meanwhile, after going quiet for several months, Gerhard Grib-kowsky, the German banker who was once chairman of F1's holding board, was convicted in Munich of corruption. He accepted money from Bernie Ecclestone relating to the sale of the sport to CVC Capital Partners in 2006. He admitted it was a bribe; Ecclestone said it was a blackmail payment. Either way, it electrified Formula 1 and got everyone wondering whether the prosecutor's office in Munich would turn its attentions to Ecclestone.

German banker in F1 corruption scandal gets eight-year jail term
27 June 2012

Gerhard Gribkowsky, the banker from BayernLB who was once chairman of the F1 holding board, has been convicted of corruption and sentenced to eight and a half years in jail. According to Reuters this evening, "Presiding judge Peter Noll convicted BayernLB's former chief risk officer Gerhard Gribkowsky of tax evasion, bribery and breach of fiduciary trust in a court in Munich.

"Noll described the billionaire [Bernie] Ecclestone as the 'driving force' behind the payments, but said Gribkowsky, in turn, had shown 'high criminal energy'."

Prosecutor Christophe Rodler had summed up his case by saying that Ecclestone was "not the victim of extortion, but the accomplice in an act of bribery."

Gribkowsky was charged with accepting $44 million in bribes, which revolved around the sale of F1 to CVC in 2005 and specifically to a payment made by Ecclestone. Prosecutors said that the payment related to the sale by BayernLB to CVC of its 48 per cent share in the F1 business in 2005, which Ecclestone wanted to happen.

Ecclestone has not been charged by the German prosecutors and has denied any wrongdoing. He has always maintained that the payment was not bribery, but instead was to stop Gribkowsky from following through on a threat to make allegations to UK tax inspectors about Ecclestone's tax affairs relating to the family trust.

It is not clear tonight where the verdict leaves Ecclestone from a legal point of view in Germany as he now waits to learn whether prosecutors will mount a case against him, but he maintains that his version of the story is the truth, "They based their decisions on what he told them. I told them the truth," Ecclestone is quoted by Reuters as saying after the Gribkowsky verdict was announced. "I think Mr Gribkowsky told them what he thought he had to tell them. I don't think I should (face further action), but you don't know, do you?"

The development comes as CVC seeks to float the F1 business on the Singapore Stock Exchange. The flotation won't go ahead this summer as intended, due to market turmoil, but it is ready to go and there are plans to try to get it away later this year.

CVC has cut its stake in F1 from over 60 per cent down to around 35 per cent with disposals recently to major blue chip investment houses in the US and Norway.

Meanwhile, the German financial newspaper *Handelsblatt* carried a story today that internal advice within Mercedes is that it should consider withdrawing its team from F1 over this bribery scandal as it runs against the company's statutes relating to involvement with corruption.

Chapter Seven
July 2012

July is always a very busy month for F1, with three Grands Prix taking place during four intense weeks. The build-up to the British Grand Prix was marred by tragedy when Marussia's test driver Maria de Villota suffered a horrific accident while straight-line aerodynamic testing at Duxford Airfield near Cambridge.

De Villota had taken up the Marussia role amidst much fanfare as women drivers in F1 are a scarce commodity. Another is Susie Stoddart, wife of Williams minority shareholder Toto Woolf, who finally got her chance to drive an F1 car at a Williams Partner Day in October.

De Villota's accident aroused a great deal of sympathy; she lost her right eye and had to have extensive facial surgery. After a lengthy recuperation she broke cover in October, telling Spanish magazine Hola! *of her experience, including how when she came around she was speaking English to her family, rather than Spanish.*

The only fortunate aspect of the episode was that Duxford's nearest hospital is Addenbrooke's in Cambridge, where the specialist surgeons in plastics and craniofacial reconstruction are acknowledged as amongst of the best in the world.

Marussia F1 driver De Villota seriously injured in aero testing accident
3 July 2012

Maria de Villota, the Marussia test driver, has been seriously injured in a straight-line aero test session at Duxford Airfield, according to local emergency services. De Villota was in the early stages of a day of driving the Marussia car for the first time in the programme when she made contact with a truck.

An exact report of what happened has not been issued yet, but it seems she was at the end of an initial run and was manoeuvring close to the team's operations tent, when she ran into the tailgate of a support truck, which struck her helmet. The resulting injuries were described by the local ambulance service as "life threatening" and she was transferred to Addenbrooke's in Cambridge, one of the UK's leading hospitals.

Around midday it was reported that she was in a stable condition with head and facial injuries. A statement from Marussia that afternoon said, "Since Maria's arrival at the hospital at approximately 10.45 this morning, she has been receiving the best medical attention possible at the hospital, which is the region's major trauma centre. Maria is conscious and medical assessments are ongoing. The team will await the outcome of these assessments before providing further comment.

"The team's first priority at this time is Maria and her family."

An earlier statement from the team had described the accident as follows, "At approximately 09.15hrs BST this morning, the Marussia F1 team's test driver Maria de Villota had an accident in the team's MR-01 race car at Duxford Airfield where she was testing the car for the first time. The accident happened at the end of her first installation run and involved an impact with the team's support truck.

"Maria has been transferred to hospital. Once her medical condition has been assessed a further statement will be issued."

Local police added that the accident was "low speed", while an East of England Ambulance service spokesman said, "A woman has sustained life threatening injuries and following treatment at the scene by paramedics, she has been taken to Addenbrooke's Hospital for further care."

The Duxford test was a significant one, to confirm the new aerodynamic package on the Marussia, as team principal John Booth explained earlier in the week, "We have a fairly significant upgrade for this race, comprising a new rear wing, exhausts, floor and side pods. I would have to describe this as our 'first proper wind-tunnel generated upgrade of the season'; this is the first fully developed package that is not just a modification of existing elements.

"That is a big result in itself, aside from the performance step we hope it will bring us, as it means we have caught up with ourselves in terms of the diligent way in which we have approached and developed our Technical Partnership.

"We look forward to seeing what this brings, both at Silverstone and at Duxford Airfield beforehand, when we will be integrating the developments into our correlation programme. Duxford is also the first of our test driver Maria de Villota's scheduled track days. She has been waiting patiently all year for this date to come around, so we look forward to seeing her in the car for the first time."

The British Grand Prix weekend was hugely memorable, but not necessarily for the right reasons. The weather was so atrocious on the Friday that the car parks flooded and Silverstone had to ask many fans to stay away on the Saturday. It was a major blow to the prestige and self-image of the Northampton circuit, which in other respects was hosting a very successful event. One of the few F1 venues which sells out for all three days of the race weekend, Silverstone surpassed itself this year with the stoicism of the fans and their passion for the sport. They came to see a British winner, but in the end witnessed a great battle between Fernando Alonso and Mark Webber.

Webber and Red Bull hunt down Alonso for brilliant Silverstone victory
8 July 2012

Mark Webber chose the perfect strategy and paced his race to perfection to catch and pass Fernando Alonso in the closing stages and clinch his second British Grand Prix victory. It was the ninth win of Webber's career and his second of 2012. Webber's Red Bull teammate Sebastian Vettel completed the podium. The result moved Webber to within 13 points of Alonso, confirming him as the Spaniard's closest championship rival. The double podium finish also extended Red Bull's advantage at the top of the constructors' championship table.

After a weekend of heavy rain, Silverstone surprisingly remained dry throughout the race, which was run entirely on slick tyres with track temperatures fluctuating between 29 and 34 degrees. A further surprise was that the hard compound tyres proved to be faster than the softs. Ultimately, it was the final stint that proved decisive as Webber, who had started the race on the softs, ended on the hards, while Alonso was the other way around.

The greater structural strength of the hard tyres was important through the lateral loads in the high-speed corners of sector 2 in particular, while drivers found that the soft tyres understeered more. Pre-race expectations that they were up to a second faster than the hards proved inaccurate.

Ferrari had started Massa on softs and had data from his runs which indicated that the softs would perform reasonably well at the end, but Webber's pace on hards was too much for Alonso, who had not been able to build enough of a lead over the Australian in the early part of the race to maintain his position at the end. Webber stayed in touch with Alonso throughout the first two stints, never allowing him to get too far ahead, and then was able to catch and pass him with one decisive move around the outside of Brooklands corner with three laps to go.

"I have a few wins now, but this one is taking a little bit to sink in," Webber said. "It didn't look like a spectacular race with Fernando initially, but it was on. There was a little bit of strategy involved, particularly pacing stints on tyres.

"I knew he was running a different way, and I thought after the first stint he was in very good shape to close the win out, but it came our way in the last stint and I am absolutely over the moon."

Alonso had controlled the race throughout as he kept a steady gap ahead of the Red Bull duo. However, the superior speed and durability of the prime tyres turned the race in Mark Webber's favour as he took the lead with just four laps remaining. Vettel came close to making it a Red Bull 1-2 after an early pit stop put the double world champion in contention for the win. He had earlier been stuck behind Michael Schumacher in a train of cars, but opted for the early stop after seeing the performance of the prime tyres. In the clear air he was able to jump from fifth to third.

Lewis Hamilton was the only other driver in the top ten to start on the prime tyres. But he was not able to exploit the advantage, also being caught in a queue of traffic behind Schumacher. When the traffic did clear during the first phase of pit stops he was 18 seconds off Alonso. He held the lead briefly, but Alonso quickly regained first place on fresher tyres. Hamilton eventually finished the race in eighth place.

Felipe Massa put in arguably his best drive of the season and his highest finishing position since Korea in 2012 to hold off a fast-charging Kimi Raikkonen and take fourth place. Massa looked racy throughout as he hassled Schumacher in the early stages, taking third place, but losing that position to Vettel after the pit stops.

Raikkonen headed home Lotus teammate Romain Grosjean as the pair gained another good haul of points for the team after swapping fastest laps in the closing stages of the Grand Prix. Grosjean, in particular, produced yet another very good performance to overcome an early front-wing change and pass Schumacher and Lewis Hamilton.

Schumacher and Hamilton had difficult races, starting from third and eighth and finishing seventh and eighth respectively, both lacking pace throughout. Bruno Senna and Jenson Button completed the top 10 of a lively race. Button made up four positions on the opening lap to make up for his poor qualifying, but did not have the pace to progress any further.

In the early stages Pastor Maldonado and Sergio Perez were in points scoring positions. But an overtaking manoeuvre around the outside by Perez quickly ruined their days as Maldonado lost control and continued his run of assisting other drivers in early retirements. Maldonado managed to finish the race, but in a lowly 16th. Perez described the Venezuelan as "stupid" and said that he and other drivers felt that he shouldn't be in F1, with such driving.

Kamui Kobayashi compounded a bad day for Sauber when he locked up on the way into the pits and struck a member of his team. Kobayashi continued to 11th place, while the mechanic went to the medical centre for attention.

The three podium finishers all got trophies, but the fans deserved a medal for putting up with difficult conditions, muddy car parks and traffic problems all weekend and were rightly rewarded with a great race.

British Grand Prix
Silverstone 52 laps

1. Webber	Red Bull-Renault	1h25:11.288
2. Alonso	Ferrari	+3.060
3. Vettel	Red Bull-Renault	+4.836
4. Massa	Ferrari	+9.519
5. Raikkonen	Lotus-Renault	+10.314
6. Grosjean	Lotus-Renault	+17.101
7. Schumacher	Mercedes	+29.153
8. Hamilton	McLaren-Mercedes	+36.463
9. Senna	Williams-Renault	+43.347
10. Button	McLaren-Mercedes	+44.444
11. Kobayashi	Sauber-Ferrari	+45.379
12. Hulkenberg	Force India-Mercedes	+47.856
13. Ricciardo	Toro Rosso-Ferrari	+51.241
14. Vergne	Toro Rosso-Ferrari	+53.300
15. Rosberg	Mercedes	+57.394
16. Maldonado	Williams-Renault	+1 lap
17. Kovalainen	Caterham-Renault	+1 lap
18. Glock	Marussia-Cosworth	+1 lap
19. Pic	Marussia-Cosworth	+1 lap
20. De la Rosa	HRT-Cosworth	+2 laps
21. Karthikeyan	HRT-Cosworth	+2 laps

Drivers' Championship Standings

1. Alonso	129 pts
2. Webber	116
3. Vettel	100
4. Hamilton	92
5. Raikkonen	83
6. Rosberg	75

Constructors' Championship Standings

1. Red Bull-Renault	216 pts
2. Ferrari	152
3. Lotus-Renault	144
4. McLaren-Mercedes	142
5. Mercedes	98
6. Sauber-Ferrari	60

Amazingly, Alonso was in control of the drivers' championship table as we approached the halfway stage in the championship, which seemed almost miraculous considering how far off the pace the team was at the start of the season. It was all about consistency at this stage: Alonso was clearly in the prime of his career, extracting the maximum from every opportunity, while Ferrari was also working well on strategy and pit stops, taking all the points available. McLaren brought updates to the German Grand Prix that would start to turn its season around, going on a winning streak, while the Red Bull hit its stride from Singapore onwards. But at this stage of the season it was all about Alonso.

Meanwhile, Toto Wolff increased his influence over the Williams F1 team by stepping up to an executive position on the board. The Austrian had been a minority shareholder of the company since 2009, and the new plan was that he would "assist" Sir Frank Williams in his role as team principal. Clearly over time he had come to gain Williams' trust and, as the company went through changes with Patrick Head retiring and anointed successor Adam Parr being moved on, the decision was that Wolff would understudy Williams, who had just turned 70.

One of his tasks over the coming years will be to find strong partners to take the team forwards. It is over-reliant on the money from Venezuelan oil company PDVSA. It had become clear on a visit the Williams team's motorhome, that Wolff was now a central figure. Together with his wife Susie, he works the room methodically and spends a lot of time with current and prospective sponsors.

Parr was the CEO of the business until his departure earlier this year. An abrasive figure, it is believed that Bernie Ecclestone was not keen to have to deal with him any longer and with Wolff expanding his influence, Williams changed course and parted company with the Cambridge graduate, who he had originally anointed as his successor.

Fernando Alonso wins German Grand Prix as Red Bull courts controversy
22 July 2012

Fernando Alonso won the German Grand Prix from pole position, his third win of the season. It was another stunning drive under intense pressure by the Spaniard, who increased his lead in the drivers' championship to 34 points. It was the 30th win of Alonso's F1 career, one less than Nigel Mansell, and his second consecutive win at Hockenheim, following on from his controversial win in 2010.

Sebastian Vettel crossed the line in second place with Jenson Button third, but afterwards Vettel was given a 20-second penalty by the stewards for passing Button by going off-track with all four wheels. This dropped him to fifth place and promoted Raikkonen to the podium.

Vettel's pass on Button recalled Alonso's move on Robert Kubica at Silverstone two years ago, where he went all four wheels off the track to pass. At that race the FIA Race Director ordered him to give the place back, which he could not do as Kubica pitted, so the stewards penalized him with a drive-through penalty instead. Button had got ahead of Vettel thanks to the fastest ever F1 pit stop – 2.31 seconds – which gave Button the chance to jump Vettel at the second stops.

Kimi Raikkonen got another good result in fourth with Kamui Kobayashi a candidate for driver of the day with a stunning drive from 12th on the grid to finish fifth for Sauber, ahead of teammate Perez.

It was a tense race, with the top three cars separated by less than 2.5 seconds after 60 laps of racing. The drama began an hour before the start: FIA technical delegate Jo Bauer had brought the Renault engines used by Red Bull to the attention of the stewards, claiming that the torque levels were not consistent with other races. The implication was that by changing the engine map, the team had been able to maximize the effect of exhaust blowing into the diffuser. The stewards issued a statement saying that, while they did not accept all of Red Bull's explanations, they would take no further action as there was no specific wording for the rules around this area and that therefore the two Red Bull cars would be allowed to start the race in their normal position. However, the wording of the statement hinted that this would be an area that would be closed in the near future.

At the start all the front-runners went with the soft tyres, with Vergne, Rosberg, Pic and Glock on mediums. Alonso got a good start to lead, while Schumacher attacked Vettel on the opening lap. Jenson Button gained a place to fifth, while Massa, Grosjean and Senna pitted at the end of the first lap after contact damage. All switched to medium tyres to gain data for their teammates and to play a long stint strategy.

Hamilton had a poor start and ran into trouble with a puncture on the left rear tyre on lap 3; there was a lot of debris in turn 1 from first corner tangles. It was a long slow lap into the pits for Hamilton. He radioed in that he felt they should retire, but they sent him back out with a new set of medium tyres, 64 seconds behind the race leader.

Vettel harried Alonso in the opening stint, within the DRS detection zone of under one second. Button passed Hulkenberg for fourth place on lap eight, closing quickly on Schumacher in third. He needed to pass him quickly to stay in touch with the leading pair. He passed him straight away using DRS on lap 11. Perez also had had a strong opening stint and was up to fifth place by lap 14 after the first cars started to make stops. This netted him eighth place after his own stop.

Some, like Webber and Hulkenberg, went with medium tyres while Schumacher and Raikkonen went with softs. Both of them passed Hulkenberg in one move on lap 16 as the Force India driver struggled on the medium tyres. Meanwhile, Rosberg and Hamilton were lapping quickly on the medium tyres, not having changed them since the start.

Alonso pitted for medium tyres on lap 18, having had data on them from Massa's first stint. Button stopped a lap later, also taking the medium tyres, as did Vettel, who not only lost time to Alonso by staying out the extra laps, but came out behind Kobayashi.

There was a superb battle between Raikkonen and Schumacher over fifth place, the Finn passed the German and then drove away from him, on the same pace as the leaders, but 12 seconds behind them as the race approached half distance.

Alonso was not as fast on the medium tyres as Vettel and Button, who closed up on him. By lap 29 Vettel was back within the DRS detection zone and Vettel closed right up as they came up to lap Hamilton. On lap 34 the leaders lapped Hamilton, but Vettel made a mistake and Hamilton repassed him, much to Vettel's disgust. This allowed Alonso to open a gap of over two seconds on Vettel and Button to close on Vettel. On fresher tyres Hamilton had the pace to unlap himself on Alonso, but sat behind him, apparently not wanting to influence the lead battle further.

Button pitted on lap 41, again choosing the medium tyres, as did Webber. Alonso came in on lap 42 with Vettel, who came out behind Button. McLaren's faster stop and Button's out-lap had made the difference. Now he set off after Alonso. But in pushing hard, he flat spotted his right front tyre on lap 44. It didn't seem to slow him down much as he stayed within a second of the Ferrari, while Vettel dropped to two seconds behind. But with four laps to go Button's tyres began to show signs of losing performance, he had been the first of the three leaders to pit for the second time.

Vettel passed him, but went off-track with all four wheels in the process, which Button complained about over the radio and the stewards did the right thing by giving Vettel a 20-second penalty.

"The rules state that you can't go off the track to gain an advantage," said Button. "The thing is, there would have been more opportunities for him before the end of the race as my rear tyres were damaged. That's because I had to push hard to try and catch Fernando, which meant I had nothing left for the end of the race. We pretty much ran out of rubber two laps before the chequer.

Vettel accepted the stewards decision, which drops him a further eight points behind Alonso in the championship, but said, "It was a difficult one, I didn't know if he was on the inside or not," said Vettel. "The last thing you want is contact. I can't see him from the side of the car so I tried to give enough room and went wide. We were all struggling with our tyres and I think that was the case for Jenson and that's why I passed him."

German Grand Prix
Hockenheim 67 laps

1. Alonso	Ferrari	1h31:05.862
2. Button	McLaren-Mercedes	+6.949
3. Raikkonen	Lotus-Renault	+16.409

4. Kobayashi	Sauber-Ferrari	+21.925
5. Vettel	Red Bull-Renault	+23.732*
6. Perez	Sauber-Ferrari	+27.896
7. Schumacher	Mercedes	+28.960
8. Webber	Red Bull-Renault	+46.900
9. Hulkenberg	Force India-Mercedes	+48.100
10. Rosberg	Mercedes	+48.800
11. Di Resta	Force India-Mercedes	+59.200
12. Ricciardo	Toro Rosso-Ferrari	+1:11.400
13. Massa	Ferrari	+1:16.800
14. Vergne	Toro Rosso-Ferrari	+1:16.900
15. Maldonado	Williams-Renault	+1 lap
16. Petrov	Caterham-Renault	+1 lap
17. Senna	Williams-Renault	+1 lap
18. Grosjean	Lotus-Renault	+1 lap
19. Kovalainen	Caterham-Renault	+2 laps
20. Pic	Marussia-Cosworth	+2 laps
21. De la Rosa	HRT-Cosworth	+3 laps
22. Glock	Marussia-Cosworth	+3 laps
23. Karthikeyan	HRT-Cosworth	+3 laps

*after 20-second penalty added

Drivers' Championship Standings

1. Alonso	154 pts
2. Webber	120
3. Vettel	118
4. Raikkonen	95
5. Hamilton	92
6. Rosberg	76

Constructors' Championship Standings

1. Red Bull-Renault	238 pts
2. Ferrari	177
3. McLaren-Mercedes	157
4. Lotus-Renault	156
5. Mercedes	105
6. Sauber-Ferrari	78

The top three cars separated by less than three seconds with a handful of laps to go; it was the ideal scenario for F1 racing and this is what happened in Germany. All three leaders had followed the same strategy of soft/medium/medium tyres, but this was a weekend that showed a lot about how far many teams have come in getting on top of the Pirelli tyres, which were described by some as a "lottery" early in the season.

The tyre selection was the same as in Melbourne and four other events this season. However, even though the racetrack and its demands on the tyres were comparable with Melbourne, some teams were still struggling to balance tyre temperatures and this is affecting their strategies and how much impression they can make on the race.

Meanwhile, both the FIA technical staff and rival teams believed that Red Bull had an unfair advantage both in traction and aerodynamics in Germany from an engine map that changed the amount of torque the engine produced at medium revs. Although FIA technical delegate Jo Bauer flagged up his findings as a contravention of the rules, the stewards let Red Bull race on in Germany. However, following meetings held during the week after the race, a clarification was made, which came into force in Budapest.

Hamilton holds off hard-charging Lotuses to claim victory in Hungary
29 July 2012

Lewis Hamilton won his second Grand Prix of the season despite a sustained challenge from the Lotus drivers Kimi Raikkonen and Romain Grosjean, who both joined him on the podium. It was his 19th career victory and one of the most important as it gets him back in the game in the championship, taking 15 points out of Alonso's lead by cutting it to 47 points. Webber remains second in the table with Vettel third after a mixed day for Red Bull with both cars forced to stop three times.

Hamilton dominated the qualifying session on Saturday and led most of the race today, but he had to soak up huge pressure from Raikkonen, in the closing stages in particular, after the Lotus team played a blinder on strategy to get the Finn into clear air in the middle stint on soft tyres, allowing him to jump Vettel and Grosjean for second place. On fresher tyres, but with an erratic KERS, he hounded Hamilton in the closing stages, but the British driver managed to hold on to his tyres without needed the extra stop taken by Button, Vettel and Webber.

It was brilliant from Raikkonen, and another great showing by Lotus with both drivers on the podium. They have been saying for some time that they just needed a strong qualifying session to get their first win as their race pace is so strong – and today they almost got it. With their second double podium of the year they are now just one point behind second-place McLaren in the constructors' championship.

Grosjean and Raikkonen both went for soft tyres in the middle stint, which was an attacking strategy, while McLaren were touch-and-go on tyre wear with Jenson Button forced to adopt plan B and stop three times. McLaren's Woking-based strategy team, under the management of sporting director Sam Michael at the track, made the call for Hamilton to stay out and try to win the race and the driver did the rest, a very impressive, measured performance by the 2008 champion.

"It's always good to come away with a win," said Hamilton. "I am 100 per cent focused and I have been on it all year. Hungary has been good to me. We always have such a great turnout here. There are a lot of Finns here and it's great to see Kimi up here. I used to play computer games with him.

"This weekend shows that the championship is still all to play for. But if we can continue with this kind of performance we can close up. We need consistency. Today I got the best start I've had all year. This is a good stepping stone for us after the tough races we've had."

The first half of the race saw Hamilton having to contain Grosjean as the Lotus driver went for a second set of option tyres following his first stop to try and snatch the lead from the Briton. However, Hamilton was able to keep him at bay on his prime tyres and maintain his lead after the second and final stops.

Jenson Button made a good start to snatch third place from Sebastian Vettel after the German was forced wide while attacking Grosjean. And he maintained the position during the middle period of the Grand Prix on the medium tyres as Vettel hassled him constantly on the soft compounds.

Later in the race both Vettel and Button had to make a third stop as their tyres could not complete the final 30 laps and they finished in fourth and sixth respectively with the two-stopping Ferrari of Alonso in fifth. Alonso had a fairly quiet race, but kept ahead of his main title contender Mark Webber to increase his championship lead and make it 23 consecutive points-scoring finishes. Webber finished in eighth, behind Bruno Senna who had another good Sunday after showing impressive pace all weekend. Felipe Massa and Nico Rosberg completed the top ten of an uneventful Grand Prix. Rosberg made a good start from 13th, but today's result is another disappointing one for Mercedes, compounded by Michael Schumacher retiring for the sixth time in eleven races.

The majority of the grid began the race on the soft tyre compound with Webber the only car in the top 20 to opt for the medium tyres. And his quest for a two-stop race was helped by a tremendous start that saw him move up to seventh from his 11th place qualifying position.

Hamilton pulled away from the line well and managed to open up a comfortable gap in the opening laps. Grosjean maintained his second place after holding off Vettel into turn 1, with Vettel losing time and dropping to fourth place behind Button.

As the cars approached their first stops, Hamilton led Grosjean by 2.5 seconds and the duo began to pull further ahead of the Button-Vettel battle. Button was the first of the leaders to pit on lap 16 for the medium tyres and crucially exited the pits just ahead of a battle between Sergio Perez and Paul di Resta. When Vettel pitted for another set of softs he returned to the track just behind Button and went about setting the fastest laps of the race to close the Briton down.

As Hamilton pitted from the lead Grosjean briefly led the GP before pitting for a set of used soft tyres. He immediately began to claw Hamilton in during the second phase of the race as he consistently set fastest laps.

As the race neared the second pit stop phase Vettel began to hassle Button for third place, becoming very aggravated in the process. When Button pitted the German was able to put in two very fast laps and take third place after being helped by Senna holding up the British driver.

Vettel now found himself on the tail of Grosjean who was held up by a longer running Alonso, but it was Raikkonen who quickly became a candidate for the race win as he managed to make his scrubbed soft tyres last much longer than anyone else and put in fastest laps which were consistently around 1.5 seconds faster than the other leading cars. He then made use of his much fresher tyres to reel in Hamilton in the final 20 laps of the race.

The Sauber pairing of Sergio Perez and Kamui Kobayashi struggled to make any ground on their poor qualifying performances, finishing 14th and 18th respectively. Williams had another mixed Sunday with Senna once again keeping his nose clean and gaining another points finish in seventh place, while Pastor Maldonado will find himself in front of the race stewards after making contact with Paul di Resta and receiving a drive-through penalty. Maldonado is still yet to score a championship point since his race win at Spain in May.

Hungarian Grand Prix
Budapest 70 laps

1. Hamilton	McLaren-Mercedes	1h41:05.503
2. Raikkonen	Lotus-Renault	+1.032
3. Grosjean	Lotus-Renault	+10.518
4. Vettel	Red Bull-Renault	+11.614
5. Alonso	Ferrari	+26.653
6. Button	McLaren-Mercedes	+30.243
7. Senna	Williams-Renault	+33.899
8. Webber	Red Bull-Renault	+34.458
9. Massa	Ferrari	+38.300
10. Rosberg	Mercedes	+51.200
11. Hulkenberg	Force India-Mercedes	+57.200
12. Di Resta	Force India-Mercedes	+1:02.800
13. Maldonado	Williams-Renault	+1:03.600
14. Perez	Sauber-Ferrari	+1:04.400
15. Ricciardo	Toro Rosso-Ferrari	+1 lap
16. Vergne	Toro Rosso-Ferrari	+1 lap
17. Kovalainen	Caterham-Renault	+1 lap
18. Kobayashi	Sauber-Ferrari	+2 laps
19. Petrov	Caterham-Renault	+2 laps
20. Pic	Marussia-Cosworth	+2 laps
21. Glock	Marussia-Cosworth	+3 laps
22. De la Rosa	HRT-Cosworth	+3 laps

Drivers' Championship Standings

1. Alonso   164 pts
2. Webber   124
3. Vettel   122
4. Hamilton   117
5. Raikkonen   116
6. Rosberg   77

Constructors' Championship Standings

1. Red Bull-Renault   246 pts
2. McLaren-Mercedes   193
3. Lotus-Renault   192
4. Ferrari   189
5. Mercedes   106
6. Sauber-Ferrari   80

Chapter Eight
August 2012

What can F1 learn from the Olympics?
13 August 2012

With the closing of the 2012 Olympics in London the "Greatest Show on Earth" has ended. It has been an amazing two weeks of sport, particularly for those of us who live in the host nation and have seen another side to our country. These were the "Happy Games"; in fact, to borrow a couple of adjectives from the British national anthem, "Happy and Glorious" would be the best way to sum up the London 2012 games.

So what can Formula 1 learn from the last two weeks? Is there anything that could be adopted to make F1 better, any methodologies that would suit our very own "world class" sporting event?

These last two weeks were all about sport, and we'll never forget that. The way these games were organized and presented had "sport" at the heart of everything. Yes, many of the competitors were professionals, earning millions back home in their professional leagues and series, but in these Olympics the cynical and the mercenary were put to one side in pursuit of pure sporting excellence.

There is a balance to be struck and London 2012 struck it perfectly; for all the spirit of "togetherness" and the heart-warming enthusiasm of the athletes, fans and volunteers, winning was still very much the driving force of competition. The coveted gold medal at the end of four years of hard training is what all the serious athletes were in London to achieve. The public naturally looks to the medals table to see who is doing the best and where their country stands.

No one is naive enough to think that the Olympic motto, "it's not the winning, it's the taking part" covers anything more than the few stories of fighting through adversity, overcoming racial or gender barriers to compete for the sake of being there. So winning is the main thing, but it's not everything.

In recent years the Olympics has shown that it is possible to compete at the highest level and engage the public in the process. London's triumph was the way the fans were drawn in, right from the start with the wacky opening ceremony, to the very end when the final medals were handed out.

People love "people stories": the triumphs and the tragedies, the comebacks, the failures, the elation and the despair. London 2012 gave fans a chance to engage, to feel part of it. Sport was both the spectacle and the end in itself – human beings pushing themselves to do amazing things in the name of competition. But as they did so they allowed thousands in the stadiums and millions around the world to share in their experience, and that is the lesson F1 can learn from the games.

Our sport is the world's largest year-round sporting event with a huge and passionate global fan base. But its popularity and accessibility is part of the problem – it is hard to engender such enthusiasm week in and week out, compared to an event that occurs only once every four years. The sport also takes fans' money without giving much back; the way F1 has gone racing in new countries without trying to build a lasting legacy shows how much there is to do in engaging with fans and building F1's following into new generations and new markets.

Of course, the sport needs to embrace emerging markets for many reasons: to offer new opportunities for manufacturers and sponsors and to "inspire a generation" of youngsters in that country to race, so one day one of them may become their country's first F1 champion. But the way we go about starting up in a new country (normally in Asia and the Middle East where they pay the highest sanctioning fees) is often too cynical – country X will pay the most so we'll race there, end of. When they run out of money, move on to the next place with deep pockets. This is spelled out very clearly in F1's flotation prospectus.

F1 can learn from the London Olympics, first by evaluating carefully what a new host country can bring to the sport besides money. Then in engaging the local people, thinking about the legacy it is building in a country, working closely with the organizers on long-term projects, focusing on building a following rather than simply pocketing the cash and moving on to the next showground.

In terms of other ideas, Bernie Ecclestone was impressed by a visit to the Beijing Games in 2008 and felt that the idea of gold, silver and bronze medals was something F1 could take from the Olympics. He was unable to garner enough support from within the sport so it has not happened and I don't think it's any more likely today. Medals work brilliantly for the Olympics, but F1 has already got a perfectly good podium ceremony, and big trophies and champagne spraying are the heart of that.

The 2012 Olympics proved that Britain can put on a world-class event with no problems – there was anxiety about whether the UK could pull it off after the bid was won and especially after organizers saw what Beijing laid on. Visitors to the events were treated to the best of British professionalism and enthusiasm. That mix is often hard to strike.

F1 is organized with great professionalism, especially when you witness the inner workings of FOM, as some of us on the inside are lucky enough to see. But the good-natured enthusiasm of the volunteers and the security staff at London 2012 was in sharp contrast to what we experience at a lot of F1 venues, like Spa, where black-shirted heavies present a cold and menacing front.

Some people have even brought up the idea of motorsport having a place in the Olympics. I don't agree with that, I don't think mechanized sports have a place in the games. Powerboating was once included, in Great Britain in 1908, but was dropped from the next event. Anyway, Formula 1 already has enough going for it. What the Olympics has shown is that F1 could do a lot of things a lot better.

One of the most interesting stories in JA *on* F1*'s new "Innovation" section, launched at the start of August in association with our partner Tata Communications, concerned the use of the technology behind the Electronic Control Unit – essentially the "brain" of an F1 car – in a children's hospital heart unit. This is a great example of what is called "Applied Technology" – using technology that has been pioneered in one sector for another purpose altogether. It was a heart-warming example of how to make Formula One relevant in the modern world.*

How the brain of an F1 car is being adapted for use in children's hospitals
20 August 2012

As a result of a chance conversation between a McLaren engineer and a paediatrician, Birmingham Children's Hospital has been trialling the ECU in an intensive care ward. The idea is that the F1-derived unit – which normally measures oil pressures, brake temperatures and the like – can also measure all the key signs from a young patient: sensing trends and detecting developing problems earlier than the electronics previously used by the NHS.

The trial utilizes a lightly adapted version of the F1 ECU to measure things like heart rate, oxygen levels and blood pressure. Inevitably, it is far more capable than the units currently used in hospitals, for example, taking a heart cardiogram 125 times a minute, instead of once an hour. This allows doctors to pick up signs of deterioration in a child's condition much earlier by detecting subtle shifts, which the current system would not register.

The ECU is the result of F1's desire to know as much as possible in real time about what is happening on the race car. There are over 120 sensors on an F1 car, recording over 500 parameters that are transmitted live via telemetry back to the pits and also to the teams' factories in the UK and Europe. The ECU, a standardized unit used by all the F1 teams, manages the data and the control systems. In the four years since McLaren Electronic Systems started as ECU supplier, no car has retired from a race due to ECU failure, which gives a level of confidence for medical staff, no doubt.

The *Mail on Sunday* spoke to Dr Heather Duncan, a consultant paediatrician at BCH, who described the trial as "a transformational breakthrough"; she is hoping to find additional funding to continue the trial and encourage other hospitals to trial the system too. "Formula 1 engineers do lots of real-time monitoring during races and look at performance and modelling to see when they should change tyres and have pit stops," she said. "They're predicting, essentially, which is something we don't do very much in healthcare.

"Although we can always see what is happening at the bedside, we can't see trends over time. This software lets us do this – and it could improve a child's chances of survival.

"At the moment it's intuitive for a racing engineer, but less so for clinicians.

For example, breathing rate kept coming up as 'revs per minute'. So there's a bit of tweaking to do."

It's easy to be cynical about stories like this, but the application of F1 technology to other areas of life is an important by-product of the drive for innovation, which makes F1 what it is. As the team bosses fight each other over how to control costs and what F1 should be all about, they could do with taking more account of stories like this one.

One of the things we like to do regularly on the JA *on* F1 *site is to write "think pieces" and to take a longer term view on all matters F1; this is partly a function of having been in the sport for a long time, but also because it's something that the readers really appreciate and it always provokes an interesting debate in the comments section. This is in many ways the lifeblood of the* JA *on* F1 *community.*

I always enjoy speaking to people who come into F1 from the business world. They bring a different perspective into what can often be quite a short-sighted environment. One such person is Lotus F1 team owner Gerard Lopez, who was one of the original investors in Skype and who has stakes in a wide variety of technology and internet businesses. He is concerned with what he sees is the short-term thinking of many of his peers at the top of F1 teams. He feels that because their focus is primarily on where the next few tenths and hundredths of a second will come from, they lose sight of where the sport is going to be five, ten and fifteen years from now.

The biggest danger to F1: short-term thinking?
23 August 2012

The summer break has dragged on, with all F1 factories shut down for two weeks since the last Grand Prix. But that does not mean that nothing has been happening. Behind the scenes F1 is moving forward on several fronts, at the same time as keeping an eye on the prosecutor's office in Munich for any signs of a follow up to the conviction of Gerhard Gribkowsky, who said he had accepted a "bribe" from F1 commercial boss Bernie Ecclestone.

The teams are closing in on a deal to secure their involvement for the medium term – the next eight years. The new Concorde Agreement is pretty much sorted out, but the outstanding issue concerns the sporting regulations and particularly cost control. And here the danger is that the teams revert to type and think short-term rather than long-term.

Before the break I interviewed Lotus F1 boss Gerard Lopez for a *Financial Times* feature. One of the subjects in our interview was cost control and it was interesting to hear his take, as a man with extensive business experience outside the sport, on the way the teams have been tying themselves up in knots over the Resource Restriction Agreement.

He made a very interesting point about how people whose sole focus is on finding fractions of a second, struggle to see long term, and I think he's right. "Some of the stuff that happens [in F1] is a bit strange," says Lopez. "But there is so much at stake in terms of performance. We are talking about tenths and hundredths of a second. So it's always edgy because the moment you give something up in a contract, you think you are losing something on the track. And the moment you lose something on the track you feel that you have the potential to lose sponsors or prize-money. So there is an economic angle to whatever decision gets taken.

"The problem is everything is so tight that negotiation becomes really tough. And that's what marks this sport. When you think in terms of tenths of a second, how does that combine with long-term thinking? Long term is years. Tenths of a second is what defines winning and losing and every contract that we discuss has some sort of impact on performance."

The FOTA split over the issue of cost control and because of the lack of trust between the teams, and this loss of perspective is at the heart of it. It's easy to see how competitive individuals find it hard to change their focus from short- to long-term. But change they must if F1 is to secure the right formula for the future. A sport with a turnover in billions should not see teams in financial trouble. The payments to the 12 teams in the current Concorde Agreement are well over $600 million, not divided equally of course, but it's still a lot of money. Teams will always call for more money, while the sport's owners will want to keep as much of it as possible. Controlling costs, like a proper business, has to be the solution, as long as it's the same for everyone.

Another problem that all the stakeholders have been wrestling with this summer is that while Ecclestone's Formula One Management business is in charge of the Concorde Agreement, which is essentially a commercial contract, the FIA is in control of the sporting regulations, of which cost control is part. Some teams argue that they need to be controlled by the same body. So who should regulate the new RRA?

The answer needs to be for the long term – like the thinking that needs to go behind it.

Hot on the heels of this discussion was another item, which was all about the future of motorsport and sustainability. During an interview we did with the FIA president Jean Todt in April 2011, he had announced that the EU had asked the FIA to come up with an electric car series, to help promote electric vehicles and to encourage the fast-tracking of new technologies to improve their range and efficiency.

In August, having been through a tender process, the FIA announced details of an exciting new series due to start in 2014, which would be based on tracks in city centres, with a young promoter who has worked in GP2. This new series is not a threat to Formula 1, nor will it have much to do with it, as the races will all be run in cities with no F1 connections like Rio de Janeiro, with Los Angeles, Vancouver and New York also expressing an interest.

FIA announces Formula E – is this the future of motorsport?
28 August 2012

The world of electric motorsport has taken a step forward after the FIA announced that it has awarded the promoter contract for the new Formula E series to a group called Formula E Holdings, involving French company Formulec, former UK science minister and champion of green racing Lord Drayson and GP2 entrant Alejandro Agag. Additional funding will come from Spanish entrepreneur Enrique Banuelos.

The series, which will feature ten teams each with two drivers, will start in 2014 with a race in Rio de Janeiro after some demonstration runs in 2013. The prototype car, produced by Formulec, will have lithium ion batteries, a maximum speed of 220kmh and will run for 25 minutes between charges. Entrants will be able to use a Formulec car, but are also allowed to design and build their own cars to FIA regulations. This leaves room for Toyota, Honda and other interested manufacturers to enter the series.

The FIA hope that the creation of this new series will establish its green credentials and take some of the heat off F1, at least for a while. One of the sport's ideological struggles of the past year or two has been the debate about how far down that road F1 should go with its new 2014 engine formula. Some parties, like Renault, are keen to really push the boundaries and move far away from the gas guzzling V8s used today. Others believe that F1 should remain all about conspicuous consumption, despite the rising costs and the obvious evidence that the world is running out of oil.

An uneasy compromise has been reached with the V6 1.6 litre turbo engines, which are already being dyno-tested by Renault, Mercedes and Ferrari. These will be 30 per cent more efficient than the current units, will have a large proportion of regenerative energy from braking and will run on electric only in the pit lane.

Talk of the new engines not sounding like proper racing engines has been a big part of the debate, with many parties once again guilty of short-term thinking. Engine sound will be one of the key things the Formula E promoters must get right from the outset, using synthesized noise.

However, the arrival of Formula E allows FIA to have something to point at to highlight its work in this area of environmental concern as it is their response to pressure from the European Commission chiefs, among others, for the governing body to do more to provide the platform for manufacturers to push innovation in technologies around electric vehicles. Racing has long been proven to be a very effective test bed for the automotive world.

The Formula E races will take place in cities that are leading the sustainable motoring agenda: to maximize the population reach and to underline those cities' desires to promote environmentally friendly motoring.

FIA president Jean Todt said, "This new competition at the heart of major cities is certain to attract a new audience. We are pleased with this agreement with Formula E Holdings as they bring a very strong experience in motorsport. This spectacular series will offer both entertainment and a new opportunity to share the FIA values and objectives of clean energy, mobility and sustainability with a wider and younger audience as well."

It will be interesting to see whether the FIA is able to persuade the promoter of F1, Bernie Ecclestone's FOM, to find a way to showcase Formula E in front of its huge global audience and help spread its influence more quickly, or whether it will have to stand on its own feet.

Will battery powered cars be the future of electric motorsport? I put that question recently to Sir David King, former chief scientific adviser to the UK government, now engaged in work on the future of mobility and transport. He pointed to an experiment in Korea, which he thinks will provide the future model for motorsport. "The weight of the batteries required to do 15 laps is too much," he said. "So I think the online vehicle technology, which is a very exciting new technology, only recently developed, is the most likely.

"In Seoul, a primary coil is installed an inch down under the tarmac of the road. In your car is a secondary coil. There's no electricity coming from the primary until your car is over it, so there's very little energy loss: 93 per cent energy transferred to the secondary coil. And the car is driven on that energy. You have a small, low weight battery in the car and that battery is always fully charged until you drive off the track. Then you use the charge left in the battery.

"I know that sounds like Scalextric. But I think the future of F1 is going to take up these amazing new technologies."

It's a fascinating theory and one we will watch out for. Meanwhile Formula E will start a process of shifting the perception of the way men (and women) race cars and we will see where it leads us.

During the long summer break the influential Italian paper Gazzetta dello Sport *published a mid-season rating for each of the F1 drivers, with Ferrari's Fernando Alonso coming out on top, just ahead of Lewis Hamilton and Kimi Raikkonen. In contrast Ferrari's other driver, Felipe Massa, was placed at the bottom of the table, with a stark assessment that he had not done enough to earn a contract renewal with the Scuderia.*

The Italian media is very fond of what its calls the "pagelle" – marks out of ten after every event. It's a well-established part of Italian sports media coverage and has been copied here and there in the UK media and elsewhere. But in Italy it carries a bit more weight. So it was well worth reporting and JA on F1 readers had a lot to say about the ratings.

Fernando Alonso, who at that stage of the season was leading the championship in a less than competitive car, came out top with a 10, having won three races in an open season. "The merit is above all the Spaniard's: he has managed to get 101 per cent out of the car, no serious mistake, no below par race," said the citation.

Hamilton was second on 8.5, the Gazzetta *noting that "if he had translated the three poles into three wins it would be a different championship."*

In contrast the Gazzetta *didn't spare Massa's blushes, "25 points against the 164 of Alonso, who has beaten him 11 times out of 11. A few signs of a revival in recent races, but it's not enough to get him re-signed [for 2013]. Perhaps it's time for a change of scene..."*

Less than three months later Ferrari announced that Massa had been handed a one-year contract extension. The little Brazilian had a rally in form in September and October at just the right moment and received a lot of support from Alonso. But after the way he had performed in 2011 and 2012 he could truly count himself fortunate. Few other teams would have renewed a driver who had performed so poorly for so long.

The full rundown of the mid-season ratings was as follows:

10:   Alonso

8.5:   Hamilton

8:   Raikkonen

7:   Webber, Vettel, Rosberg, Grosjean

6.5:   Di Resta, Maldonado

6:   Schumacher, Perez, Kobayashi, Hulkenberg, Kovalainen, Glock, De la Rosa, Pic, Petrov

5.5:   Senna

5:   Button, Vergne, Ricciardo, Karthikeyan

4.5:   Massa

My own ratings were:

9.5:	*Alonso*
8.5:	*Hamilton*
8:	*Raikkonen*
7.5:	*Vettel, Webber*
7:	*Grosjean*
6.5	*Rosberg*
6:	*Perez, Schumacher*
5.5:	*Kobayashi, Button, Di Resta, Hulkenberg,*
5:	*Maldonado, Senna, Kovalainen, Petrov, Ricciardo, Glock, Pic, De la Rosa*
4.5:	*Massa, Vergne*
4:	*Karthikeyan*

Chapter Nine
September 2012

The month started with the F1 circus reconvening after the summer break in Spa, Belgium for one of the drivers' favourite races. It also led to one of the most bizarre episodes of the season: Lewis Hamilton's Twittergate saga. McLaren dominated the weekend with Jenson Button taking pole position and the race win.

But Hamilton didn't have a great weekend, by any standards. First he went the wrong way in qualifying on aerodynamic set-up, selecting the higher downforce option and ending up well behind teammate Button, then he got into a twist with his Twitter feed, using the expression "WTF" to highlight his frustration, before swiftly deleting the tweet and rephrasing it.

On Sunday morning he went even further, committing one of the faux pas of the year by tweeting a photo of a telemetry printout showing data from his and Button's qualifying laps. "Jenson has the new rear wing on, I have the old. We voted to change, didn't work out. I lose 0.4 tenths [of a second] just on the straight" was the body of the tweet.

"I'd just like to rephrase some things I said," he later tweeted by way of explanation, but not before his words had been read from Sydenham to Sydney. The genie is always out of the bottle, however fast you try to pull it back in. Social media is a great and powerful tool through its direct contact with fans, but it can also catch you out.

Many fans think it is a very good thing that the drivers' Twitter feed sits outside of team control because it has a chance to be more honest and less corporate-spun self-expression. It is considered to be closer to the drivers' true feelings.

McLaren are one of the most advanced teams when it comes to social media and it's given them a fresher image as a result, but clearly their intervention today to tone down Hamilton's tweets was considered necessary, given the blue chip sponsors attached to the team.

Button dominates Spa as Grosjean is banned for start-line pile up
2 September 2012

Jenson Button drove a faultless race to secure his second victory of 2012 at Spa, as championship leader Fernando Alonso and Lewis Hamilton retired after a nasty first-lap pile up. The crash was triggered by Romain Grosjean, who moved over on Lewis Hamilton and was launched over Fernando Alonso and Sergio Perez, causing the retirement of all four cars. It was another in a series of first-lap incidents, which have stretched the patience of the stewards to breaking point.

They handed Grosjean a one-race ban for the Italian Grand Prix, leaving Lotus looking for a substitute driver for Monza. Pastor Maldonado was also punished for a jump-start and an avoidable collision. He will move back ten places on the grid in Monza.

It was a race full of incident and overtaking, but Button stayed clear of all of it with a lights-to-flag victory ahead of Sebastian Vettel and Kimi Raikkonen. Avoiding the carnage at La Source, Button made very good use of a one-stop strategy to put himself back in the hunt for the world championship with his 14th career win.

Alonso's first non-score of the season means that Vettel is now only 24 points off the championship leader after leapfrogging Mark Webber, who finished sixth.

Button was on good form in Spa, after a mixed season so far. He has recently found a good way to work with the Pirelli tyres, balancing the temperatures front to rear and getting the fronts to work as he wants them. If he can stay consistent on them, he can easily claw back points on the others, given the raw pace of the McLaren at the moment.

"I'm sorry to all the fans if it wasn't very exciting at the front," said Button. "However, winning a grand prix is never easy: you've always got to look after the tyres and keep an eye on the gap behind. Today's race was particularly tricky to read, in fact, because lots of cars were on different strategies so you never knew exactly where you stood ... Turn 1 looked pretty crazy – in my mirrors, I could see cars all over the place. For me, it was all pretty straightforward though.

"It was unusual to be able to run a one-stop strategy. We got to lap 12 and the team asked me how the car was feeling; I told them that the balance was getting better and better, so we were able to get to lap 20 before pitting."

As predicted, strategy was the crucial factor in this race with both Button and Vettel opting for a one-stop race. They were able to make their option tyres last near half-distance and then pull away from the field on the hard compounds. It quickly became apparent that the prime tyres were the right choice on Sunday as Nico Hulkenberg, who started on them, found himself in third place following the first-lap carnage. After overtaking Raikkonen for second many of the cars behind were prompted to make an early stop and switch to primes. This opened the door for Vettel to gain some clear air and put himself in a position for a podium. He, arguably, produced his best drive of 2012 as he put to bed any claims that he cannot race through the pack by making numerous passes around the outside of the Bus Stop chicane.

Raikkonen was unlucky to be held up following both his pit stops and made a tremendous move past one-stopping Schumacher on the entrance to Eau Rouge. He had spent six laps tucked up behind the German driver as he could not match the Mercedes engine, and losing some of his KERS functionality early on did not make this any easier. Schumacher eventually had to switch to plan B and make a second stop in the closing laps. Raikkonen was followed home by Hulkenberg, who managed to match the leaders' pace throughout the race to keep Massa and Webber behind him in the closing stages. The sole Ferrari of Massa had a strong race in fifth and kept the team within touching distance of Lotus in the constructors' championship.

Schumacher was able to salvage seventh following his unplanned second stop, but it could have been much more in his 300th GP after he had sat in third position before the first round of stops. Mercedes' tyre woes continued and Nico Rosberg also had to make an unscheduled pit stop to make it to the end.

The two Toro Rosso cars of Jean-Eric Vergne and Daniel Ricciardo headed Paul di Resta home to complete the top ten. The trio had made good progress in the first lap, but slowly slipped down the order as faster cars made their way through the field, Di Resta battling with a KERS problem.

Belgian Grand Prix
Spa Francorchamps 44 laps

1. Button	McLaren-Mercedes	1h29:08.530
2. Vettel	Red Bull-Renault	+13.624
3. Raikkonen	Lotus-Renault	+25.334
4. Hulkenberg	Force India-Mercedes	+27.843
5. Massa	Ferrari	+29.845
6. Webber	Red Bull-Renault	+31.244
7. Schumacher	Mercedes	+53.374
8. Vergne	Toro Rosso-Ferrari	+58.865
9. Ricciardo	Toro Rosso-Ferrari	+1:02.982
10. Di Resta	Force India-Mercedes	+1:03.783
11. Rosberg	Mercedes	+1:05.111
12. Senna	Williams-Renault	+1:11.529
13. Kobayashi	Sauber-Ferrari	+1:56.119
14. Petrov	Caterham-Renault	+1 lap
15. Glock	Marussia-Cosworth	+1 lap
16. Pic	Marussia-Cosworth	+1 lap
17. Kovalainen	Caterham-Renault	+1 lap
18. De la Rosa	HRT-Cosworth	+1 lap

Drivers' Championship Standings

1. Alonso	164 pts
2. Vettel	140
3. Webber	132
4. Raikkonen	131
5. Hamilton	117
6. Button	101

Constructors' Championship Standings

1. Red Bull-Renault	272 pts
2. McLaren-Mercedes	218
3. Lotus-Renault	207
4. Ferrari	199
5. Mercedes	112
6. Sauber-Ferrari	80

It was interesting to speak to a few of the drivers privately after the race in Belgium and to hear that some of them welcomed the stewards' tough stance on Romain Grosjean, banning him from the next race in Monza. One or two said that the ban should have been longer. Clearly there is a problem this season with two drivers in particular: Grosjean and Pastor Maldonado. Their peers are upset with their repeated incidents involving other drivers and don't feel safe racing against them.

Grosjean has been involved in incidents at the start in Australia, Malaysia and Monaco among seven incidents in total and, like Maldonado, has clearly been punished by the stewards this weekend as a way of making them take a long hard look at themselves.

A racer's instinct is one thing, but it's costing their teams valuable points and in Spa it directly affected the drivers' championship as it took out the points leader, Fernando Alonso. Maldonado was handed a five-place grid penalty at the next race in Monza for jumping the start and another five-place penalty for causing an accident with Glock at the restart. This was on top of a three-place grid penalty yesterday for blocking Hulkenberg.

Some suggested that he and Grosjean might soon receive loyalty cards from the stewards!

Alonso escape shows urgent need for driver cockpit protection
3 September 2012

Sometimes the goal of an innovation in F1 is not in pursuit of better performance, but rather of safety. There have been plenty of examples of this and now the F1 teams and the FIA are working closely together to come up with a solution to the problem of driver vulnerability in the cockpit.

F1 has been lucky in recent years to avoid injury as a result of several accidents that could have harmed or killed the driver due to his exposure in an open cockpit. We had another on Sunday. Fernando Alonso's point of view as Romain Grosjean's car smashed across the top of his chassis in a violent accident at the start of the Belgian Grand Prix, with the car passing less than a metre from his head, makes for terrifying viewing and has redoubled efforts to find a solution that could be engineered into the new generation F1 cars in 2014 without unbalancing the design.

Alonso was relieved to escape without serious injury, as he turned his car to the right to take the corner and Grosjean's car hit him amidships, "I'm lucky that I can be in the car in five days at Monza because, looking at the image, we were turning in so you could have a problem with your hands or even your head because the car was so close," he said. "I think we broke everything on top of the car. It was lucky in that aspect."

Work on driver protection began in earnest after the incidents in 2009 where Felipe Massa in F1 and Henry Surtees in F2 were struck by objects, fatally in Surtees' case. The breakthrough, when it comes, will be adopted across other single-seater categories, like the HANS device (which protects a driver's neck in the event of head-on impact). On Saturday there was a nasty accident in the GP3 race in Belgium, when Robert Cregan, son of Abu Dhabi circuit boss Richard Cregan, was struck on the helmet by his left rear wheel after a heavy impact with a barrier. He has since been released from hospital.

The FIA and the F1 Technical Working Group of engineers have been looking at two main options: canopies made of polycarbonate, similar to those used on F-16 fighter jets, and more recently a forward roll structure, which is now the main avenue being pursued.

The main problems with canopies are around visibility (they get dirty), what happens if they jam and weight distribution (they add a lot of weight high up on the car, where a low centre of gravity is desirable). Canopies were extensively tested by the FIA Institute last year, "The aim was simple: to fire a Formula One wheel and tyre, together weighing 20kg, at 140mph into, first, a polycarbonate windshield and, second, a jet fighter canopy made from aerospace-spec polycarbonate, and measure what happens (all close-up observations being recorded by strategically positioned high-speed film cameras)," said the institute's Andy Mellor.

The roll structure, like the canopy, has recently been tested with loads being fired at it to simulate an impact. The main challenge for the innovators of F1 will be to produce a structure which sits forward of the driver to protect him, but which also allows him unrestricted visibility

1

2 3

1 › Sebastian Vettel fought Fernando Alonso for the right to become a three-times world champion. But the rumours continued that they would become Ferrari teammates one day.

2 › Romain Grosjean was in the headlines for the wrong reasons in 2012, causing a series of start-line accidents of which the most spectacular was this one at Spa.

3 › The stewards gave Grosjean a one-race ban hoping he would learn from his mistakes, his fellow drivers agreed with the tough punishment.

4   5

6   7

8

4 › Lewis Hamilton and Jenson Button had been the world champion dream team at McLaren since 2010, but the relationship soured. Button wasn't happy that Hamilton tweeted confidential data.

5 › Lewis Hamilton's move to Mercedes was the story of the year. After six seasons with McLaren he wanted a fresh challenge and his manager Simon Fuller saw the opportunity at Mercedes.

6 › Sergio Perez was the main beneficiary of Hamilton's defection from McLaren. The 22-year-old Mexican caught the eye with a string of podiums in the Sauber and now has a great chance to shine with McLaren.

7 › SKY TV really made their presence felt in their first year as the UK's main broadcaster of live F1 coverage. At some races they had over 60 people on the ground. But they were beaten to the biggest story of the year – Hamilton's Mercedes move – by the BBC.

8 › Fernando Alonso had arguably his best year in F1, leading the points standings for much of the season and challenging for the championship despite the Ferrari not being on the same pace as the Red Bull or the McLaren.

9   12

10   11

9 › Mark Webber had a stronger season in 2012 than 2011, winning again in Monaco and Silverstone and he had the luxury of turning down a Ferrari drive for 2013.

10 › Red Bull started the season on the back foot after a major rule change took a lot of the downforce away from its car, but the team bounced back strongly in the second half of the season.

11 › Sebastian Vettel had some setbacks, including retirement from the lead in Valencia, but he was untouchable in the closing stages of the season.

12 › Sebastian Vettel has achieved much in his first 100 Grands Prix at the age of 25.

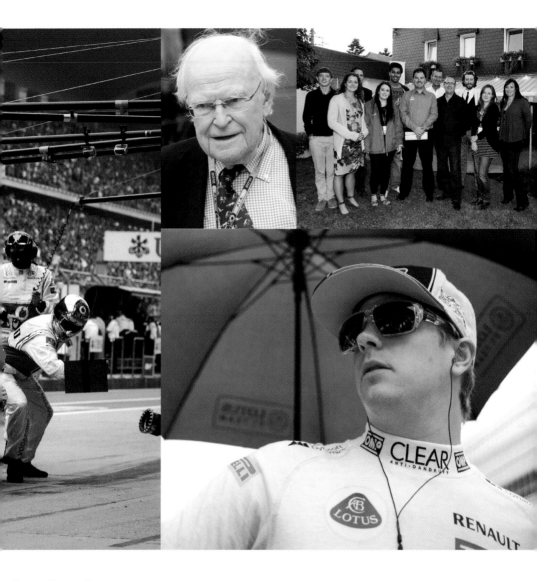

13   14   15

16

13 › Pit stops have become a mini-Grand Prix in themselves, between mechanics. In Germany McLaren did a stop in under 2.5 seconds.

14 › F1 lost one of its most celebrated figures with the death of FIA Medical Delegate Professor Sid Watkins, who did more than anyone to improve safety in F1.

15 › JA on F1 had its strongest year, increasing its audience, adding a new Innovation section, supported by Tata Communications and organising the "Ultimate F1 Road Trip" to the Belgian GP at Spa in conjunction with Shell.

16 › Kimi Raikkonen made an impressive return to F1 after two years in rallying. The Finn was ultra consistent and despite the lack of outright qualifying pace from the Lotus, he was in contention for the drivers' championship.

17

18   19   20

17 › Felipe Massa had another very disappointing season until the weeks leading up to contract renewal time, when he rediscovered his form and managed to get another contract for 2013. It will be his eighth season with the Scuderia.

18 › Bernie Ecclestone had another busy year, sorting out commercial deals with the F1 teams for the next eight years, corralling everyone towards a new Concorde Agreement and facing a judicial threat from Germany over the Gribkowsky affair.

19 › Michael Schumacher was pushed into retirement by Mercedes signing Lewis Hamilton. The 43-year-old seven-times world champion had few highlights in his three-year comeback, but he said he had "learned how to lose".

20 › Jean Todt was under pressure to exert his authority as President of the FIA as the F1 teams looked to him to help resolve their cost control wranglings. He wanted more money for the FIA.

One of the leading figures in the F1 Technical Working Group is McLaren's Paddy Lowe, "Obviously, a driver ideally wants nothing in the way, but in the same way we drive a road car with pillars, you just get used to it, don't you?" he said, after the Belgian Grand Prix weekend. "We started the project a year ago. Personally, I think it's inevitable that something will happen because it is the one big exposure we've got. How many times have you looked at things including today and thought ... that was lucky? One day it won't be lucky and we'll all be sitting there going: 'We should have done something about that.'"

The subject comes up fairly regular in drivers' meetings and they seem to be reconciled with the fact that some kind of protection will be adopted soon.

Hamilton strolls in Monza Park as Alonso and Vettel clash
9 September 2012

Lewis Hamilton was never threatened as he dominated a dramatic Italian GP in Monza ahead of inspired displays from Sergio Perez and Fernando Alonso. It was Hamilton's third win of the season and the 20th of his career as well as one of the most dominant. Once he'd got clear at the start, he was able to control the race on a one-stop strategy.

"I was cruising," admitted Hamilton. "The last 20 laps I had a 14-second gap. At the time Felipe was behind and even though I was cruising, he was going slower than me and then I heard that Fernando had overtook [sic], so then I pulled out a little bit more time and matched his time just to keep it relaxed, and then Sergio started catching me at a second a lap. So probably the last four laps I started to push a little bit more, just to maintain a little bit more of the gap."

Perez fought his way through from 12th on the grid to second, while Alonso started tenth and ended up third. He survived a scare when Sebastian Vettel put him on the grass at over 186mph as they battled midway through the race. Vettel was given a drive-through penalty, but the Spaniard is likely to continue the discussion with his fellow champion over the incident behind closed doors.

There was quite a bit of unreliability: Vettel suffered a repeat of the alternator failure that forced him to retire in Valencia and hit him again in practice in Monza. Jenson Button had a fuel pick-up problem, which robbed him of second place.

It was a great day for Alonso as he put himself back in the driving seat of the world championship, 37 points clear as the season heads out of Europe. It was a good day too for McLaren as Hamilton moved into second place in the drivers' championship and the team closed the gap from Red Bull to just 29 points in the constructors' championship. This is McLaren's first hat-trick of victories since 2008 and they will continue to be the team to beat for the remainder of the season. However, if Alonso continues to move through the field as he did today it will take another streak of victories from Hamilton to overhaul him in the face of the Spaniard's consistency. In contrast, neither of the Red Bulls made it to the finish, Mark Webber pulling out two laps from the end after losing rear grip and suffering a wild slide.

But is there a sting in the tail for McLaren? The victory for Hamilton in Ferrari's backyard comes amid increasingly strong rumours that the Briton is heading for Mercedes next season, leaving behind the team that brought him to F1 and took him to the 2008 title.

The leading cars were able to complete the race with just one stop without any of the predicted problems. Perez used the Sauber's kindness of a set of hard prime tyres in a 30-lap opening phase and did the remaining 23 laps on the option tyres, moving through the field in the process and closing on Hamilton in the final few laps.

With Hamilton out of sight for much of the race there were several good battles behind him, with Alonso making his way past four cars on the opening lap. He then hunted down Vettel and Massa and looked set for a second-place finish. When Massa let the championship leader through with ten laps remaining, his first podium since 2010 began to slip away. Massa had a very good getaway from the start line and went into the first turn alongside Hamilton, but had to slot in to second. He held this position for the first phase of the race in his strongest showing of the season, but a superb drive by next year's potential Ferrari driver Perez got the better of him before the finish.

Behind them, Kimi Raikkonen and the Mercedes duo had a fairly uneventful race as Mercedes made two stops and could not match the pace of those ahead. It had always been the plan for Mercedes to make an extra stop with their cars being harder on the tyres than the three leading teams.

Raikkonen stopped once on lap 17 and did 36 laps on a set of hard tyres; he was catching Massa at the end and finished just one second behind him. Another lap and he would have taken fourth. He now lies third in the championship on 141 points, one less than Hamilton – quite an astonishing comeback after two years in rallying.

Towards the end it looked very much like a one-two result for McLaren as Jenson Button also drove a very strong race. But it was not to be, as he pulled over and out of the race with a fuel pick-up issue in the closing stages. Second place for the Briton would have put McLaren just 11 points behind Red Bull.

One final point about the three drivers who stood on the podium today – they were the three "victims" of Romain Grosjean's start-line pile-up last weekend in Spa. Funny how things turn around!

Italian Grand Prix
Monza 53 laps

1. Hamilton	McLaren-Mercedes	1h19:41.221
2. Perez	Sauber-Ferrari	+4.356
3. Alonso	Ferrari	+20.594
4. Massa	Ferrari	+29.667
5. Raikkonen	Lotus-Renault	+30.881
6. Schumacher	Mercedes	+31.259
7. Rosberg	Mercedes	+33.550
8. Di Resta	Force India-Mercedes	+41.057
9. Kobayashi	Sauber-Ferrari	+43.898
10. Senna	Williams-Renault	+48.144
11. Maldonado	Williams-Renault	+48.682
12. Ricciardo	Toro Rosso-Ferrari	+50.316
13. D'Ambrosio	Lotus-Renault	+1:15.861
14. Kovalainen	Caterham-Renault	+1 lap
15. Petrov	Caterham-Renault	+1 lap
16. Pic	Marussia-Cosworth	+1 lap
17. Glock	Marussia-Cosworth	+1 lap
18. De la Rosa	HRT-Cosworth	+1 lap
19. Karthikeyan	HRT-Cosworth	+1 lap
20. Webber	Red Bull-Renault	+2 laps

| 21. Hulkenberg | Force India-Mercedes | +3 laps |
| 22. Vettel | Red Bull-Renault | +6 laps |

Drivers' Championship Standings

1. Alonso	179 pts
2. Hamilton	142
3. Raikkonen	141
4. Vettel	140
5. Webber	132
6. Button	101

Constructors' Championship Standings

1. Red Bull-Renault	272 pts
2. McLaren-Mercedes	243
3. Ferrari	226
4. Lotus-Renault	217
5. Mercedes	126
6. Sauber-Ferrari	100

The Monza weekend had been dominated by the story, broken by the BBC's Eddie Jordan a few days before, that Lewis Hamilton was close to agreeing terms to race for Mercedes in 2013. McLaren said that this was news to them and that they had "no plan B" in place. Hamilton said only that he was in advanced negotiations with McLaren.

On race day in Monza, I got a strong indication from a reliable source that the move was on and that some kind of agreement had been reached, pending Mercedes' sign-off on a new eight-year commitment to F1, paving the way for them to accept the commercial offer from Bernie Ecclestone and sign the 2013 Concorde Agreement.

Hamilton set to move to Mercedes
11 September 2012

Lewis Hamilton's demeanour and that of his team after victory in the Italian Grand Prix bore all the hallmarks of a divorce that has already been agreed.

Minimal celebrations on the pit wall and beneath the podium, a team photo for appearances' sake with an implacable looking Hamilton and Ron Dennis declining to join in.

Despite appearances, team boss Martin Whitmarsh said after the race that suggestions of a deal already done were "fantasy" and insisted that the door was still open if Hamilton wants to stay. However, driver contracts often get signed during race weekends and there were strong indications that the situation may have been closed out before everyone left Monza.

Hamilton looks like he is moving on, perhaps the only way he can become his own man, certainly the only way he and XIX Entertainment can fully cash-in on his status, box office power and image rights. And that is a big part of what this is about. Mercedes is one of the world's most powerful brands, while McLaren makes F1 cars and small volume sports cars. This deal will take Hamilton's name and image well beyond the boundaries of F1. If Hamilton did not want this, why would he have signed up with XIX?

Also McLaren drivers have to work within strict guidelines with team sponsors. Mercedes need Hamilton, and this deal will give him greater freedom. The suggested deal with Mercedes and its sponsors is very big and will have a significant impact, both on the competition in F1 over the next three years and the driver market in the nearer term.

Mercedes had to do this: as one of only two "works" teams in F1 they had to get a champion on board, especially with Michael Schumacher winding down towards retirement again. There is risk if they don't go on to win; but it's a risk worth taking.

Ron Dennis's fellow McLaren shareholders were all in Monza this weekend, from Friday onwards: Bahrain's Sheikh Salman and long-time shareholder Mansour Ojjeh could be observed in discussions with Whitmarsh over the next steps in a painful negotiation with a driver whom the team has nurtured since childhood.

Eddie Jordan, apparently prompted by both XIX and Bernie Ecclestone, lobbed the grenade in on Wednesday, saying that Hamilton was on the point of signing for Mercedes. It was a final call to McLaren to improve the deal on offer or lose their man.

There were some signs from McLaren of a reluctance to meet the financial terms, but also a weariness with the whole pantomime of "Life with

Lewis". The tweeting of the set-up sheet in Spa was a symbolic watershed in a relationship that has veered off-track since the wide-eyed enthusiasm of 2007.

The biggest problem for McLaren is how to replace Hamilton without losing significant performance. He's worth £25 million a year because he's one of the fastest drivers in the world and whoever sits in the car next year is unlikely to be able to match that speed. Whitmarsh said yesterday that he does not have a plan B.

Paul di Resta senses an opportunity, but will he be able to match the numbers on the stopwatch that Hamilton does? And will McLaren want both their drivers to be managed by the same person? Di Resta confirmed his deal with Jenson Button's manager Richard Goddard this weekend, replacing Lewis' father Anthony, who is suing Di Resta for wrongful dismissal and loss of earnings.

F1 is an incestuous world, with such complex intertwined relationships, but there is great goodwill between Goddard and Whitmarsh. Goddard looked very pleased all weekend in sharp contrast to the careworn faces of the McLaren management.

Kimi Raikkonen is the only driver who could get close to Hamilton's performance – he is only a single point behind him in the championship – but he seems happy at Lotus and he wasn't terribly happy last time he drove for McLaren. His qualifying pace has yet to be rediscovered, but he's racing very strongly. He would work well with Button and form a strong team, but he's come back to F1 to enjoy himself and the sponsor commitments would be a huge sticking point. Button would refuse to do more than his fair share for Vodafone, Mobil and the rest to compensate.

Speaking of Vodafone, there have been suggestions that discussions are taking place with Sergio Perez: Vodafone has been looking for years into expanding its reach in Latin America, and particularly Brazil, via Perez's backers Telmex and America Movil. So this could provide a strong business case for a move. However, Perez is a Ferrari Academy driver and that might be a significant hurdle.

There have also been suggestions of a trade with Mercedes on Nico Rosberg, with Michael Schumacher staying on to partner Hamilton. But one senses that Mercedes were only waiting to see if they could get Hamilton signed before making their next move, and now may start gently leaning on the seven times champion to ease him into retirement.

Hamilton at Mercedes, if and when confirmed, is good news for Bernie Ecclestone, as it keeps Mercedes involved and committed, despite strained relations between the two parties recently over Mercedes' share of the sport's revenues in comparison with Ferrari, Red Bull and McLaren. It could be Mercedes' turn to do some winning in F1.

Ecclestone has got what he wants, but is known to be suspicious of Simon Fuller and XIX Entertainment. Such a group having so much power and control over one of his biggest stars is a situation he will be monitoring carefully.

This looks like the final push for Mercedes – Ross Brawn knows what it takes to win and has followed the tried and tested formula: he has built up his technical team, they have their own engine facilities and a clear plan – now it looks like they have the driver. All the pieces are in place and Mercedes must deliver the title in the next three years. Fail with this group and there would be pressure from Daimler shareholders to call time on the F1 adventure.

The deal that took Hamilton to Mercedes was announced two weeks later.

Not long after Monza, F1 lost one of its most celebrated figures, Professor Sid Watkins, who had done as much as anyone to make F1 safer and to ensure that fatalities were a thing of the past. All of F1 was united in its grief about the Prof's passing: a Book of Remembrance was open in the paddock at the Singapore Grand Prix and most of the drivers, team principals and other insiders who had known him over the years, wrote their messages. Even though he started in F1 after the Prof had retired, Sebastian Vettel dedicated his win in Singapore to the Prof, a very nice touch from a classy sportsman.

The great Prof Watkins passes away
12 September 2012

One of F1's greatest figures has died this evening; Prof Sid Watkins, who was 84, passed away in a London hospital. The neurosurgeon from Liverpool, who was brought into F1 by Bernie Ecclestone to improve safety and medical standards, did more than anyone else in that field, getting F1 to the stage it is today: a high-octane adrenalin sport in which dangerous accidents are survivable.

The FIA medical delegate for 26 years, Prof Watkins introduced correct techniques for getting drivers out of cars after accidents, led moves to improve crash structures and other safety measures and saved the lives of many well-known F1 names. He attended serious accidents for Gerhard Berger, Martin Donnelly, Nigel Mansell and Mika Hakkinen among others as well as the fatal accidents of Gilles Villeneuve and Ayrton Senna, who was a close personal friend.

The Prof features prominently in the documentary film *Senna*, released in 2011. He appeared late last year along with the film-makers on the panel that met with BAFTA voters and had a major hand in the film winning the 2011 BAFTA for best documentary.

But he also saved less well-known people. In the early 1990s, I was on a long-haul flight back from a Grand Prix when a man unconnected with racing collapsed on the downstairs deck of a BA 747. A group of us went in search of the Prof, finding him asleep upstairs on the business-class deck. Sid woke up immediately, came downstairs and performed a tracheotomy on the man, saving his life.

He began work in F1 in 1978. One of the first tragedies he encountered was the death of Ronnie Peterson after a crash at Monza – an incident that inspired him to push for better medical facilities. By the 2000s the Prof's influence was clear for all to see and the following decade was the first in which not a single F1 driver died. Watkins went on to found the Brain and Spine Foundation and was the first president of the FIA Foundation, which is dedicated to research in motorsport safety.

Since news of his death broke, tributes from the F1 community have poured in for the Prof with McLaren chairman Ron Dennis saying: "Today the world of motor racing lost one of its true greats: Professor Sid Watkins.

"No, he wasn't a driver; no, he wasn't an engineer; no, he wasn't a designer. He was a doctor, and it's probably fair to say that he did more than anyone, over many years, to make Formula 1 as safe as it is today.

"As such, many drivers and ex-drivers owe their lives to his careful and expert work, which resulted in the massive advances in safety levels that today's drivers possibly take for granted.

"But, more than that, Sid was a dear friend of mine, and I'll miss him bitterly. To his widow Susan, and to his family, I extend my sincerest condolences. He was a truly great man, and the world of motor racing simply won't be the same without him."

Jenson Button tweeted: "Rest in Peace Sid Watkins … Motorsport wouldn't be what it is today without u. Thank you for all you've done, we as drivers are so grateful." Rubens Barrichello's tweet said: "It was Sid Watkins that saved my life in Imola 94. great guy to be with, always happy … tks for everything u have done for us drivers. RIP."

Martin Brundle also paid his own personal tribute: "Motorsport has lost a true visionary + character with death of Prof Sid Watkins, 84. Great man; funny too. Saved my left foot being amputated."

The FIA has also issued an official statement with its president Jean Todt hailing the legacy Watkins leaves behind. "This is a truly sad day for the FIA family and the entire motorsport community. Sid was loved and respected in equal measure by all those who knew and worked with him. We will always be grateful for the safety legacy that he has left our sport."

Gérard Saillant, FIA Institute President, added: "Sid was a true gentleman of our sport and always a pleasure to work with. He will be sorely missed by everyone who knew him, from doctors and drivers to officials and fans. Sid's influence will live on for many years to come."

Anyone wishing to learn more about the life of the Prof should read his memoirs: *Life at the Limit: Triumph and Tragedy in Formula One.*

In the build-up to the Singapore Grand Prix Sauber's Sergio Perez spoke this evening about his desire to get into a top team, claiming that he is "ready" to fight for wins and championships. At the same time he said that he had not had any approaches from top teams, despite speculation that McLaren are interested in him as a possible partner for Jenson Button. "It's only my second year in Formula One, but I feel ready to do a good job with a top team, to fight for the championship. In that respect I feel ready," said the 22-year-old Mexican, who is the third youngest driver in F1 after Jean-Eric Vergne and Charles Pic.

Perez has scored three podiums this season and all have attracted praise from engineers of rival teams, particularly the performance in Monza two weeks ago, where he finished second on a reverse strategy compared to his rivals. "In the position that I'm in, when I have a good result – because I'm fighting for the points and sometimes I can get some good podiums – it's always the time when the rumours start," Perez added.

"But then you have a bad race and there are no more rumours and they are changing to the driver who had a good race. So in that respect I'm not really worried; I know that I have a very strong car for the next seven races so I hope I can deliver very strong performances."

When asked directly, "Have any approaches had been made [from major teams]?" Perez said, "No".

A week later, after he was announced as the new McLaren driver, he admitted that he had felt he had to put the media off the scent as it was such an important moment in his career.

Hamilton's loss is Vettel's gain in Singapore
23 September 2012

Sebastian Vettel took his second win in Singapore and the second of this 2012 campaign after pole sitter Lewis Hamilton dropped out at one-third distance with a gearbox failure. The Red Bull driver had jumped Pastor Maldonado at the start and was too fast for Jenson Button in the second McLaren. When Hamilton pulled off the road on lap 23, the way was clear for Vettel to control the race and, despite two safety car periods to allow for accident damage to be cleared away, he steered the Red Bull home for the 23rd win of his career. Button finished second with championship leader Fernando Alonso third.

Paul di Resta was a candidate for driver of the day with fourth place in the Force India, just 3.8 seconds behind Alonso at the finish, which came after two hours, rather than 61 laps, due to the delays under the safety cars.

Of the main title contenders, only Vettel gained ground on Alonso, closing the gap to 29 points, while Hamilton fell behind Kimi Raikkonen and now sits 52 points (more than two race wins) adrift of Alonso with six races to go. If Alonso averages third placed finishes in all the remaining races, Hamilton will need to win them all to beat him.

Coming after Button's retirement in Monza, two technical failures in two races is a worrying picture for McLaren. Hamilton had commanded the race from the start and looked trouble free during the first stint. However, his gearbox started to misbehave as he crossed the line at the end of lap 22 and when exiting turn 3 he found himself with a box of neutrals and was forced to retire.

Vettel's win, his first since Bahrain, plus a tenth-place finish for Mark Webber means that Red Bull have extended their lead in the constructors' championship to 37 points over McLaren. "It's great to get the win today," Vettel said on the podium. "I'd like to dedicate it to Professor Sid Watkins. It's thanks to all the work he did to bring safety advancements to the sport that we can race on circuits like this. Looking to the race, Lewis had to retire which is a shame for him. I know how it feels and have been in that position before. I think we could have had a tight battle. I felt very good on the harder tyres and we had a lot of pace."

Following Hamilton's retirement, Vettel took control of the race and was only under pressure during the two safety car periods, which caused the race to be cut by two laps at the end. The first safety car was caused by a collision with the barriers for Narain Karthikeyan, while the second involved Michael Schumacher missing his braking point and driving over the back of an unfortunate Jean-Eric Vergne. The stewards decided to penalize Schumacher with a ten-place grid penalty at the next race in Japan. They pointed out that Schumacher accepted blame and that this was a second offence (he also hit Senna in Spain in a similar way this year), which counted against him.

Prior to the race there had been a lot of debate about whether to make two or three stops, but the safety car periods enabled a two-stop strategy and a sprint finish. In this phase Vettel showed the pace he had in practice and pulled a nine-second lead by the finish.

Button pressured Vettel throughout, only looking to secure his second-place finish in the closing laps. The two came very close at one point under the safety car as Button tried to heat his tyres while Vettel did the same to his brakes. Button later complained to his team, saying that Vettel was too "stop-start" under the safety car, but he declined to pick up the thread when the pair were interviewed on the podium after the race and the incident was not investigated.

Button was also able to make his first stint last four laps longer than Vettel, and had there been no safety car he would have had fresher tyres at the end of the second and final stints to pressure Vettel for the win. That was the plan, however, it's debatable whether he would have had the pace.

Alonso drove a typically astute race, on a weekend when the Ferrari was not competitive, to claim his 81st career podium. He kept his nose clean behind a sometimes-erratic Maldonado, who lost places at the start. The Ferrari did not have the pace to significantly trouble Red Bull or McLaren this weekend, but Alonso was once again able to extract the full potential from the car and collect a significant haul of points. Maldonado was having a good battle with Alonso for third place until he was forced to retire with hydraulic failure.

As last year in Singapore, Paul di Resta was on fine form, taking a career-best fourth place. Like the cars around him he started out with the intention of stopping three times, but was able to make it work with two stops and was helped by the safety car and by Nico Rosberg in fifth holding up cars behind him.

In the second Ferrari Felipe Massa made a good recovery from a poor qualifying after having to make a pit stop on the first lap following a puncture. He was in last position, but picked his way through the traffic and had a particularly strong final stint on the option tyres. He came very close to Bruno Senna across the short bridge and it took a spectacular save with opposite lock to remain on track. He ended the race in eighth position.

At the foot of the constructors' championship Timo Glock finished 12th for Marussia, putting them in pole position for tenth place. The team that finishes the season in this position is guaranteed millions in prize money and travel benefits. As neither Marussia, Caterham nor HRT have scored a point, this finish – the best of any of the "new teams" who entered F1 in 2010 – could swing it Marussia's way. Failure would be a major blow to Caterham who have invested heavily this year.

Singapore Grand Prix
Marina Bay (2-hour limit reached)

1. Vettel	Red Bull-Renault	2h00:26.144
2. Button	McLaren-Mercedes	+8.959
3. Alonso	Ferrari	+15.227
4. Di Resta	Force India-Mercedes	+19.063
5. Rosberg	Mercedes	+34.759
6. Raikkonen	Lotus-Renault	+35.700
7. Grosjean	Lotus-Renault	+36.600
8. Massa	Ferrari	+42.800
9. Ricciardo	Toro Rosso-Ferrari	+45.800
10. Webber	Red Bull-Renault	+47.100
11. Perez	Sauber-Ferrari	+50.600
12. Glock	Marussia-Cosworth	+1 lap
13. Kobayashi	Sauber-Ferrari	+1 lap
14. Hulkenberg	Force India-Mercedes	+1 lap
15. Pic	Marussia-Cosworth	+1 lap
16. Kovalainen	Caterham-Renault	+1 lap
17. De la Rosa	HRT-Cosworth	+1 lap
18. Senna	Williams-Renault	+2 laps
19. Petrov	Caterham-Renault	+2 laps

Drivers' Championship Standings

1. Alonso	194 pts
2. Vettel	165
3. Raikkonen	149
4. Hamilton	142
5. Webber	133
6. Button	119

Constructors' Championship Standings

1. Red Bull-Renault	298 pts
2. McLaren-Mercedes	261
3. Ferrari	245
4. Lotus-Renault	231
5. Mercedes	136
6. Sauber-Ferrari	100

A week after his retirement from the Singapore Grand Prix, the worst kept secret was confirmed: Lewis Hamilton was cutting the umbilical cord with McLaren and heading off on his own to Mercedes. The move was actually announced by McLaren, who got their retaliation in first by announcing Sergio Perez alongside Button for 2013. Although they praised the young Mexican's talent and potential, it was clear that in losing Hamilton they were losing one of the fastest, if not the fastest, drivers in F1. They are sure to miss that extra couple of tenths his speed in qualifying gives to the team.

Hamilton turns back on McLaren and signs for Mercedes
28 September 2012

Lewis Hamilton has cut his 14-year umbilical cord to McLaren and announced he will join Mercedes at the end of the season on a three-year deal. It's a huge coup for Mercedes and a major shot in the arm for its ambitions of winning consistently in Formula 1: the 2008 world champion will replace Michael Schumacher in the team's 2013 line-up, reuniting him with his old karting teammate Nico Rosberg. Sauber's Sergio Perez will replace Hamilton at McLaren.

Intriguingly, however, there was no mention in the Mercedes press release of what Schumacher will do now, despite an expectation that Hamilton's arrival would prompt the 43-year-old into permanent retirement.

What there was confirmation of, however – and which clearly paved the way for the Hamilton deal – is that Mercedes have committed to F1 and signed the new eight-year Concorde Agreement. Niki Lauda, who is said to have played a key role in convincing Hamilton of the Mercedes "project", has also joined the team's board of directors as non-executive chairman.

An hour or so earlier McLaren, having to face up to life without the driver they have nurtured since the age of 13 and took all the way to the world championship, were the first to confirm news of Hamilton's departure and duly announced that in his place will come Mexican youngster Perez to partner Jenson Button next season, the team crediting the 22-year-old's "string of giant-killing performances" for the decision to sign him on a "multi-year deal" from Sauber.

But while Martin Whitmarsh expressed confidence in McLaren's statement that Perez is "perfectly poised to develop into a world championship challenger", the stark reality hitting home for the team and its shareholders this morning is that they have just lost a driver who's a proven champion and 20-time race winner.

"It's entirely appropriate that I should take this opportunity to pass on our thanks to Lewis Hamilton. He wrote a huge chapter of his life and career with us, and was, and always will be, a fine member of an exclusive club: the McLaren world champions' club ... It goes without saying that we all wish him well for the future, just as it also goes without saying that we hope and believe that Sergio, too, will become a member of that exclusive club before too long."

It is Mercedes who will certainly feel they have got the better end of the deal, having signed one of the top three stars on the grid and one of the biggest names in world sport. Speaking in the press release issued by this new team, Hamilton admitted it was time for a change and that, crucially, he believes he can win more world championships with his new employer. "It is now time for me to take on a fresh challenge and I am very excited to begin a new chapter racing for the Mercedes AMG Petronas Formula One Team. Mercedes-Benz has such an incredible heritage in motorsport, along with a passion for winning, which I share," Hamilton said.

"Together, we can grow and rise to this new challenge. I believe that I can help steer the Silver Arrows to the top and achieve our joint ambitions of winning world championships."

Team chief Ross Brawn, who has overseen a major restructuring at Mercedes to get them in position to win races on a consistent basis over the coming years, is likely to see the arrival of a world champion in his prime as the final piece in a similar jigsaw to that of Ferrari with a young Michael Schumacher in the late 1990s.

"The arrival of a driver of Lewis's calibre is a testament to the standing of Mercedes-Benz in Formula One and I am proud that Lewis shares our vision and ambition for the success of the Silver Arrows," Brawn said. "I believe that the combination of Lewis and Nico will be the most dynamic and exciting pairing on the grid next year, and I am looking forward to what we can achieve together.

"Over the past three years, we have been putting in place the foundations and building blocks that are needed to compete regularly for the world championship. Behind the scenes, we have assembled a team that is technically stronger, more experienced and better resourced. The potential is now there to match any other team on the grid, which is the minimum standard for a Mercedes-Benz works team. Our task is now to translate that potential into on-track performance for next season and beyond."

Although media reports in the week before Monza suggested that McLaren had upped their basic offer to Hamilton to try and get him to stay, the 27-year-old is set to earn more at Mercedes. His earning potential will be further increased with the freedom to strike his own personal sponsorship deals and maximize his image rights – a major factor behind his decision to hire XIX Entertainment as his management last year in the first place.

Speaking to reporters this afternoon, however, Whitmarsh said that McLaren's offer to Hamilton would have made him the highest paid driver in F1. "We have made a financial offer which is better than anyone in Formula 1, other than himself, receives today, and that is something that I am comfortable with," he said.

Nonetheless it is believed that the deal to bring Hamilton to Mercedes was already in place by the end of the Italian GP, with Brawn and the Mercedes F1 hierarchy waiting for the sign-off on their F1 future from the main Mercedes board in Stuttgart before going ahead – this duly arrived on Wednesday.

This looks like the final push for Mercedes – Ross Brawn knows what it takes to win and has followed the tried and tested formula: he has built up his technical team, they have their own engine facilities and a clear plan and now it looks like they have the driver. All the pieces are in place and Mercedes, confident they will be in a position to take advantage when the new engine regulations come into place in 2014, know they now have to start delivering over the next few seasons.

That will now be without Germany's star sportsman Schumacher, his departure a relative footnote in Hamilton's arrival in contrast to the fanfare that greeted his shock decision to come out of retirement in the winter of 2009 to spearhead what he and the team had expected to be a push for the title by now.

"I have had three nice years with the team which unfortunately did not go as well as we all would have wanted on the sporting side," Schumacher said today. "I wish Lewis well and for the team to achieve the success we worked so hard for in the build-up. I would like to thank the team for their trust and all the guys for their unconditional commitment. I will now concentrate on the next races."

One of the more inspirational stories of the year was former F1 driver Alex Zanardi's triumph in the Paralympics in September, winning two gold medals. The 45-year-old came close to losing his life when he was involved in a horrific crash during his second stint in the American-based Champ Car series at Germany's Lausitzring in 2001, an accident which saw him lose both of his legs. Yet since then his story and return to top-level sporting competition has been little short of remarkable. He has made a second career for himself in Paralympic sport and especially hand cycling.

Fittingly he won at Brands Hatch, a track he had once sped around in an F3000 car.

Chapter Ten
October 2012

October was a crunch month in terms of the behind-the-scenes negotiations over the new Concorde Agreement. There had been a lot of horse-trading going on during summer as the teams, the FIA and the commercial rights holder tried to finalize the new agreement for 2013–20 with particular emphasis on the rule-making process, cost control and the new generation 2014 engines.

This culminated in a meeting on 22 October in Paris, at which all parties were present and a new structure for rule making was presented, on which all three parties would have one-third of a say. The twist was that only six teams would hold seats, with no obligation to represent the views of the missing teams. Those six teams would be Red Bull, Ferrari, McLaren, Mercedes, Williams plus one rotating seat for the highest placed other team in the championship, which this year is Lotus.

But at the back of the grid, the concern was survival and particularly worries over the cost of the 2014 new generation engines, which were mooted to be three times as expensive as the current V8s.

Marussia F1 boss warns 2014 engines a threat to sustainability of the F1 grid
2 October 2012

Marussia team president Graeme Lowdon fears that the implementation of the costly 2014 engine regulations will put the futures of a number of Formula 1 teams on the line. Despite the in-development 1.6 litre, turbocharged V6 engines and accompanying energy efficient systems being less than 18 months away from their scheduled introduction, the new engine formula continues to prove a divisive issue with concerns over the cost of the technology for customer teams in particular.

In recent days Bernie Ecclestone, a long-time critic of the 2014 rules, renewed his calls for the engines to be scrapped, suggesting that FIA president Jean Todt may can them altogether or at least delay their introduction. "I listened to the noise of the engines in [Ferrari's headquarters at] Maranello the other day, the new engine and the old engine, and even Luca di Montezemolo said it sounded terrible and didn't like it," Ecclestone told the *Hindustan Times*, going on to suggest that FIA president Jean Todt "will get rid of it".

The continued uncertainty over Cosworth's 2014 plans, and the recent suspension of Craig Pollock's independent engine firm PURE's operations over funding, has created the prospect of there being only three engine suppliers to serve the whole grid when the new-spec engines come in for 2014. And with the several fold increase in the development cost of the drastically new designs set to be passed on to the customer teams, Marussia chief Lowdon admits he has real concerns over the sustainability of the grid.

Speaking in an interview with the October edition of the *JA on F1* podcast Lowdon said: "Looking back over the last two or three years, one of the things that's really been surprising is just how much the goalposts have moved in terms of things like cost control or resource restrictions and things like that.

"Also uncertainty over engines for 2014, which I think is potentially one of the biggest threats to the sustainability of large numbers of the teams on the grid, and that really shouldn't be the case ... Introducing any new step is good for a sport – you need to be innovative, you need to be relevant, that's absolutely for sure. But it has to be done with sustainability at the heart of it.

"We're all running businesses, we have responsibilities to our employees and there's an awful lot of investment, time, effort and devotion that goes in from a lot of people. We owe it to those people to ensure that this sport is sustainable and has a long and bright future."

Expressing concern that the 2014 engines will only increase the notion that spending more money is the only way to success in F1, Lowdon added: "I think most fans aren't too worried whether it's a V4, 5, 6, 7, 8, 9, 10 – who cares? It has to be fast, it has to make a noise and preferably be environmentally friendly, although I think there's an awful lot that the teams can demonstrate in other ways with carbon footprint and the like.

"But the key thing is we have to maintain and create great competition, that's what people want to watch. My own view is that we owe it to the sport to promote a regulatory framework that has the fans at the centre of it. That is ultimately what pays the bills."

Any about turn in the 2014 plans would certainly require a delicate approach given that both Mercedes and Renault have committed their futures to the sport in part due to the opportunities presented by the new more environmentally friendly technology. Mercedes, in particular, having only last week signed up to the new eight-year Concorde Agreement and lured Lewis Hamilton to spearhead its assault on the world titles, is confident its F1 team will be very well placed to take advantage of the new format.

The saga of Felipe Massa and the second Ferrari seat reached its endgame this week when he was given a one-year extension to his deal. It has always seemed to me that the team want Massa to stay and were looking for a reason to retain him, despite his many abject performances over the two years of his most recent contract. An upturn in form for the Brazilian around the time of the Japan and Korea Grands Prix proved the catalyst for the renewal. But before it was done, there were some interesting messages flying around from Ferrari, which were linked to rumours that refused to go away that the team had some kind of understanding with Sebastian Vettel for the end of his 2014 contract.

First Alonso should win the title, then we won't hire a teammate who bothers him: Montezemolo
3 October 2012

Last Friday, somewhat lost among all the furore over the announcement of the Hamilton-Mercedes transfer, there was an important note made by Ferrari president Luca di Montezemolo in a Q&A session at the Paris Motor Show. It was the session where he confirmed that Ferrari would need to shut down its wind tunnel in either December or January for calibration checks. In the same session, Montezemolo talked about Fernando Alonso and Felipe Massa and there were a couple of important lines to note, for better understanding the full picture when the time comes for the team to announce who will drive alongside Alonso in 2013.

The first point was that he described Alonso as "the strongest driver Ferrari has ever had," which is quite some claim. But then he responded to Alonso's line from Singapore that, "If the team decides to change Felipe, anyone who arrives has to be better than Felipe. I've seen a lot of names written, and I don't know if they have been written with the head or the heart. With all the names you hear, if you compare what Felipe has done in Formula 1 and what these little names have done in Formula 1 …"

Montezemolo said, "He's right that there aren't any 'phenomenons' in circulation. But first Fernando should win the world title and then we will certainly not put anyone alongside him who would bother him. It is the case that the decisions on drivers are taken by us, obviously sharing them with him. Massa has been very strong in the last two races. I'm taking a few days to reflect."

This is interesting on a couple of levels: first by agreeing with Alonso that the possible candidates for the seat are "little names" – this would make for some uncomfortable questions if and when then should hire a Di Resta or a Hulkenberg. Also the use of the word "share" is interesting. In Italian he said of the decisions "*ovviamente condividendole con lui*," which literally means "obviously sharing them with him." I take that to mean that they will share their decisions with him, rather than that he would have a share in making the decision, but there is an intriguing ambiguity in the words he used.

Meanwhile, Massa said this week: "The best way to deal with this situation is to race without thinking about the future. My future is important, but now what counts are results. I feel good. At Suzuka we can be very competitive because there are plenty of fast corners which suit the F2012."

There is a feeling that one of the two Force India drivers has a shot at the Ferrari drive. There's been a suggestion at large for a few weeks now that one of them is on some sort of option for a one-year deal, a kind of "prove yourself" opportunity. The team seems to be in no hurry to decide, but the market is now shifting into gear with the logjam of Hamilton/ Schumacher/Perez now cleared, so it may not be too long before we learn what Ferrari plans to do.

Ferrari is rallying in the constructors' championship thanks to 26 points from Massa in the last three races. They are now in third place, 14 points ahead of Lotus and 16 behind McLaren.

Vettel cruises to victory in Japan and blows championship wide open
7 October 2012

Sebastian Vettel became the first back-to-back race winner in 2012 at the Japanese Grand Prix, cruising to an easy win after a start-line accident eliminated championship leader Fernando Alonso for the second time in four races. Felipe Massa scored a potentially vital second place, as far as his Ferrari career is concerned, from tenth place. It was his first podium for two years, although Ferrari celebrations will be muted as their hopes of winning the drivers' championship took a massive blow today. Kamui Kobayashi finished third, his first F1 podium, to the delight of the Japanese fans, the first home podium for a Japanese driver for 22 years.

It was Vettel's third win of the season and the 24th of his career. It was also his third Japanese GP in the last four years and it means that he has cut Alonso's championship lead to just four points with five races to go. His winning margin was a massive 20 seconds and several times he had to be told to slow down by his engineer.

With Red Bull hitting peak form in its car development and rumours of a double DRS device on the car this weekend, there is a momentum about Vettel's campaign that Alonso will find extremely hard to halt. "We had a good start which was important because there was a crash," said Vettel. "I saw a Ferrari was out and I worked out it must have been Fernando. When you dream at night you dream about being able to drive a car like this … It was an important step today. We don't know what happens in the next race, but it was good to take the points today."

Kimi Raikkonen moved into third place in the championship on 157 points, amazingly just 37 off the front, thanks to his sixth place, with Hamilton five points behind the Finn.

The start was explosive: Fernando Alonso was eliminated by an incident into turn 1, as he squeezed across to the left and tagged Raikkonen, getting a puncture that put him into a spin. He was out for the second time in four races, so too was Nico Rosberg. Alonso questioned why Raikkonen had not lifted off, but accepted that it was a racing incident. Raikkonen had been involved in hurting him for the second time in the weekend, after the Lotus driver's spin in qualifying had ruined his chances of starting on the front two rows.

Meanwhile, Webber's race was ruined by Grosjean driving into the back of him into turn 2. Webber had to pit, switched to the hard tyres and decided to go for a one-stop strategy from there as a safety car was sent out. The race was restarted before Webber was ready and he rejoined 20 seconds behind the pack. Grosjean was given a ten-second stop/go penalty by the stewards, which he served on lap 8. It was a suitably tough penalty for Grosjean, the stewards clearly sending him a message that they were unhappy he had not learned from the one race ban after Spa.

After ten laps Vettel led by almost six seconds from Kobayashi, with Button up to third from eighth on the grid, Massa fourth, Raikkonen fifth, Perez sixth, Hamilton seventh, Hulkenberg eighth, Maldonado ninth and Riccardo tenth. Heikki Kovalainen was up to 11th.

The first stops came on lap 14 with Raikkonen, Hulkenberg and Button pitting for hard tyres. Kobayashi came in a lap later. Kobayashi and Button were held up by Riccardo, as Massa took his chance to pit and rejoined ahead of the pair of them, up to second place; clever strategy giving him a chance to make a big gain. Perez chased Hamilton who got ahead of him at the stop, but came out of the kink too quickly on lap 20 and was eliminated after the two almost collided. Button meanwhile was struggling with a gearbox issue, ironic given that he had been forced into a change before this race and took a five-place penalty as a result. But it stabilised and he was able to continue pushing.

At the halfway stage the order was Vettel, ten seconds clear of Felipe Massa who was running well in second place, the Ferrari lapping consistently, and with Kobayashi not making any ground on him, the top three looked fairly static.

Raikkonen pitted on lap 31, Hamilton a lap later and he rejoined alongside the Lotus, holding his line into turn 1 and taking seventh place. Button stayed out longer than Kobayashi trying to jump him, but his pit stop wasn't fast enough due to the right rear wheel taking longer than usual to go on, so Button came out behind.

Massa pitted on lap 37, with Vettel a lap later, the race completely under control. Vettel had a 17-second lead over Massa by lap 40, but had to be told to slow down by his engineer, who was worried about him overheating his tyres.

The main interest of the end of the race was whether Jenson Button could catch and pass Kobayashi. McLaren had managed the strategy so that Button would have the fresher tyres for the end of the race. He closed right up on the final lap, but couldn't pass him. It was Sauber's fourth podium of the season. Lewis Hamilton was fifth, ahead of Raikkonen and Hulkenberg. Mercedes ended up without any points again, Rosberg out at the start and Schumacher unable to pass Ricciardo for tenth place at the end of the race.

Japanese Grand Prix
Suzuka 53 laps

1. Vettel	Red Bull-Renault	1h28:56.242
2. Massa	Ferrari	+20.639
3. Kobayashi	Sauber-Ferrari	+24.538
4. Button	McLaren-Mercedes	+25.098
5. Hamilton	McLaren-Mercedes	+46.490
6. Raikkonen	Lotus-Renault	+50.424
7. Hulkenberg	Force India-Mercedes	+51.159
8. Maldonado	Williams-Renault	+52.364
9. Webber	Red Bull-Renault	+54.675
10. Ricciardo	Toro Rosso-Ferrari	+1:06.919
11. Schumacher	Mercedes	+1:07.769
12. Di Resta	Force India-Mercedes	+1:23.400
13. Vergne	Toro Rosso-Ferrari	+1:28.600
14. Senna	Williams-Renault	+1:28.700
15. Grosjean	Lotus-Renault	+1 lap
16. Kovalainen	Caterham-Renault	+1 lap
17. Glock	Marussia-Cosworth	+1 lap
18. Petrov	Caterham-Renault	+1 lap
19. De la Rosa	HRT-Cosworth	+1 lap

Drivers' Championship Standings

1. Alonso	194 pts
2. Vettel	190
3. Raikkonen	157
4. Hamilton	152
5. Webber	134
6. Button	131

Constructors' Championship Standings

1. Red Bull-Renault	324 pts
2. McLaren-Mercedes	283
3. Ferrari	263
4. Lotus-Renault	239
5. Mercedes	136
6. Sauber-Ferrari	116

Mark Webber called for Romain Grosjean to face another driving ban after he was taken out by the Frenchman at the start of the Japanese Grand Prix, the seventh such incident Grosjean had been involved in this season. Webber called Grosjean a "first lap nutcase" and added, "The rest of us are trying to fight for decent results. Maybe he needs another holiday. He needs to have a look at himself, how many times can you make the same error? It's embarrassing at this level."

Grosjean received a one-race ban after causing a pile-up in Spa, but today's incident shows that either he has not learned or he has some in-built problem when it comes to the instinctive phase of the racing driver's art – the chaotic race starts. Many ex-drivers in the paddock argue that this is not something that can be trained into him.

Grosjean said, "After the ban I am very careful at the start. I kept my line trying to avoid any contact with Perez, who was on my left. I was focusing on that and I didn't see the delta speed with Mark ... Trying to avoid any contact was my main objective, but it didn't work, it's a stupid crash."

Meanwhile, Kamui Kobayashi celebrated his podium finish in his home Grand Prix with his many fans. Despite his success in this race, the popular Japanese driver was not sure of his place in the Sauber team for 2013. Kobayashi has been under pressure recently to secure a podium for the team, especially after his teammate Sergio Perez had managed to get three of them in the first 13 races. This has propelled Perez into the big league with a long-term McLaren contract secured from 2013.

For Kobayashi, however, prospects of retaining his seat have been quite shaky in recent weeks and it is not clear whether his performance in Japan will save his seat or whether the team has already decided to move on and this will be merely a sweet memory. There are other drivers sniffing around the Sauber team, which has been one of the revelations of 2012 with its class-leading aerodynamics.

With the technical rules set to stay relatively unchanged in 2013, the Sauber is a highly prized seat. One rival for Kobayashi is Nico Hulkenberg, who looks likely to be disappointed by Ferrari as they look set to retain Felipe Massa for another year.

Sauber CEO Monisha Kaltenborn noticeably played down the effect this result could have on Kobayashi's chances of staying. She kept referring to the fact that, "We know him very well," which didn't sound too promising.

A week later the teams were gathered in Yeongam for the Korean Grand Prix, which is by some considerable margin the least popular race on the calendar among the people who work in the sport. Huge travel distances from the capital Seoul, lack of interest from the local population and seedy hotels are among the reasons that this Grand Prix weekend is considered something to be got through, rather than enjoyed.

However, it still pays the same 25 points as the rest of the races and that is what the title contenders were focused on.

Vettel takes championship lead with dominant win in Korean Grand Prix
14 October 2012

Sebastian Vettel won the Korean Grand Prix and took the lead in the world championship – he is developing a significant momentum as the season reaches its denouement. His victory came despite some late race drama as his team warned him that the right front tyre could let go at any time – it was down to the cord. It was Vettel's second Korean GP win, his fourth of 2012 and his third victory in a row this year, a real game changing result that gives him and Red Bull the initiative with four races to go.

How quickly things change: five races ago, after the Hungarian Grand Prix, Vettel was 42 points behind Alonso. Alonso finished 14 seconds behind Vettel today, an average of 0.25 seconds per lap off the Red Bull pace. Vettel now has a six-point lead at the top of the drivers' table. The momentum of the Red Bull team at the moment seems irresistible. The team also increased its lead in the constructors' championship to 77 points with Mark Webber finishing in second place, having started the race from pole position.

It was the 25th victory of Vettel's F1 career in just 97 race starts, putting him equal with Jim Clark and Niki Lauda. It was the second occasion in three races where he has won despite not starting on pole position. "Very pleased. I'm very happy. We had a good start and a good launch, so I was able to get by," said Vettel. "It was quite tight in the first stint, but the second stint was more comfortable ... The championship has gone up and down. We have to focus on ourselves, we need to have our best possible results and we go from there."

Fernando Alonso wasn't able to compete with the Red Bulls today and had to settle for third place, with Ferrari ordering his teammate Felipe Massa, who was faster than Alonso here, to "back off" in the second half of the race and he came in fourth. Ferrari moved into second place in the constructors' championship ahead of McLaren thanks to the recent strong results of Massa.

McLaren had a terrible day all round with Jenson Button eliminated at the start and Lewis Hamilton scoring just a single point in tenth place. For the second race in a row Hamilton had a car that wasn't balanced properly and struggled for pace, due to a problem with the rear anti-roll bar breaking (the same problem Alonso had in qualifying in Monza). A problem with a damper was identified in Japan, so this is a disappointing pattern for McLaren. Hamilton was forced into a three-stop strategy.

As the cars went off on the formation lap, Button, the two Saubers, Di Resta, Vergne and De la Rosa had all decided to start on the prime soft tyres, aiming for a longer first stint.

At the start Vettel managed to get a better getaway and, starting on the inside, was able to get ahead of Webber and into the lead by turn 1, while Alonso jumped Hamilton for third, maintaining his impeccable start record this year. Behind them Button was hit by Kobayashi, who steamed up the inside, smashing his right front suspension, "Idiot" said Button on the radio. Rosberg was also involved in the incident, puncturing his radiator. Perez made up three places at the start.

On the opening lap Vettel led from Webber, with Alonso third, Hamilton fourth, Massa fifth, Raikkonen sixth, Hulkenberg seventh, Grosjean eighth, Perez ninth and Schumacher tenth.

In the first five laps, the pace of the top four was similar, but after six laps the Red Bulls started to lap 0.5 seconds a lap faster. By lap 10 the gap to Alonso opened out to 3.5 seconds as the Red Bulls really began to stretch their legs.

Hamilton was the first of the leaders to come in on lap 14, with Hulkenberg and Grosjean also pitting. Hamilton came out behind Perez who was on the harder tyres. Vettel and Alonso pitted on lap 16, Alonso coming out just ahead of Perez, who attacked him on the first straight, Hamilton managed to pass him and a lap later so did Massa.

Vettel's pace at the start of the second stint was very strong and he increased the lead over Webber, while Alonso and Hamilton closed up slightly. Perez ran long, battling Raikkonen for sixth prior to his first stop. On lap 18, Hamilton radioed in that the second set of tyres were not going to last long, as his pace dropped into the 1m 46s, whereas the cars in front were in the 1m 44s. This meant that Massa passed him on lap 20 for fourth place, while Raikkonen attacked him three laps later. The pair had a great battle for a few laps.

Hamilton pitted on lap 26, only 12 laps after the first stop. This put him out of joint strategy wise. There was a slight delay on the right front and he rejoined ahead of Ricciardo. This released Raikkonen into fifth place. Webber pitted for the second time on lap 32, the first of the front-runners once again. Alonso came in two laps later, with Vettel pitting on lap 35 from the lead.

Webber closed the gap up to Vettel through the second stops while Alonso rejoined 4.5 seconds behind the second Red Bull. Teammate Massa was able to stay with him comfortably. Alonso also lost time in traffic, but Massa was told by his engineer to sit a second or two behind him to preserve his tyres. Massa believed that he could get ahead of Webber if released, but Ferrari were thinking about maximising points for Alonso with Vettel set to take the championship lead off him for the first time.

Meanwhile, Hamilton was forced on to a three-stop strategy, but didn't achieve the pace he expected. Grosjean and Hulkenberg caught him on lap 40 and, as Grosjean tried to pass, he went off track, allowing Hulkenberg to pass the pair of them for sixth place with a brilliant move in what was another very strong drive by the German.

Hamilton pitted again on lap 43 for a 12-lap sprint on supersofts. He rejoined in tenth place, behind Vergne in the Toro Rosso.

In the closing stages Red Bull were concerned about wear on the front tyres, the right front in particular, with both Vettel and Webber repeatedly told to take care. Vettel, in particular, was told to be very careful when loading it up under braking for the big stops.

Korean Grand Prix
Yeongam 55 laps

1. Vettel	Red Bull-Renault	1h36:28.651
2. Webber	Red Bull-Renault	+8.200
3. Alonso	Ferrari	+13.900
4. Massa	Ferrari	+20.100
5. Raikkonen	Lotus-Renault	+36.700
6. Hulkenberg	Force India-Mercedes	+45.300
7. Grosjean	Lotus-Renault	+54.800
8. Vergne	Toro Rosso-Ferrari	+1:09.500
9. Ricciardo	Toro Rosso-Ferrari	+1:11.700
10. Hamilton	McLaren-Mercedes	+1:19.600
11. Perez	Sauber-Ferrari	+1:20.000
12. Di Resta	Force India-Mercedes	+1:24.400
13. Schumacher	Mercedes	+1:29.200
14. Maldonado	Williams-Renault	+1:34.900
15. Senna	Williams-Renault	+1:36.900
16. Petrov	Caterham-Renault	+1 lap
17. Kovalainen	Caterham-Renault	+1 lap
18. Glock	Marussia-Cosworth	+1 lap

| 19. Pic | Marussia-Cosworth | +2 laps |
| 20. Karthikeyan | HRT-Cosworth | +2 laps |

Drivers' Championship Standings

1. Vettel	215 pts
2. Alonso	209
3. Raikkonen	167
4. Hamilton	153
5. Webber	152
6. Button	131

Constructors' Championship Standings

1. Red Bull-Renault	367 pts
2. Ferrari	290
3. McLaren-Mercedes	284
4. Lotus-Renault	255
5. Mercedes	136
6. Sauber-Ferrari	116

Pirelli were somewhat mystified by the radio messages at the end of the race regarding Vettel's tyres. They examined the tyres after the race and found that they were fine, marginal in terms of how much longer they would have gone on for, but they still had life left in them. Perhaps the engineers just wanted to slow him down to avoid taking any risks. But it is one of Vettel's signatures to try to set the fastest lap of the race in the closing stages.

After Korea, Williams held a Partner Day at Silverstone, with all three of its drivers, Maldonado, Senna and Bottas as well as development driver Susie Wolff. She is the wife of shareholder and prime mover in the Williams team Toto Wolff and this was her big day, her chance to drive the 2011 Williams F1 car for the first time.

It was a clever idea to open the team up to sponsors, suppliers, guests and media. We produced the UBS/JA on F1 Podcast #9 (see page 238) from the event, including a moving interview with Susie Wolff and an insightful one with her husband. It was the first time

a woman had driven an F1 car since the horrific accident of Maria
de Villota at Duxford in July, a point lost on no one.

Susie Wolff: "I was thinking of Maria as I drove the F1 car for the first time"
17 October 2012

Susie Wolff today put women F1 drivers back on the agenda when she completed two 75-minute track sessions at Silverstone, driving a Williams FW33 from last year. Wolff's opportunity was the showcase event in Williams' F1 Partner Day, which also saw Bruno Senna at the wheel of Keke Rosberg's 1982 championship-winning car and Pastor Maldonado driving Damon Hill's 1996 title winner.

Susie Wolff has extensive DTM experience, but this was her first time in an F1 car and it passed off well in her two runs, though she admitted that thoughts of F1's other female test driver, Maria de Villota, who was badly injured in an accident in the Marussia F1 car in July, had hung over her big day, "When I went out for the first time in that car it was a very special feeling," said Wolff. "It's incredible, you can't put into words what it's like. You prepare for it, but shifting up through the gears at incredible speeds … it's phenomenal.

"Without a doubt Maria was in my thoughts today and I was out there for both of us. I know she would have done just as good a job in the car. So it was important to go out there and do a good job and show that her accident was a freak and to show that women are capable of driving in F1."

Shortly before the transfer to India, for one of F1's more exotic Grands Prix, came the news of the postponement of one of the races F1 people had been most looking forward to in 2013 – the inaugural New Jersey Grand Prix. F1 insiders suggested that the selling of the race to potential partners in the riverside track project had proved difficult and that the organisers were regrouping in order to secure the funding to ensure a successful 2014 event.

This news had been coming for some time. F1's CEO Bernie Eccle-stone had flagged up some problems over finance and building in

September, but he remains as keen as the rest of the F1 paddock to see the race against a Manhattan skyline take place in 2014.

On arrival in Delhi, one of the more bizarre stories of the year came to light: Ferrari placed themselves at the centre of a political storm when they put the flag of the Italian navy on the nose of the car, a strong statement of support for two sailors who were under arrest for the suspected murder of two Indian fishermen in a botched anti-piracy raid. F1 rules strictly prohibit political gestures by teams. Ferrari argued that their gesture was not political, but the Indian media and some politicians disagreed and it got pretty hot for a while for Ferrari's boss on the ground at the track, Stefano Domenicali.

Of course it violated FIA rules, but a way was found to take the sting out of it when an Indian FIA member held a meeting with Ferrari and declared himself satisfied with their reasoning.

Ferrari deny navy flag gesture has any political message
26 October 2012

Ferrari is at the centre of a deepening political row in India over its decision to run both cars in the Indian Grand Prix with the flag of the Italian navy, the Marina Militare. Two Italian sailors, Salvatore Girone and Massimiliano Latorre, have been held in India since February having been arrested in connection with the shooting of two Indian fishermen, who were allegedly mistaken for pirates.

The matter has been drawn out because of a row over jurisdiction, according to Italian news agency ANSA, "Italy says it should have jurisdiction for the case as the officers were aboard an Italian vessel in international waters, but the Indian authorities do not agree ... The Italian government also believes that, regardless of who has jurisdiction, the marines should be exempt from prosecution in India as they were military personnel working on an anti-piracy mission."

Ferrari president Luca di Montezemolo told Italian network SKY Tg24 that the flag gesture at the Grand Prix "is the contribution that Ferrari can make to this story ... We only want to make a small contribution, with great respect for the Indian authorities, so that a solution might be found through dialogue."

Meanwhile, foreign minister Giulio Terzi said that Ferrari's gesture "shows the support of the whole country for our sailors." Speaking to reporters today in Rome, Terzi also said the two sailors "will return home. I'm not able to give a date, but they will come home."

However, a spokesperson in the Indian ministry of external affairs, Syed Akbaruddin, said that the gesture by Ferrari at this weekend's Italian Grand Prix is "using sporting events to promote causes which are not of a sporting nature and is not in keeping with the spirit of sports."

Vettel takes dominant Indian victory, but Alonso won't give up
28 October 2012

Sebastian Vettel cruised to victory in the Indian Grand Prix ahead of Fernando Alonso, with Mark Webber finishing third. The title is now a two-horse race between Vettel and Alonso. The German driver leads by just 13 points with three races to go.

In a fairly uneventful race, Vettel survived a late scare with a floor stay to take his fourth consecutive race victory. Vettel's car began to produce sparks due to a loose skid block in the final dozen laps, giving Alonso some false hope, but the German managed to cope with the problem and even set his fastest lap on the final lap of the race.

Vettel led every lap, for the third race in succession – equalling a record of Ayrton Senna's from the late 1980s. That stat tells you everything you need to know about the momentum Vettel and Red Bull enjoy, but Fernando Alonso limited the damage with a dogged drive for second place and says he is even more confident now of winning the world title.

"I'm very pleased with today's result," said Vettel. "I pushed hard early on to open a gap. With hard tyres Ferrari and McLaren were very strong." He was able to make his first stint, on the option tyres, last very long, giving himself the chance to look after his RB8 and cruise to the flag. He seemed unaware of any problems at the end of the race, "I don't know about [the sparking], there were a lot of cars throwing sparks, there was nothing I was told was a problem or that I could feel."

Up until lap 20 it had looked to be another one-two for Red Bull, but a KERS issue for Webber allowed Alonso to close up and pass the Australian and minimise the points lost to the race winner. The two had been in a tight battle in the second phase of the Grand Prix and a resilient Webber had initially managed to put a gap between the two, but it was to be undone by the Ferrari's much superior straight-line speed in the extended DRS-zone.

"It was a fight all race through because we could not lose more points, we are still convinced we can win [the title]," said Alonso. "Today is a Red Bull day again, but our day has to arrive in Brazil.

"Seb has won four consecutively, but before long this will finish and when it does we must take the opportunity. We remain optimistic. Today was a KERS problem for Mark, the same can happen to Seb, so we must be ready. I remain 100 per cent confident that we will fight for this championship and we will win it."

Webber subsequently came under pressure from Lewis Hamilton, but the McLaren ran out of laps to make it on to the podium. McLaren's rapid pit stops reached new levels today when the crew were able to change all four tyres and the steering wheel for Hamilton in just 3.3 seconds.

Prior to the race Red Bull knew that their start was key, even more so than normal, as the very long back straight could leave them susceptible to the McLarens and Ferraris when DRS was enabled. However, the Red Bull duo pulled away with ease during the first phase of the race.

Behind, both Jenson Button and Alonso managed to jump Hamilton in the first lap after they drove three abreast down the back straight and through the following two turns. But Alonso quickly took second place with the use of DRS on the fourth lap and Hamilton made the same move just two laps later. Button maintained fifth position for the remainder of the race, losing time to those ahead after being held up by a long-running Romain Grosjean. Button went on to set the fastest lap of the race, even though he was the first of the leading cars to pit, seven laps before Vettel.

Felipe Massa and Kimi Raikkonen took sixth and seventh place respectively after a race-long battle. Massa had shown good pace in the first phase of the race, hassling Button for fifth place, but he could not sustain the pressure on the prime tyres. Raikkonen did get past the Ferrari; he pitted one lap earlier and passed him, only to be quickly overtaken again in the DRS-zone.

Nico Hulkenberg, Grosjean and Bruno Senna completed the top ten and each had a strong race. Senna, in particular, scored a much needed point as he showed the kind of pace that we saw in free practice, passing Nico Rosberg late on. He spent much of the race in a battle with teammate Pastor Maldonado, only for the Venezuelan to receive a puncture after being tagged by Kamui Kobayashi. Maldonado was one of three drivers to receive a puncture during the Grand Prix, with Jean-Eric Vergne and Michael Schumacher also having punctures through similar incidents.

For all the drama and colour of this fabulous event, the fact was that Vettel was unbeatable all weekend and he was never seriously troubled as he took his 26th career victory and provided another impressive stat – no other driver has led a lap in India in its two-year history.

Indian Grand Prix
Buddh International Circuit 60 laps

1. Vettel	Red Bull-Renault	1h31:10.744
2. Alonso	Ferrari	+9.437
3. Webber	Red Bull-Renault	+13.217
4. Hamilton	McLaren-Mercedes	+13.909
5. Button	McLaren-Mercedes	+26.266
6. Massa	Ferrari	+44.674
7. Raikkonen	Lotus-Renault	+45.227
8. Hulkenberg	Force India-Mercedes	+54.998
9. Grosjean	Lotus-Renault	+56.103
10. Senna	Williams-Renault	+1:14.975
11. Rosberg	Mercedes	+1:21.694
12. Di Resta	Force India-Mercedes	+1:22.815
13. Ricciardo	Toro Rosso-Ferrari	+1:26.064
14. Kobayashi	Sauber-Ferrari	+1:26.495
15. Vergne	Toro Rosso-Ferrari	+1 lap
16. Maldonado	Williams-Renault	+1 lap
17. Petrov	Caterham-Renault	+1 lap
18. Kovalainen	Caterham-Renault	+1 lap
19. Pic	Marussia-Cosworth	+1 lap
20. Glock	Marussia-Cosworth	+2 laps

| 21. Karthikeyan | HRT-Cosworth | +2 laps |
| 22. Schumacher | Mercedes | +5 laps |

Drivers' Championship Standings

1. Vettel	240 pts
2. Alonso	227
3. Raikkonen	173
4. Webber	167
5. Hamilton	165
6. Button	141

Constructors' Championship Standings

1. Red Bull-Renault	407 pts
2. Ferrari	316
3. McLaren-Mercedes	306
4. Lotus-Renault	263
5. Mercedes	136
6. Sauber-Ferrari	116

Four seats on the 2013 grid were confirmed in the days after the Indian Grand Prix as first Kimi Raikkonen was retained at Lotus, then Nico Hulkenberg's move to Sauber was confirmed and finally the two youngsters at Toro Rosso were given a second year.

Kimi Raikkonen will drive for the Lotus F1 team again next season, a move which was widely anticipated after no real sign that he was in the running for a seat at Ferrari, McLaren Red Bull or Mercedes, all of whom have confirmed their drivers this summer. There is no word in the statement about the future of Lotus's other driver Romain Grosjean. Raikkonen's comeback from two years away in rallying was very impressive and was capped with a stunning win in Abu Dhabi in November. His comeback stands in stark contrast to Michael Schumacher who only managed one podium in his three years back in the sport.

Then, with Sergio Perez moving to McLaren to replace Lewis Hamilton at season's end and Kamui Kobayashi's future at the team looking increasing uncertain, Nico Hulkenberg moved firmly into view for Sauber, particularly after rumoured suitors Ferrari opted to retain Felipe Massa. Rather like Lotus earlier that week, Sauber unusually don't confirm both of their drivers for next season together, simply stating that Hulkenberg's teammate would be revealed "at a later date". Sauber will be Hulkenberg's third different team in three seasons of racing in Formula 1, but the German appeared to have been enticed by the team's strong step forward this season.

Chapter Eleven
November 2012

November began with the publication of the FIA Sporting Regulations for next season, featuring a revised entry fee structure, which will see a significant hike in the amount teams pay to enter the Formula One World Championship. Under the new rules for 2013, the team that wins the constructors' championship will pay a basic fee of US$500,000 and then $6,000 for every point scored. The other teams will pay the same basic fee plus US$5,000 per point.

So, for example, if Red Bull have a similar season to this one next year they will end up with around 520 points, which will equate to $3.1 million on top of the $500,000 basic fee, a total of $3.6 million. This is because the FIA wants a greater share of the approximately $1.5 billion turnover the sport generates each season.

FIA president Jean Todt spoke about it to the Financial Times *this week. "FIA is a non-profit organisation, but we need to run our organisation," he said. "We need to encourage development of the sport, we need to encourage development of action for road safety. We cannot be a federation without having any revenue. So, where do we find our revenues?"*

The FIA sold its commercial rights to Bernie Ecclestone for 100 years starting in 2011, for a fee of around $350 million, which is all ring fenced in the FIA Foundation and cannot be used for the running of the FIA. Ecclestone's annual payment to the FIA is set to increase to around $20 million from a current level of around $7 million. So the FIA will have around $35 to $40 million annual income from F1 alone. Todt insists that he has not given up any of the FIA's regulatory power in exchange for the cash.

In 2012 teams shared around $675 million of F1's commercial revenues between them, but the split is not even: Ferrari gets the most as the longest standing team, with the other leading teams also *earning a lot more than the "lesser" teams such as Caterham, Marussia and HRT. Winning the constructors' championship is worth over $70 million.*

The Abu Dhabi Grand Prix has had mixed reviews over the years, due to the lack of overtaking opportunities. The world's premier motorsport facility, it seems such a shame that the architects weren't able to use the available land better to avoid the "cookie cutter" corners that prevail. However, this year's race was a classic, thanks to Sebastian Vettel's charge through the field from last place, following a mistake by Red Bull in qualifying similar to the one made by McLaren in Spain where they underfuelled the car so it was not able to return to the pits under its own power.

Vettel was able to take advantage of a rule that allows a team to take the car out of parc ferme and make changes to it, but with the caveat that they must then start from the pit lane. Red Bull changed the gearbox on Vettel's car, lengthened the top gear and tuned the car for top speed, to aid overtaking. It added an extra 5mph to his top speed and proved incredibly effective in the race.

With plenty of other overtakes, incidents and accidents, Kimi Raikkonen's win and some fascinating strategy, this was a candidate for the race of the season.

Raikkonen wins Abu Dhabi thriller as Vettel goes from last to podium
4 November 2012

Kimi Raikkonen won a thrilling Abu Dhabi Grand Prix, arguably one of the most exciting races of the season, holding off Fernando Alonso in the final laps to win for the first time since Spa 2009 and giving Lotus its first win since the 1987 US Grand Prix victory for Ayrton Senna. Raikkonen survived two safety cars, which cut his lead, to become the eighth different race winner of this 2012 championship. He went from fourth to first, Alonso from sixth to second and Vettel from 24th to third.

Amazingly, Sebastian Vettel held on to a ten-point championship lead after a stunning drive through the field, passing Jenson Button in the closing stages to take his place on the podium. He started in the pit lane, survived several scares, made an extra stop compared to the rest and still came away with a result. Lewis Hamilton controlled the first part of the race from pole position, but retired once again, as he did in a similar position in Singapore.

Raikkonen's win was built on a strong qualifying performance and a great start. He qualified fifth, which became fourth after Sebastian Vettel was penalized. The phlegmatic Finn was suitably underwhelmed when interviewed after the race. "Not much [emotion] really," said Raikkonen. "I'm really happy for the team, it's been hard times lately and I hope this can turn around the tables. I'm happy, but there's nothing to jump around about. We'll have a good party and tomorrow when we feel bad after a long night we will remember why we feel like that."

It was a thrilling roller coaster of a race, particularly exciting as far the championship contenders were concerned with Alonso and Vettel both having swings of good luck and setbacks. Vettel's final result showed the sheer performance advantage of the Red Bull over the majority of the field, as Vettel was able to twice drop to the back and still come through. It also silenced critics who think that Vettel lacks the ability to overtake.

The track temperature at the start of the race was 34 degrees, with quite a strong gusty breeze. In a stunning first lap Kimi Raikkonen jumped from fourth to second as Webber made another poor getaway from the line. Meanwhile, Alonso jumped Button for fifth place and then passed Webber for fourth on the back straight. A collision between Hulkenberg and Senna eliminated the Force India car, while Di Resta got a puncture and Vettel damaged his front wing to complete the opening exchanges.

In the opening stint, Hamilton led Raikkonen, with Maldonado third, Alonso fourth, Webber, Button, Massa, Perez, Kobayashi and Schumacher making up the top ten. Hamilton settled into a high rhythm, the McLaren lapping at 0.5 seconds faster than Raikkonen. Alonso was tucked up behind Maldonado waiting for his opportunity.

On lap 9 the safety car was deployed for only the second time in four years at Yas Marina after Nico Rosberg had a heavy accident, smashing into the back of Narain Karthikeyan's HRT. The Mercedes took off and passed over the top of Karthikeyan's car, passing close to the Indian driver's head. It was the third accident in four races for Rosberg.

Under the safety car there was a curious incident where Sebastian Vettel almost collided with the rear of Daniel Ricciardo's Toro Rosso as he weaved to heat the tyres. Vettel hit the barriers causing more damage to the front wing of the Red Bull. He pitted on lap 13 for soft tyres and a new front wing. Vettel came out behind Grosjean, who was at the back after a puncture in a quick Lotus also trying to make its way through the field.

At the restart Alonso had trouble with cold tyres and had to defend from Webber, as the leading trio broke free at the front. Vettel attacked Grosjean, but the Frenchman came back at him. Vettel finally made the pass stick on the second straight. But he went outside the white line to do it and had to give the place back then retake it.

At the front Hamilton returned to his rhythm with Raikkonen three seconds behind. Maldonado and Alonso slipped back, the Ferrari not finding the pace it had before the restart. But on lap 20 Hamilton retired from the race when his engine died. This gave Raikkonen the lead, lifted Maldonado to second and Alonso to third.

On lap 22 Alonso passed Maldonado for second place as the Venezuelan struggled with his tyres. On lap 23, with Alonso in full flight, there was a classic Raikkonen moment on the radio as his engineer offered to keep him updated on the gap to Alonso, "No! Leave me alone, I know what I'm doing!" shouted the Finn.

On the same lap, Webber made a mistake passing Maldonado and went into a spin that dropped him back behind Button, Massa and Perez. As the pit stop approached, Button passed Maldonado for third and Perez passed Massa for fifth.

On lap 27, Massa and Webber made contact, as Webber went off the track to overtake. Massa spun and immediately pitted for medium tyres. Alonso came into the pits on lap 29, moving to the medium tyres.

Vettel caught Webber on lap 31 and the Australian was told, "If Sebastian gets a run don't fight him," but Red Bull pitted Webber at the end of the lap just in case, releasing Vettel, who was now second, on tyres which had done 15 laps. Pirelli estimated that the soft tyres could do 36 laps, so Vettel was pushing his luck to try 40.

After the stops, Raikkonen led on the medium tyres, from Vettel, Alonso, Button, Grojean. There was a significant gap between these two which meant that Vettel could push hard and if he were to run out of tyres, he would be able to stop and slot into that gap behind Button. He did so on lap 38, taking another set of used soft tyres and it worked to plan, then another safety car came out to help him again, this time for an accident involving his own teammate. Di Resta and Perez were fighting for position: Perez went off track and came back on making contact with Di Resta, which left Webber nowhere to go.

The race restarted on lap 43, with 12 laps to go, Alonso again struggling to get the tyres up to temperature. On lap 46 Vettel attacked Button for third, but wasn't able to find a way past initially. He did make it stick soon after, however, although he later admitted that Button had been very hard to pass.

One final note: Mercedes had its fourth race with no points, although Rosberg was going well before the accident and Schumacher was in the points before he got a late puncture.

Abu Dhabi Grand Prix
Yas Marina Circuit 55 laps

1. Raikkonen	Lotus-Renault	1h45:58.667
2. Alonso	Ferrari	+0.852
3. Vettel	Red Bull-Renault	+4.163
4. Button	McLaren-Mercedes	+7.787
5. Maldonado	Williams-Renault	+13.007
6. Kobayashi	Sauber-Ferrari	+20.076
7. Massa	Ferrari	+22.896
8. Senna	Williams-Renault	+23.542
9. Di Resta	Force India-Mercedes	+24.160
10. Ricciardo	Toro Rosso-Ferrari	+27.400
11. Schumacher	Mercedes	+28.000
12. Vergne	Toro Rosso-Ferrari	+34.900
13. Kovalainen	Caterham-Renault	+47.700
14. Glock	Marussia-Cosworth	+56.400
15. Perez	Sauber-Ferrari	+56.700
16. Petrov	Caterham-Renault	+1:04.500
17. De la Rosa	HRT-Cosworth	+1:11.5

Drivers' Championship Standings

1. Vettel   255 pts
2. Alonso   245
3. Raikkonen   198
4. Webber   167
5. Hamilton   165
6. Button   153

Constructors' Championship Standings

1. Red Bull   422 pts
2. Ferrari   340
3. McLaren   318
4. Lotus   288
5. Mercedes   136
6. Sauber   124

Lewis Hamilton's retirement while he was leading the race in Abu Dhabi was a major talking point, as it had been in Singapore. McLaren's season was unravelling. Having had the fastest car in the field at the start of the season, again in the summer and with Hamilton driving beautifully at Abu Dhabi, it seemed unbelievable that the team could be third behind Ferrari in the constructors' championship with Hamilton fifth in the drivers' standings, almost 100 points behind Vettel. This weekend's Grand Prix witnessed Hamilton's fourth reliability issue in five races.

Martin Whitmarsh insisted afterwards that McLaren's recent relia-bility problems were "not related or endemic, it's just one of those things", nonetheless this lack of reliability and operational mistakes have proved massively costly to Hamilton's title aspirations.

Abu Dhabi was the third time this season that Hamilton could legitimately complain that certain victory had been prised from his grasp through no fault of his own. The other two were in Spain, when he was stripped of what had been a dominant pole for McLaren fuel irregularities and demoted to the back of the grid, and Singapore, when he suffered a gearbox failure.

Had he won those three races, he would currently have 71 points more (not including the four points he did score for eighth place in Barcelona). Those additional points, combined with the negative knock-on effect for his rivals' scores, would eradicate much of Hamilton's current 90-point deficit to Sebastian Vettel and mean he was very much still in the title hunt heading to the penultimate race of the season.

McLaren also paid a big price for its early-season pit stop problems, before new sporting director Sam Michael and his group put in place a more reliable and faster pit stop process.

We did some analysis on Hamilton's season: it certainly showed how different things could have been if the team had enjoyed the same reliability and operational record as Ferrari or Lotus, for example. Although the nature of F1 makes it impossible to quantify exactly how many points have been squandered through car failures and team mistakes, the list of examples and considered estimations on likely finishing positions and points losses below serves as an illustration of how Hamilton's overall points tally has been severely compromised:

__China__ – Qualified second, but started seventh due to gearbox change penalty. Finished third. __Estimated points lost: 3__

__Bahrain__ – Running third, but ended up eighth following two slow pit stops. __Estimated points lost: 8–10__

__Spain__ – Qualified on pole, but demoted to back of the grid for McLaren fuel infringement. Finished eighth. __Estimated points lost: 21__

__Monaco__ – Running third, but suffered slow pit stop and lost positions first to Alonso, who stops a lap later, and the even later-stopping Vettel. Finished fifth. __Estimated points lost: 2–5__

__Europe__ – Slow pit stop when running third dropped him to sixth, behind eventual race winner Alonso. Spun out on final lap from third after collision with Pastor Maldonado while struggling with tyre wear. __Estimated points lost: 15 (based on likely position ahead of Maldonado in closing stages without pit-stop delay)__

__Singapore__ – Running first when gearbox failed. Result: DNF. __Estimated points lost: 25__

__Korea__ – Rear anti-roll bar failure early in race played havoc with *tyre wear. Dropped down order from fourth. Result: 10th.* **Estimated points lost: 11**

Abu Dhabi *– Leading the race by three seconds when fuel pressure problem ground car to a halt. Result: DNF.* **Estimated points lost: 25**

Estimated total of points lost: 110

At a Williams' partner day at Silverstone last month I sat down with Toto Wolff, who has moved into a more front-line role at the team this year following the departure of Adam Parr. Wolff is an engaging character and an increasing presence at Williams as Sir Frank hands more of his duties over to him. Wolff had some strong views on a consistently controversial topic that has been hanging over F1 all season – the new 2014 turbo engine regulations.

Bernie Ecclestone recently cast doubt over whether the new engine format would ultimately see the light of day, but Wolff is adamant that, although he feels F1 should never have started down that road in the first place, the journey is now irreversible – particularly as the team's own engine supplier, Renault, recommitted to the sport on that premise. "My own personal view is that it should have never happened," he explained. "It was agreed to make a new engine without having properly analysed how much the engine would cost in terms of research and development and in terms of running it later on. But the engine manufacturers have started developing their business. All of them are pretty much on the way. They have spent millions and millions to develop it; some of them don't even have benches for the old engines any more.

"Renault made it a condition of their staying in the sport that a new engine is developed, so my honest opinion is that it's quite late to change that decision. I support our engine manufacturer's position, which is in favour of the new engine."

On the eve of the Austin Grand Prix, the first of two "match points" for Vettel to clinch the championship, we looked at which of the two contenders for the drivers' title had done a better job.

Vettel v. Alonso: who has done a better job?
15 November 2012

And so it comes to this: two races in eight days to decide the outcome of the 2012 world championship. It's been a long road to this point, but which of the two drivers has done a better job? Here we present an analysis of what has got us to this point over the course of the season.

The margin between them is small at 10 points. But it will be all over this weekend if Vettel wins with Alonso fifth or lower. It could also be settled if Vettel is second with Alonso ninth or lower or if Vettel is third and Alonso is out of the points. However, experiences this season with Red Bull's alternator problems and the two start-line accidents in Spa and Suzuka, which cost Alonso so dearly, tell us that there are no foregone conclusions. This is motor racing and anything can happen.

A few weeks ago we looked at the battle between Fernando Alonso and Sebastian Vettel for the right to be the only three-times world champion in the field next season. Other newspapers, magazines and websites have followed suit, and in particular there's a good, comprehensive piece this week by Andrew Benson on the BBC F1 website that's well worth reading.

Today, 1978 world champion Mario Andretti, who serves as an ambassador of the new US Grand Prix at Austin, had his turn in comparing the merits of the two rivals: "I have a very high opinion of Fernando and I often send him messages. He is a driver to appreciate for his determination and intelligence. For Ferrari he's been doing the impossible. It will not be easy for him to take points off Vettel, but I'm not giving up." Meanwhile, of Vettel he says, "I've met him, he's a great kid and a top class driver. He will be one of the greats."

Ferrari has not won a race or been on pole since Germany in July. Their efforts now may be too little too late, but Ferrari has been straight-line aero testing this week with Jules Bianchi in Spain, trying out revised versions of solutions which were seen in Abu Dhabi as well as other new ideas, no doubt. Ferrari's development has been its Achilles heel this season: the car has been through some positive development stages, but the team was unable to sustain the rapid growth which Red Bull managed to bring through, largely due to inefficiencies in the wind tunnel at Maranello following its upgrade from 50 to 60 per cent. This sort of painful infrastructure upgrade is one that has also cost Mercedes this season, although they hope that the pain is now behind them as they seek to build Lewis Hamilton a winning car for next year.

No doubt if Red Bull wins both titles there will be dark murmurings in the aftermath about them spending far more money than the others to achieve it. And it is a great shame for the sport that the teams have failed to agree on a formula for cost controls.

The bottom line is that both Vettel and Alonso have driven superbly – as have Lewis Hamilton and Kimi Raikkonen – but we should consider two areas of comparison in particular: car pace relative to the fastest qualifier and results relative to qualifying position.

In terms of pure car pace, if we look at the fastest lap from both drivers in qualifying at the 18 rounds so far, Vettel has had the faster car on 12 occasions. Taking an average of the gap to pole for the 18 races, Vettel has been 0.43 seconds off pole while Alonso has been 0.6 seconds off. So the big picture is that the Red Bull hasn't been much faster this year.

However, in the five races since Monza, Vettel has had an average qualifying advantage over Alonso of 0.5 seconds. Looking at the season as a whole, Vettel has had an advantage of 0.26 seconds, factoring in the days when Alonso was faster. Breaking that down further: of the races that Vettel has had the faster car he has been on average 0.57 seconds faster in qualifying. Of the six races where Alonso had the faster car, he has qualified 0.358 seconds faster than Vettel.

In terms of who has done a better job in races – looking next at how they converted their qualifying positions into results, Vettel converted pole into a win on three out of five occasions. He made up places from his grid slot on eight occasions, gaining a total of 22 places from his grid slot in races where he started behind pole. (In Abu Dhabi, of course, he made up another 22 places after being forced to start from the pit lane.) He lost places from his grid slot on two occasions (three places in Canada and Germany), then had two technical retirements and a collision in Malaysia.

Alonso, in contrast, made up places on 12 occasions, gaining a total of 48 places in races where he started behind pole. He also had two DNFs and two races where he lost places from his starting slot (Canada and Silverstone). He had two poles and converted one to a win.

Alonso's average gain of four places compared to Vettel's 2.75 places gained is one of the main reasons why the Spaniard is still in the championship hunt today.

Hamilton wins in Austin as title battle goes to the wire
18 November 2012

Lewis Hamilton continued his strong record in North America by winning an exciting race in Austin, Texas. Although Red Bull clinched the constructors' championship, the result means the drivers' championship battle rolls on to the final race of the season in Brazil, as Sebastian Vettel was beaten into second place while his title rival Fernando Alonso completed the podium, from seventh on the grid.

Losing the extra seven points a win would have given him, the result sees Vettel increase his championship lead over Alonso by just three points, to 13, while Red Bull have become the first Formula One team to win their first three constructors' championships in consecutive years.

After a race-long battle, played out in front of a crowd of 117,000 fans, Hamilton piled relentless pressure on Vettel and eventually made his way past on lap 42 to claim his fifth victory in North America. Vettel had led the Grand Prix throughout, but after losing time behind Narain Karthikeyan in sector 1 of the decisive lap, he could not keep the McLaren driver far enough behind him in the long DRS zone. Although he came back at Hamilton in the final 14 laps, the German was unable to get close enough to attack him.

"When Seb was delayed by a back-marker, I knew I had to grab my chance," said Hamilton. "So I turned the engine up to maximum revs and pushed like crazy. Along the back straight I went to the outside, but Seb closed the door, so I moved to the inside, and he came back towards me. I was very lucky. It was very close … What made the difference today between Seb and me? I wanted it more, that's what!"

This is Hamilton's fourth victory of 2012, making a total of 21 in his career. Amazingly, it is the first time that these three champions have found themselves together on the podium.

It had looked from an early stage as though Alonso would secure the points required to take the fight to Brazil, as the Ferrari driver made his way from seventh to fourth at the first corner, no doubt aided by being able to start from the clean side of the grid. This came about as a result of a gearbox penalty that Ferrari forced on Felipe Massa. The Brazilian had out-qualified Alonso, but by taking the five-place grid drop it promoted Alonso to seventh. Alonso's challenge was further strengthened when Mark Webber retired on lap 17 with an alternator problem, from third position. Moving from fourth to third meant another three points for the Spaniard.

All three podium finishers were candidates for driver of the day in their own individual ways. In the run-up to the stops Hamilton closed to within half a second of the race lead, giving him a slim chance of a manoeuvre in the DRS zone. But Vettel responded well and built a three-second gap prior to the tyre change. We have seen this tactic from Vettel a number of times during the final stages of the season – he romps away in the opening laps, only to be caught slightly and then re-open that gap in the five laps leading to his stop. This way of drawing in the second-placed car saves his tyres while ruining those of the car behind, allowing him to put the hammer down at the end of the tyre life and rebuild his lead. But Vettel was unable to pull a sufficient lead and Hamilton showed McLaren's long run pace from practice to set up an epic title decider next weekend.

Hamilton drove what his father Anthony described as his finest Grand Prix, using his experience to ensure he had a strong first sector and allow himself a chance in the DRS zone. In what could be his last victory for McLaren he gave the Woking team a reminder of the speed they will be missing in 2013. For his part, Alonso came through the field to minimize the points' loss to his title rival, helped largely by a very good first corner. He struggled to match the pace of those ahead in the first phase of the race, but after the stops set a fastest lap which was only marginally beaten by the two ahead.

Behind the top three, Felipe Massa reacted to his forced penalty with great character and put in his strongest performance of the year thus far, making his way through a large group of cars from 11th during the first phase of the race, setting numerous fastest laps on the way to fourth, eventually finishing just six seconds behind Alonso. He was followed home by Jenson Button, the Briton opting to start the race on the prime tyres from 12th on the grid and use a long first stint to bring himself back into contention. He was also able to make use of his short run on the option tyres to find his way past the Lotus pairing. Had Button not dropped back into a large group of cars at the beginning of the race he would have found himself with a fighting chance of a podium.

Kimi Raikkonen led Romain Grosjean home, the latter recovering from a spin, which forced an early stop due to a heavy flat-spot. They once again showed strong race pace and Raikkonen had an exhilarating battle with Button as the two ran side by side for much of a lap, before the Briton eventually took the position.

The top ten was completed by Nico Hulkenberg and the Williams pairing, headed by Pastor Maldonado. The trio had a very good race with Hulkenberg running fifth during the early phases. The double points finish for Maldonado and Senna will be highly beneficial to their hopes of race seats on 2013.

At the other end of the spectrum is Mercedes. The Brackley-based squad suffered its fifth consecutive race without scoring a point and was the only team forced in to making two stops solely down to tyre degradation. Once he's done celebrating this win, Hamilton will be aware that there is a huge job to do to make them competitive.

United States Grand Prix
Circuit of the Americas, Austin 56 laps

1. Hamilton	McLaren-Mercedes	1h35:55.269
2. Vettel	Red Bull-Renault	+0.675
3. Alonso	Ferrari	+39.229
4. Massa	Ferrari	+46.013
5. Button	McLaren-Mercedes	+56.432
6. Raikkonen	Lotus-Renault	+1:04.425
7. Grosjean	Lotus-Renault	+1:10.313
8. Hulkenberg	Force India-Mercedes	+1:13.792
9. Maldonado	Williams-Renault	+1:14.525
10. Senna	Williams-Renault	+1:15.133
11. Perez	Sauber-Ferrari	+1:24.341
12. Ricciardo	Toro Rosso-Ferrari	+1:24.871
13. Rosberg	Mercedes	+1:25.510
14. Kobayashi	Sauber-Ferrari	+1 lap
15. Di Resta	Force India-Mercedes	+1 lap
16. Schumacher	Mercedes	+1 lap

17. Petrov	Caterham-Renault	+1 lap
18. Kovalainen	Caterham-Renault	+1 lap
19. Glock	Marussia-Cosworth	+1 lap
20. Pic	Marussia-Cosworth	+2 laps
21. De la Rosa	HRT-Cosworth	+2 laps
22. Karthikeyan	HRT-Cosworth	+2 laps

Drivers' Championship Standings

1. Vettel	273 pts
2. Alonso	260
3. Raikkonen	206
4. Hamilton	190
5. Webber	167
6. Button	163

Constructors' Championship Standings

1. Red Bull-Renault	440 pts
2. Ferrari	367
3. McLaren-Mercedes	353
4. Lotus-Renault	302
5. Mercedes	136
6. Sauber-Ferrari	124

Hamilton's win had a real feeling of closure about it – he had wanted to sign off his McLaren career by giving them a win and this was the best possible way to do it.

The US Grand Prix was one of the best races of the season, as it was all about a furious duel for the lead and a great overtake to win it. It was a huge success on many levels and it seemed that in Austin, F1's tenth different venue in America, the sport had found a spiritual home. It was noticeable that there were a lot of heavy hitters in the Austin paddock, from CEOs of sponsors to numerous F1 circuit bosses. CVC was very active as well, entertaining investors. After the visit of News Corp's James Murdoch to Abu Dhabi and his tour of the F1 broadcast facility, there was a strong feeling that behind-the-scenes deals were afoot that could lead to some big changes in the ownership of the sport.

But the talking point for many fans was the decision by Ferrari to deliberately penalise Felipe Massa by breaking a seal on his gearbox, thereby attracting a five-place grid penalty, to help his teammate Fernando Alonso. It was cynical and an act of desperation, but it was also within the rules. It required some deeper analysis.

On Ferrari's "tactical" gearbox penalty 19 November 2012

One of the major talking points from the US Grand Prix weekend was the decision by Ferrari on Sunday morning to deliberately break a seal on the gearbox of Felipe Massa's car, so that he would get a five-place grid penalty which would move teammate Fernando Alonso one place up the grid and on to the clean side of the grid for a better start. Practice starts during the weekend had shown that the dirty side of the grid was so lacking in grip that the car would lose up to a second in the 350-metre run to turn 1, equivalent to two positions.

Much has been said and written about Ferrari's tactic in the last 24 hours, but it's worth looking in more detail at the background and technical detail of this to better understand whether the rules need to be re-written to avoid similar actions in future.

Ferrari used Article 28.6 (e) to give their own driver a tactical penalty on Sunday. This states that: "a replacement gearbox will also be deemed to have been used if any of the FIA seals are damaged or removed from the original gearbox after it has been used for the first time."

Each box must last for five Grands Prix. An FIA seal is placed in several areas of the gearbox, "to ensure that no moving parts, other than those specifically permitted ... can be rebuilt or replaced."

These seals may only be broken with the approval of the FIA in order to make limited repairs, for example, replacing a damaged gear ratio with a similar one, O-rings and oil seals. But nothing can be done to the transmission itself and the use of a new gearbox incurs a five-place grid penalty.

Ferrari were transparent about the fact that there was nothing wrong with Massa's gearbox and they will have been equally open with the FIA about it. In fact, they will have gone through the procedure carefully with the FIA's Charlie Whiting and Jo Bauer to ensure that they satisfied the regulations. They broke the seal on the cross-shaft, which is at the back of the gearbox and drives the final drive.

Ferrari team principal Stefano Domenicali confirmed that the team waited until the last moment to break the seal, so as not to allow time for Red Bull to react and do the same with Mark Webber, who was starting third. However, Red Bull team boss Christian Horner said that they never even considered it.

This is the second race in succession where a team fighting for the championship has done something unusual in order to gain an advantage. In Abu Dhabi Red Bull Racing were penalised for not having enough fuel in Sebastian Vettel's car in qualifying. He was sent to the back of the grid, but Red Bull used Article 34.5 of the Sporting Regulations to change his car and optimise it for overtaking in the race. So he was able to gain an advantage from what should have been a severe penalty. The rule states, "If a competitor modifies any part on the car or makes changes to the set-up of the suspension whilst the car is being held under parc ferme conditions the relevant driver must start the race from the pit lane."

Both actions were within the rules and, as things stand, both rules are in the 2013 Sporting Regulations.

A lot of effort goes into thinking through various scenarios and wording these regulations. For example, on the rule regarding teams using eight engines in a season, Ferrari was one of the prime movers in adding a detail whereby if an engine is replaced after qualifying with another from the permitted eight, the unit removed cannot be used again that season for qualifying and race. This was to avoid teams producing special "qualifying engines".

There's no doubt that what Red Bull did in Abu Dhabi and what Ferrari did in Austin played badly with fans. Ferrari's move not only affected their own driver, Massa, it also meant that several drivers who had qualified on the clean side of the grid, were forced to start on the dirty side. The most affected were Raikkonen, who lost three places from fourth, Senna who moved to tenth and lost two places at the start, and Hamilton who lost a place from second. In contrast, Maldonado moved on to the clean side in ninth and still lost four places, while Hulkenberg moved to sixth and picked up a place at the start.

Anthony Hamilton and Jenson Button reflect on the changing world of Lewis Hamilton
20 November 2012

Lewis Hamilton's father, Anthony, has given a revealing insight into how his relationship with his son has evolved over the last couple of years and why the move to Mercedes is another example of him flying the nest.

Hamilton Senior's presence at McLaren's post-race celebrations of Lewis's brilliant victory in Austin pointed towards father and son having firmly been reconciled this year after a period in which their relationship, publicly at least, has appeared more distant.

The pair had been famously like a double act as Lewis came through the motorsport ranks and into his record-breaking early years of F1. However, that started to change in early 2010 when the McLaren driver decided to stop having his career managed by his father before eventually appointing XIX to look after his affairs.

Appearing on the BBC Radio Five Live Chequered Flag podcast during McLaren's celebrations of his son's victory on Sunday, Anthony acknowledged that Lewis had felt a desire to "have his own space", implying that the 27-year-old had belatedly experienced his teenage "tantrum years". "To be honest it hasn't been so much (me) not being part of the set-up, it's been Lewis having his own space, us having our own space, and Lewis is now going to have his own space next year. It's what kids do isn't it?" Hamilton said.

"The unfortunate thing for young racing drivers is that they don't have the opportunity to go through the tantrum years. I've been fortunate – actually maybe I've been unfortunate, I'm not sure! – none of my kids went through the terrible teens. When you're a racing driver, or a kart racer or a single-seater racer you don't have time to go off the rails, you've got to stay on the rails.

"So it's been interesting. But the family are great as we always have been and we have all found our feet in life … eventually."

The comments from Hamilton – who described Sunday as "Lewis's greatest ever race" – regarding the Mercedes move come at a time when fresh questions over its logic are being raised given the Brackley team's current travails. While Hamilton was beating Sebastian Vettel to his fourth win of the season on Sunday, his new employer was faring far worse with Michael Schumacher enduring what he bluntly described as a "disaster" as he slipped from fifth on the grid to 16th at the chequered flag, having had to make two pit stops due to high rear tyre wear.

Ironically, since Hamilton's move to the team was announced in the week before the Japanese GP, Mercedes has failed to score a single point in five races.

Perhaps with that statistic in mind, his current teammate, Jenson Button, continues to assert that Hamilton is making an error in leaving McLaren. Asked in the same podcast if Hamilton's victory had been good for the team as a whole, Button replied: "Especially for him. He's leaving us – I still think it's the wrong decision, but it's his own." He added: "It's always great having a very quick teammate like Lewis. He pushes you hard and we've had some good battles over the last three years. But things change, you move on, and I'm excited about working with Checo."

Vettel is triple world champion as Button wins dramatic Brazilian GP finale
25 November 2012

Sebastian Vettel has become only the third man in history – and the youngest – to claim three consecutive Formula One World Championship titles after an exhilarating season finale in Brazil, which saw Jenson Button claim victory. In a three-year spell of dominance, Vettel also becomes only the ninth three-time world champion, along with Schumacher, Fangio, Senna, Prost, Piquet, Lauda, Brabham and Stewart.

Vettel overcame a first lap collision which dropped him to 17th, three pit-stops and a broken radio, which meant the team wasn't expecting him for one of his stops, to take sixth place and join Michael Schumacher and Juan Manuel Fangio as triple-consecutive World Champions, as his fellow contender, Fernando Alonso, finished second in the race and three points behind Vettel at the climax.

"Only two guys have done that before, you need to be in the right place at the right time, but I also believe that you make your own luck," said an exhausted Vettel after the race. "One of the great things about F1 is you can compare your era to the past. We are in São Paulo where Ayrton Senna came from and where he is buried and to come here and win for the third time ... what we achieved today is what we've been working for since I arrived (at Red Bull). You do this job because you love the sport and the excitement. The hardest thing is winning after winning."

In his final race, Michael Schumacher took seventh place and the first points' scoring finish for Mercedes in six races.

The title looked like it could have been settled on the very first lap as a slow starting Vettel was squeezed by teammate Webber, then tapped in to a spin by Bruno Senna at turn 4, which damaged bodywork on the left side of Vettel's car, then hit the rear-right of the Red Bull quite heavily. At this stage Alonso was already in fourth place, which soon became third, and for a short time it seemed as though he might achieve the impossible.

It looked inconceivable that Vettel had not sustained any serious damage but, like in Abu Dhabi, he was able to keep his cool and make his way from last place and into the points. For Alonso, all he could do was keep it on the black stuff on his way to second, but it was not enough to stop the charging World Champion from gaining the necessary points.

The race lead changed hands throughout as the McLaren duo of Button and Lewis Hamilton both took turns at the front, but they could not keep a hard charging Nico Hulkenberg behind. As others were forced in for a change to intermediate tyres Button and Hulkenberg were the only drivers to stay out and hope for a break in the conditions. Luck was on their side and they found themselves with a 45-second lead as those behind had to switch back to dry tyres. However, this lead was to be undone by the deployment of a safety car for debris on the circuit, which bunched the pack up and reopened the possibilities for the world title.

At this point Hulkenberg led the race, after taking first place from Button around the outside of turn 1 and pulling away from the McLaren pairing. The Force India driver excelled in the wet conditions on slick tyres, but after a half-spin he lost the lead to Hamilton and had to hunt him down as the rain started to fall heavily again. On Lap 52, as Hamilton was caught in traffic behind Heikki Kovalainen, Hulkenberg sensed his opportunity and tried to out-brake the race leader. But, braking late and off the racing line, he slid in to Hamilton and forced the Briton out of his final race for

McLaren. Hulkenberg subsequently received a drive-through penalty, dropping him to fifth position and dreams of what could have been in his final race for Force India.

Button was the man to gain from the collision in front and he was able to control the race from then on, taking his third victory of the season and 15th of his career. Completing the podium was Felipe Massa, in the process helping his team secure second in the constructors' championship, worth an estimated $10 million in extra prize money compared to third. He has had a fine finish to the season and his change in form has been very much key to Ferrari retaining that spot ahead of McLaren. Massa sat comfortably in second as the race neared the end, but, as expected, he let Alonso through to take the maximum points available.

Behind the top three, Mark Webber also had an eventful race running wide trying to overtake Vettel following the safety car and then spinning at Junção. However, he was able to recover and secure his most common position, finishing fourth for the sixth time this year.

Completing the top ten were Jean-Eric Vergne, Kamui Kobayashi and Kimi Raikkonen. Vergne, in particular, produced a very strong drive from a 17th place start to take his fourth points' scoring position in his debut year. Kobayashi had battled with Vettel and Massa during the middle phase of the race, but spun after a brush with Schumacher and dropped to ninth. Raikkonen, meanwhile, seemed to get lost after running off the track at Junção and tried to rejoin through an escape road, which turned out to be a dead-end.

In a crucial race for the three tail-end teams, Caterham were able to clinch tenth position as Vitaly Petrov finished 11th ahead of Marussia's Charles Pic. With Pic moving to Caterham in 2013 and a substantial amount of money gained by finishing tenth, today's result could have been due to savvy gamesmanship by the young Frenchman.

Brazilian Grand Prix
Interlagos 71 laps

1. Button	McLaren-Mercedes	1h45:22.656
2. Alonso	Ferrari	+2.754
3. Massa	Ferrari	+3.615

4. Webber	Red Bull-Renault	+4.936
5. Hulkenberg	Force India-Mercedes	+5.708
6. Vettel	Red Bull-Renault	+9.453
7. Schumacher	Mercedes	+11.900
8. Vergne	Toro Rosso-Ferrari	+28.600
9. Kobayashi	Sauber-Ferrari	+31.200
10. Raikkonen	Lotus-Renault	+1 lap
11. Petrov	Caterham-Renault	+1 lap
12. Pic	Marussia-Cosworth	+1 lap
13. Ricciardo	Toro Rosso-Ferrari	+1 lap
14. Kovalainen	Caterham-Renault	+1 lap
15. Rosberg	Mercedes	+1 lap
16. Glock	Marussia-Cosworth	+2 laps
17. De la Rosa	HRT-Cosworth	+2 laps
18. Karthikeyan	HRT-Cosworth	+2 laps
19. Di Resta	Force India-Mercedes	+3 laps

Drivers' Championship Final Standings

1. Vettel	281 pts
2. Alonso	278
3. Raikkonen	207
4. Hamilton	190
5. Button	188
6. Webber	179
7. Massa	122
8. Grosjean	96
9. Rosberg	93
10. Perez	66
11. Hulkenberg	63
12. Kobayashi	60
13. Schumacher	49
14. Di Resta	46
15. Maldonado	45
16. Senna	31
17. Vergne	16
18. Ricciardo	10

Constructors' Championship Final Standings

1. Red Bull-Renault   460 pts
2. Ferrari   400
3. McLaren-Mercedes   378
4. Lotus-Renault   303
5. Mercedes   142
6. Sauber-Ferrari   126
7. Force India-Mercedes   109
8. Williams-Renault   76
9. Toro Rosso-Ferrari   26
10. Caterham-Renault   0 (best finish: 11th place)

And so an exceptional year of F1 came to an end with an appropriately thrilling conclusion.

This season was a pleasure to cover: light(ish) on politics, strong on racing and on characters. I liked the ebb and flow of the year: the fact that different teams had a chance to shine, with Williams winning in Spain, Sauber challenging for the win in Malaysia and Force India leading in Brazil. It was a season that showed the cast of characters in F1 is deeper than just the two or three leading teams.

You had to feel for Fernando Alonso: he had given his all like a gladiator, but one with a smaller sword than his opponent. Alonso was on a higher level this year than at any other time in his career. He slipped a little in qualifying later in the season, eclipsed by Felipe Massa, and gave himself a lot of work to do on race day in the final few rounds.

But his starts and his race management were exceptional all year. It would be wrong to say that Ferrari didn't develop their car; after all it was over a second off the pace in Melbourne. But they didn't develop it enough and that began to tell in the final third of the season. Of course, that's not the only reason why Alonso lost the title. He lost it because of his two non-finishes, in Spa and Suzuka, where he tangled with a Lotus driver. One of these was not his fault, in the other he risked a lot and lost out. Such are the fine margins in Formula One.

Sebastian Vettel also had his non-finishes this year, but these were

173

due more to reliability. Yes he had a tangle with a backmarker in Malaysia, which meant he didn't score any points there, but his alternator failures robbed him of a win in Valencia and points in Monza, so it evens out in the end.

The Red Bull was the fastest car at times this season, notably in the Asian races in October, but not the fastest car of the season. That honour goes to McLaren, it's just that they were unable to exploit it. Lewis Hamilton should have won the 2012 world championship. His driving this year was of the highest standard; gone were the errors and anger of 2011, to be replaced by some sublime speed.

The McLaren was the fastest car at the start and end of the season and in the middle too. It was eclipsed by the Red Bull in early summer and in October, but apart from that it was the car of the year. However, operational errors and reliability failings in the autumn cost Hamilton over 100 points and his shot at the title.

Take nothing away from Sebastian Vettel's success, he deserved it and put in several performances of which his detractors thought him incapable. I was particularly impressed with his drive in Brazil. After tangling with Bruno Senna on the opening lap, losing his radio and suffering pit-stop confusions, he still managed to hold his nerve and get the result he needed to win the title. It's hard to overstate how tough that is mentally. He had a lot to lose on that final day of the season. It helped that Alonso didn't have the pace to challenge for the win, but there was still a lot for Vettel to deal with at Interlagos and he proved himself a worthy champion.

I said at the start of the 2012 season that with six world champions in the field whoever won the title would deserve it. That view was underlined after seven different drivers won the first seven races, and the final round just confirmed it. The 2012 champion was thoroughly deserving of his third title in a row.

Other talking points from the season were the crashes involving Romain Grosjean and Pastor Maldonado. Grosjean was at it again in Brazil, trying to force his was past Pedro de la Rosa when both were on a hot lap in qualifying. Already on a final warning after his ban for the Spa pile-up, he was fortunate not to be penalised by the stewards for that. He crashed again on race day, summing up his season. Kimi Raikkonen had carried the Lotus team all year, scoring in excess of 200 points and, with a more consistent performer in the other car, Lotus might have been able to challenge Ferrari and McLaren for second or third place in the table.

Maldonado, like Grosjean, wowed us with his speed in qualifying at times this year, but his race performances were also inconsistent. The Williams was one of the best cars this year and for the team to end up down in eighth place in the standings is a bitter disappointment. Perhaps in recognition of this, both Maldonado and Grosjean were still waiting for confirmation of their seats for 2013 as the F1 circus left São Paulo.

Another worrying concern for F1 in 2012 was the rise of "pay drivers", taking up the seats in increasingly important teams. I wrote during the year about how the sport is storing a problem up for itself in five years time with no sign of stars coming through to replace Alonso, Hamilton and Vettel. As the season closed there were still seats available at several teams and it will be interesting to see how many pay drivers there are on the grid when next season starts.

For 2013, with no major rule change from this year, I expect the McLarens to start and continue strongly, but I wonder if the drivers will be able to qualify consistently enough to mount a title challenge. Red Bull must be favourites again with Vettel, but the effort they put in takes a lot out of the race team, especially the mechanics, who were exhausted after another punishing year of late nights. Adrian Newey's cars are very fast, but also complex to work on and the risk for Red Bull is motivation and fatigue. This is what Christian Horner and his management group must guard against.

Meanwhile, Ferrari and Alonso should challenge again, but cannot afford to produce another car that misses the mark. Motivation is high at Ferrari, but the inspiration is lacking and this will be a very high-pressure winter in the technical department at Maranello.

And what of Lotus and Mercedes? Lotus built a good car in 2012 and Kimi Raikkonen did a wonderful job with it, but can they raise their game to win consistently? And can Mercedes produce a car for

Lewis Hamilton and Nico Rosberg to get regular wins? All the pieces are in place now, but the worrying lack of progress on fundamental issues like tyre wear in 2012 raise doubts. Like Maranello, the technical department in Brackley will feel the heat this winter.

Chapter Twelve
Strategy Reports

The most popular content strand on the *JA on F1* website, the UBS Race Strategy Briefings and Reports, now in its second season, continued to enjoy a massive reach among F1 fans this year. The unique in-depth content is written with input and data from several of the leading F1 teams' strategists and from Pirelli.

The content is posted on jamesallenonf1.com and is also distributed via a network of partner websites around the world, reaching 10 million unique users in 10 languages. The interactivity and engagement of the audience remains exceptionally high for this strand, with an average of 140 comments and interactions from readers on every post.

This year we also provided a realistic Race Strategy Calculator, complete with a tyre model that was designed by one of the F1 team strategists. It allowed fans to change variables of tyre choice and pit-stop laps to see if they could find the fastest strategy for each race.

Here are the Strategy Reports for all the Grands Prix in 2012, reproduced in the hope and expectation that they will provide further insight into the way the races were won this year and that they will be useful for future reference.

Australian Grand Prix
Melbourne, 18 March 2012, 58 laps

As the first race of the season the Australian Grand Prix is always something of a test case for how race strategies have been affected by a new generation of tyres and rule changes, such as the one banning the exhaust blown diffuser.

This weekend we saw clearly that the 2012 Pirellis are more suitable race tyres for F1 than last year's: they allow the drivers to push a bit more and they wear differently from the 2011 versions, which would wear quickly along the shoulder, whereas the 2012 models wear evenly across the tyre. This is positive as it makes them slightly more predictable, though performance still drops sharply if you stay on them too long.

Expectation before the start was that the leading drivers would do a two-stop race, starting on used soft tyres, taking a second set of used softs at the first stop around lap 19 and then pitting for medium tyres around lap 39.

McLaren controlled the race from the front row of the grid and the victory was only threatened 22 laps before the end, when the safety car neutralized the field and removed Button's lead, with Vettel right behind him. Lewis Hamilton didn't have the pace to stay with Button and some bad luck with strategy cost him second place. Both drivers had to be careful on fuel saving as well according to the team boss Martin Whitmarsh, due to starting with an aggressively low fuel load.

The start was the decisive moment. Hamilton had qualified on pole, but Button immediately gained the strategic advantage over his teammate by winning the start, which meant that he had first call on when to pit. He made his first stop on lap 16 and moved on to the medium tyres. This meant Hamilton had to come in a lap later. Hamilton's tyres were already going off significantly and he lost 3.4 seconds on lap 16 and on his in-lap to the pits on lap 17. He lost a further 1.4 seconds on his out-lap. Worse still, he rejoined behind Raikkonen and Perez, who was on the medium tyres and one-stopping. By the time he passed Perez he was 11 seconds behind Button. More significantly, Vettel had gained seven seconds on him through this period. The world champion also stopped at the ideal moment – lap 16 – before the tyre performance dropped off and was now just two seconds behind Hamilton. This time lost for Hamilton would prove decisive at the second stops. Vettel had opted for the soft tyres, while Hamilton and Button were on mediums.

The double-stop

With an 11-second gap between Button and Hamilton at the end of the second stint and the tyres going off on both cars, the McLaren team decided to pit both at the same time, on lap 36. Their in-laps were identical, but Hamilton's out-lap was three seconds slower than Button's, meaning he was vulnerable to Vettel.

People have questioned the wisdom of pitting the two cars on the same lap. It's something that McLaren have been working on, as it's hard to achieve and requires a well-drilled pit crew to have the second set of tyres ready to go. But being able to double-stop has significant strategic advantages in multi-stop races, where an extra lap on fading tyres can cost a lot of time. It was an interesting decision to try it in a two-stop race.

The Red Bull team had seen McLaren stopping, but left Vettel out as he was lapping faster than the McLarens at that point. This meant that he was on target to jump Hamilton at the second stops anyway, but it was guaranteed when the safety car was deployed, as Petrov's car had broken down on the pit straight. Vettel dived into the pits from the lead and rejoined in between the McLarens, ahead of Hamilton. From sixth on the grid after a disappointing qualifying session, Vettel had made the most out of the opportunity presented to him by McLaren and Hamilton.

The total time needed for a pit stop at Albert Park is 25 seconds, which is one of the longest of the year. This is because the pit lane is long and the speed limit is just 40mph, rather than the usual 60mph, for safety reasons. This encourages drivers to do fewer stops rather than more. Even though Raikkonen, for example, had three sets of new soft tyres at his disposal, he didn't go for a three-stop sprint strategy because of the time that would be lost in the pits.

So from outside the top ten there were always going to be a few cars that would start on the medium tyres and try to get to lap 28 or 29, then switch to the softs. The front-runners would never have planned to do this as simulations showed it to be 20 seconds slower than a two-stop if you can run in clear air. It was assumed that several drivers would try to one-stop. In the event only three started on the medium tyres: Perez, Vergne and Petrov and Vergne did a two-stopper.

Mediums bring the winners' home

Going into the race the strategists knew that on one single qualifying lap the soft tyres had been 0.8 seconds faster than the mediums. But they believed that in the race the gap would probably be around 0.5 seconds. If you had a new set of options – as Raikkonen did, for example – that was a faster choice than a new set of mediums. In the event the gap between the two tyres turned out to be so close that if you only had used softs, as all the front-runners had, then a new set of mediums was better for most.

With the leaders forced to stop as early as lap 16, Perez was lapping comfortably in the 1m 33s, which convinced several strategists that the mediums were the best tyres on the day. Webber went first, followed by Button, Hamilton and Alonso. Vettel, Raikkonen and Kobayashi went for softs. The Japanese driver then underlined the Sauber's gentle action on the tyres by extending his middle stint on softs to 23 laps; longer than Alonso managed on new mediums in the Ferrari!

Perez's strategy saw him rise to second place by lap 20 before the tyres really started to go off – he dropped five places and ten seconds in three laps as the cars that had pitted for new tyres overtook him. But he made his only stop on lap 24 and drove to the flag on a set of new options. He was racing Maldonado, Rosberg, Kobayashi and Raikkonen and finished eighth, having started at the back of the grid. The Sauber's ability to run long stints on the Pirelli tyres will bring them plenty of points this year.

Malaysian Grand Prix
Sepang, 27 March 2012, 56 laps

The Malaysian Grand Prix provided us with an exciting glimpse of what we can expect in 2012 from a racing and strategy point of view. We also saw an indication of the key quality that will be required to win this year's championship – the ability to be fast on all types of tyre in all conditions. Judging from the Sepang race, even more so than Melbourne, this is something that all the teams are finding hard to manage. Hamilton, the pole sitter, for example, wasn't particularly fast in any of the conditions, while the Sauber was very quick on used intermediates and hard slicks. Williams' Pastor Maldonado was not particularly quick on intermediate tyres, but once he went on to slicks he was extremely fast. It was a fantastic race and one that Sergio Perez could and should have won; even with the driving error he made six laps from the end.

Race morning strategy predictions for a dry race had been that the hard tyres would actually prove faster in the race, with estimates of up to 0.2 seconds' advantage. In the event this proved true and the critical decision was in taking a new set of hard tyres rather than a used set of mediums. This was to be proven by the duel for the lead in the closing stages.

Perez and Sauber – the one that got away

Sergio Perez and Sauber was the fastest car/driver/tyre combination in two vital phases of this curious afternoon: in the long second stint on used intermediates and, in particular, in the final stint on slick tyres. Although driver error was in part responsible for Perez's failing to take a historic victory, Sauber's strategy, while bold early on, became very cautious as the race progressed and played a significant part in the disappointment.

As the rain fell heavily in the opening laps, Sauber pitted Perez on lap 3 for wet tyres. He was the first serious runner to make the move and everyone followed suit, though not for another two laps. On extreme wets Perez was three or more seconds faster than the leading cars and, when everyone pitted on lap 5, he moved up to third place. It was a bold move by Sauber and set up the platform for a great result.

But then they started playing it cautious. Going into the second stops – the move from full wets to intermediates – the track was drying out and, by the end of lap 13 when the safety car was withdrawn and it was obvious that intermediates were the faster tyres, Sauber left Perez out for another lap. He stopped one lap later than Alonso and two later than Button.

When Perez came out of the pits on lap 15 he was still just in front of Alonso, but was now feeling his way on new intermediates, whereas Alonso had a lap's worth of experience on them and was able to pass the Mexican straight away. Although Perez did gain a position over Hamilton, who was held in his pit box by McLaren so as not to collide with the incoming Massa, this loss of track position to Alonso was critical.

The Ferrari opened up a six-second lead over the Sauber, but as the intermediates wore down and the tyre pressures came up, Perez came flying back at Alonso, closing the gap to 1.3 seconds on lap 39. By now Ricciardo, the pioneer on slick tyres, was lighting up the time sheets and it was clearly the moment to follow.

But the Sauber strategists delayed again: they were cautious about putting their inexperienced driver on slicks too soon, they also had one eye on the weather, with the threat of more showers in the air. They lost the initiative:

Ferrari went for it, bringing Alonso in. As the leader, Alonso needed to cover off the threat from what was clearly the faster car, which he did.

This second mistake dropped Perez seven seconds behind Alonso. Sauber had chosen a new set of hard tyres; Alonso a used set of mediums. The Ferrari decision was an interesting one as many strategists weren't sure whether the mediums would last 16 laps, the distance to the flag from this point. On paper the mediums offered faster warm-up. In fact, the hard tyres proved faster to warm up on the Sauber, which was instantly quicker. Perez again caught Alonso easily and with the DRS wing activated and a tyre advantage was sure to pass him at some point in the final six laps.

However, he lost focus when the team told him to protect his position and he made a mistake, losing four seconds. There were suggestions that with Sauber so politically aligned to Ferrari and a long-standing customer of its engines, the two teams had made some kind of "arrangement", but Sauber and Ferrari denied this on Sunday night. And it does look more like a case of Sauber not wanting to throw away the chance of its best result in five years.

Nevertheless in that final stint we saw something that gives great encouragement for the season ahead. After six laps we had reached a crossover point where the hard tyres were faster than the mediums. This is something Pirelli had been hoping to achieve this year and it will make the strategies extremely interesting going forward. With lots of cars so close on performance and with so many strategic options available, it's going to be a great year of racing.

Toro Rosso – tactically astute

Toro Rosso's technical director Giorgio Ascanelli used to be race engineer to Ayrton Senna at McLaren and is one of the wiliest old foxes in the pit lane. On Sunday we saw a couple of classic Ascanelli moves: first he left Jean-Eric Vergne out on intermediate tyres as the torrential downpour hit. He had only to stay on the track as everyone pitted for full wets and he managed it. When the race director stopped the race, as Ascanelli knew he would, Vergne was in seventh place. And with the restart behind the safety car, this meant full wet tyres had to be fitted, so Vergne got a set of full wets without having to make a pit stop! It set him up for his eventual eighth-place finish.

Meanwhile, Ascanelli was at it with his other driver too. As the track dried out he decided Ricciardo should be the first to go on to the slicks. This made sense as he was 17th at the time and needed to get into the game. There was no need to risk Vergne's position, so Ricciardo rolled the dice and gained three places – not enough to get him into the points, but well worth a try. Risk and reward; it's what F1 race strategy is all about.

Chinese Grand Prix
Shanghai, 15 April 2012, 56 laps

The UBS Chinese Grand Prix was a thrilling race, despite the comfortable winning margin for Nico Rosberg in the Mercedes. Race strategy was crucial to the outcome and we also learned a lot about how F1 has changed in 2012, with the field closing up on performance so the top teams can no longer rely on building gaps over the midfield to drop nicely into after pit stops. The leading teams will have to work much harder than last year on creative race strategy and the drivers will have to do a lot more overtaking.

During Friday's Free Practice 2 it was clear that many teams have yet to master the best set-up on their cars for both qualifying and the race, going from high fuel to low fuel. McLaren appeared to have race pace that was 0.5 seconds a lap faster than Mercedes, but overnight on Friday Ross Brawn's team made some changes to the set-up to improve tyre life and at the end of the Saturday morning session Schumacher ran a handful of laps on high fuel to confirm the changes. This was not noticed by many in the paddock, but proved crucial to Mercedes' victory.

The track temperature was foremost in the minds of the team strategists as they prepared for the race: the 2012 Pirelli tyres are very sensitive to temperature changes and in qualifying it was clear that a drop of a few degrees created a disparity between different cars. The rough rule of thumb is that Mercedes likes the colder temperature, as does the Sauber, while the Red Bulls, Lotus and McLarens operate better in higher temperatures. This is a trend that is likely to continue all season, so in Bahrain the picture may look very different from China.

Two stops or three?
As with last year's Shanghai race, the key strategy decision was between two pit stops and three and the timing of them. Pre-race predictions showed that two stops was faster than three by up to seven seconds, but the danger

was that the two-stopping driver would be vulnerable in the last five laps on worn tyres. Crucially, the decision on which strategy was faster varied from team to team, depending on how fast they could run on the medium tyres. McLaren, for example, found them slower than the softs, while other teams including Mercedes, Lotus and Williams thought differently.

McLaren went for three stops, Mercedes for two; the pattern was set. One of the reasons why Hamilton, in particular, was obliged to do three stops was because in qualifying he set his fastest time on a set of tyres that had done six laps by the time he started the race. This meant he would struggle to make it to lap 13, which was the window for two stops.

Mercedes knew this and planned to exploit it. Rosberg and Schumacher were instructed to get to at least lap 13, at which point they would switch to medium tyres and do a middle stint of 21 laps, then a final stint on mediums again. Button was the greater threat to them on his three-stop strategy, based on two stints on the soft tyres, but his challenge faded with a botched final pit stop, when the left rear wheel change was delayed by six seconds. So when he rejoined, instead of being 14 seconds behind Rosberg with 17 laps to go and on tyres that were five laps newer, he was 20 seconds behind.

The pit-stop problem – not the first McLaren have suffered at critical moments this season – had a further knock-on effect in that it brought Button back out into the train of cars led by Massa and Raikkonen, who were two-stopping. Instead of gaining on Rosberg, Button could not take advantage of his new tyres, lost a second per lap to him and the race was over.

Most of Hamilton's race was spent in traffic as well, due to starting down in seventh place after his gearbox change penalty. He could never get clear of the competitive midfield cars and run in clear air, so progress through the field was difficult on the three-stop strategy he was obliged to do. A strategy like that requires plenty of opportunity to drive flat out on a clear track.

Another factor that worked against McLaren was that they had to cover Mark Webber, who made extremely early stops. This caused them to pit earlier than intended and meant that they didn't have the fresh-tyre advantage over Rosberg and the two stoppers they needed to cut through the field.

Extending the middle stint

Quite a few cars in the midfield tried the two-stop approach, based on two stints on the medium tyres, with mixed results; the key here was being able to extend the middle stint so as not to leave yourself too many laps at the end on the final set of tyres. Vettel went for it, to try to get himself up from his lowly 11th grid slot, as did Massa from 12th, Senna from 14th and the two Lotus drivers: Raikkonen from fourth and Grosjean tenth.

It is interesting to compare the results these drivers achieved, all trying to do the same thing. The starkest example of it going wrong is Raikkonen – he fell from second, with just nine laps to go, to 14th at the finish! This was partly due to worn tyres after a 28-lap final stint, but he also got off-line trying too hard to defend his position from Vettel. His tyres got dirty and this allowed other cars to pass him. He got in a vicious circle: as he defended against them the tyres got dirtier still and all hope was lost.

The reason he found himself in this position was because he pitted for his second stop on lap 26. His middle stint was only 16 laps long on the medium tyres – he blinked too early.

Conversely, Senna started on the medium tyres, did a middle stint on his new set of softs, pitted for the second time on lap 29 back to the medium and managed to gain places when the three-stoppers made their final stops. Senna's drive showed how well balanced and competitive the Williams car is this year. He managed to get a seventh-place finish. Vettel went from 11th to fifth at the finish, making the most of the strategy by pulling off a long middle stint on medium tyres.

Grosjean drove well to collect his first points of the season, but it could have been better. He managed to go four laps longer than teammate Raikkonen in the middle stint and this set him up for a great result in fifth place. He was sitting there with 12 laps to go, but made a mistake when fighting Webber and lost three places. He managed to get two of them back, which shows that he still had life left in his tyres, despite them being only three laps fresher than Raikkonen's.

Bahrain Grand Prix
Sakhir Circuit, 22 April 2012, 57 laps

The Bahrain Grand Prix was another example of close racing with uncertain outcomes dependent on race strategy, something that has already come to characterize the 2012 F1 season. Sebastian Vettel and Red Bull became the fourth different car/driver winning combination in four races, showing not only how closely matched the teams are, but also how delicate the balancing act is in getting the strategy right on the Pirelli tyres. In just four races we have already had eight different drivers on the podium, more than in the whole of 2011.

Bahrain's Sakhir Circuit provided the sternest test yet for the tyres, with plenty of high-energy corners, hard braking zones and track temperatures of around 40 degrees. Tyre degradation was very high, especially due to the heat. Degradation is a measure of the decline in lap time performance, whereas wear is the consumption of the tyre. Strategists briefed on Sunday morning that wear was not a problem – it would be possible to do a whole race distance on one set of tyres – but the drop-off in lap time was severe over 20 or so laps on the medium tyres and 14 on the softs.

So it was a question of being reactive. It was essential to have a plan in mind, whether that was two stops or three stops, but to be prepared to change it, reacting quickly to pit once you saw degradation affecting the lap times. There was also a huge benefit in having new sets of tyres, rather than used sets. Pre-race expectations were that most drivers would do three stops, with a few trying a two-stop strategy. In the event, among the top ten finishers, only Force India's Paul di Resta managed to do two stops.

Many surprises

There were many surprises in this race: the poor performance of McLaren both on the track and in the pits, for example. But the biggest was the way the Lotus cars of Kimi Raikkonen and Romain Grosjean took on the Red Bulls. They managed to beat Mark Webber fairly easily, but Raikkonen couldn't quite do enough to beat Vettel for the win. Lotus have had a good car at every race this season, but haven't quite got the strategy right. In China, for example, they tried to do a two-stop race with Raikkonen, but timed the stops wrong and on worn tyres he was vulnerable to the three-stoppers at the end of the race, falling from second place to 14th at the flag.

In Bahrain they almost got it right. The strategy planning began in qualifying, where the Finn did only one lap in the Q2 session, intending to save a new set of soft tyres. Here Lotus made a small mistake, which turned out to be a benefit as they sent him out too early and underestimated the track improvement at the end of the Q2 session. Raikkonen failed to make the top ten shootout, where Ricciardo's result shows that a sixth place start might have been possible for the Lotus. But to do that would have used up more tyres.

It wasn't their intention to miss Q3. However, the upside was that in failing to make the top ten Raikkonen had two new sets of soft tyres and two new sets of mediums, so he would do the whole race on new tyres. He also had a free choice of starting tyres. Vettel, in contrast, by going all the way to the end of qualifying and taking pole, used all his tyres except for one set of mediums and was forced to start on used softs.

How much did Raikkonen gain from this? As a rule of thumb every new set you run, compared to your rival on a used set, is worth around eight seconds per stint. Here's how the strategists work it out: degradation is 0.3 seconds per lap, so tyres used for three laps in qualifying are 0.9 seconds slower per lap than a new set. For Raikkonen this meant that he had 24 seconds available to him in the first three stints, provided he could make use of the new tyres and not lose time with mistakes or in traffic. In fact, this what got him in the game and almost won him the race.

Lotus went for the soft tyres for the start, because they have a higher working temperature than the mediums and free practice had shown the car worked well on them with high fuel. They thought they had the fastest car on Friday.

Lotus's lack of ruthlessness costs win

We've seen how the start is crucial in strategy terms and Raikkonen made a great start, showing the advantage of new softs tyres off the line, up from 11th to seventh and ahead of Rosberg and Perez. He made a mistake on lap 3 and let Massa past, taking a couple of laps to re-pass him. During this time he lost three seconds to the leader Vettel. But more significantly he damaged his front wing and so had to deal with some aerodynamic loss, which also cost him for the rest of the race.

Thanks to the new tyres he passed Hamilton, who was struggling, and he managed to extend the first stint to lap 11. By doing this he got ahead of Alonso, Webber and Button. Now he was a contender for the win.

In the second stint on new softs he was the fastest car on the track until he caught his teammate Grosjean and it was here, arguably, that he lost the chance to win. Vettel was not getting away at the front, Grosjean was on used medium tyres and Raikkonen was caught up behind him. He eventually passed the Frenchman then set off after Vettel.

On new mediums compared to Vettel's used softs he caught up quickly, but couldn't pass. With some clear air instead of the four laps he spent behind Grosjean, he might have had the platform to jump Vettel in the final stops, but instead he made his third stop on the same lap and, with Vettel using his only new set of tyres in the final stint, Raikkonen had no further tyre advantage to play and had to follow him home.

Raikkonen was disappointed after the race. He had a chance to win, just as Perez had a chance to win in Malaysia. The strategy was good enough to give him a chance, but not perfect. Perhaps with a little more ruthlessness by Lotus, moving Grosjean aside, it could have been perfect.

Two-stops allows Di Resta to equal his career-best

After a trying weekend off the track, the Sahara Force India team got a great result on Sunday with Paul di Resta finishing sixth. As the Scotsman said afterwards, this felt like a win for the midfield team. He did it despite having the slowest car of the top 12 qualifiers, with a pace offset of 0.8 of a second per lap to the Red Bulls and McLarens and 0.3 seconds to the Mercedes.

Again the strategy planning began in qualifying. The team had taken the decision not to do a lap in Q3, but instead to save tyres for the race, knowing that he was going to try to do a two-stop race. This gave him two new sets of soft tyres and one new set of mediums for the race.

The ideal two-stop race was to stop on laps 19 and 38, but even though he had new soft tyres at the start, he couldn't get further than lap 14 before the degradation became too great, relative to the three-stoppers, and he had to pit. He was the last of the top ten to do so. With everyone around him three-stopping, Force India knew their driver would be vulnerable at the end of the race on worn tyres to three-stoppers on fresh tyres, but Di Resta drove a masterful race, keeping the tyres alive at the same time as keeping the pace up.

On new softs at the start, he lost two places off the line and lost time behind Senna. However, by extending his soft tyres to lap 14 he was able to get ahead of many of the three-stoppers, including Rosberg, whom he was racing for final position.

Traffic is less of a problem for a two-stopper than a three-stopper, but Di Resta still lost time at various stages of the race, particularly the second stint where he was faster than many three-stoppers, despite looking to do a 19-lap stint compared to their 13 laps. If there was a place where he lost the opportunity to finish ahead of Rosberg, it was probably here.

With a final stint of 24 laps, he was vulnerable at the end of the race, to Rosberg, but was helped by Button's late race retirement and the fact that Alonso didn't quite have the straight-line speed to attack in the final laps. Using KERS, Di Resta could defend and hold his sixth position, equalling his career-best F1 finish.

Spanish Grand Prix
Barcelona, 13 May 2012, 66 laps

The Spanish Grand Prix was a perfect example of how a race can be won or lost on the finest of margins. Pastor Maldonado beat Fernando Alonso and won the race for Williams due to planning and a good strategy call halfway through the race, while Lotus's Kimi Raikkonen again had the car to win, but was a fraction off due to race strategy and conditions and ended up third.

There were several key moments and decisions that decided the outcome of this race. The main one was Maldonado's early second stop. But there was another before the race had even begun and it eliminated the favourite for the race win. Lewis Hamilton should have won this race comfortably for McLaren, with a 0.6 second per lap car advantage, but a mistake by the McLaren team when he did his final run in qualifying ruined his chances.

McLaren's bloomer
Due to a refuelling error, Hamilton's car did not have enough fuel to complete the lap and be legal at the end. Team boss Martin Whitmarsh has since admitted that he should have told Lewis Hamilton to abandon his hot lap as the team had realized it had not put enough fuel in his car. Had he done this Hamilton would have started the race from sixth place, with a

time set earlier in Q3. Instead McLaren did not act, Hamilton completed the lap, switched the engine off and then the team tried to argue force majeure for the error. The FIA stewards sent him to the back of the grid from where eighth was the best result achievable.

Hamilton made up four places at the start from 24th on the grid and managed to get his tyres to last 14 laps in the first stint, the longest of any front-runner. He had climbed to fourth place when he stopped and rejoined in 14th place. He made his way through the field with a combination of overtakes and a two-stop strategy which meant he did 21 laps on his second set of tyres and 31 on the final set, both of which were the hard compounds. He lost time in the second stint behind Massa; otherwise a better result might have been possible. He got ahead of Massa when the Brazilian served a drive-through penalty on lap 29 for using DRS in a yellow flag zone.

By extending the stints, Hamilton was able to make up places when the three-stoppers made their final stops. He only lost one place at the end to Vettel and almost got one back from Rosberg. It was a fine drive, but he and McLaren know that his first win of the season was there for the taking this weekend had they made a different decision in the heat of the moment in qualifying.

Getting the planning right

On Friday practice, with track temperatures above 40 degrees, the soft tyres were working well. However, expectations were that the temperature would be lower come Sunday. This led some teams to plan on saving three new sets of hard tyres for the race, as these have a lower working temperature range than the softs and would therefore come into their own in cooler conditions. It was the right call: the track was at 44 degrees on Saturday and this dropped to 32 degrees on Sunday – for the race the hard tyres proved faster. Williams and Maldonado saved three sets; Ferrari had only two new sets for Alonso.

Red Bull were also one of the teams to save three sets. However, the plan didn't quite work out for them, as they simply didn't have the pace in qualifying or the race. Sebastian Vettel was forced to use up all his soft tyres just to get through to the final part of qualifying. This meant that he had no new sets of softs for a run in Q3 and was only eighth on the grid. Both cars required a front wing change during the race. The team combined them with tyre stops, but it wasn't ideal timing tactically. Vettel also had a drive-through penalty so he did well to finish ahead of the McLarens in sixth place.

The cars are so close together this year, winning is all about getting out the front of the pack early on, as Vettel did in Bahrain and Rosberg did in China. The race was again fought out between the two cars on the front row of the grid. However, Spain was only the second time in five races (the other was Malaysia) where the car leading the first lap did not go on to win the race. This was all down to strategy. Williams believed that they had a pace advantage over Ferrari and expected the challenge for the win to come from Lotus. However, they knew they were vulnerable to Alonso's excellent starts. Maldonado duly lost the start to the Ferrari and then Alonso had enough pace in the opening two stints of the race to keep himself ahead.

Tyre life allows Maldonado to undercut Alonso
Importantly, however, the Williams had better tyre life at the end of the stints. At the end of the second stint, Maldonado closed up on Alonso, from over three seconds to half of that. Williams pitted him two laps before Alonso for the second stop and Ferrari allowed their driver to stay out and run into slower traffic. This is something they have allowed to happen before.

The call to try the undercut (pitting earlier than your opponent and using the pace of new tyres to get ahead when he stops) was made by Williams' head of strategy Mark Barnett. He brought Maldonado in on lap 24 when he was 1.5 seconds behind Alonso. Having saved the sets of new hard tyres, Barnett calculated that he would then have the tyre life to do 42 laps with one more stop to make without losing pace at the end.

The move was brilliantly executed: his in-lap was 0.4 seconds faster than Alonso's, the stop was only 0.2 seconds slower than Ferrari's, but crucially on new hard tyres his out-lap was 2.6 seconds faster and the first flying lap was also a second faster. With Alonso losing time behind Pic, Maldonado had done enough to take the lead from the Ferrari when it stopped two laps later.

As Alonso pushed hard in the Venezuelan driver's wake to stay with him in the final stint, we got a graphic example of how following another car speeds up the degradation of the tyres. Alonso wasn't able to stay with

Maldonado until the end, as the degradation caused by running in traffic was more severe than running in clear air. Alonso's tyres had done three laps in qualifying, so were the same age more or less as Maldonado's.

Why Lotus didn't win

Although they had the fastest car in race practice simulations on Friday afternoon, were third and fourth on the grid and set the fastest lap of the race on Sunday by over a second, Lotus didn't win. Why not?

Temperature has something to do with it: the drop to 32 degrees on race day took the edge off their speed (so fine are the margins now). They also made a strategy mistake at the first stop, putting the cars on to used soft tyres, rather than the hards. To compensate they pushed the stints out to make sure they'd have a chance at the end. As the temperatures rose towards the end of the race we got to see what the Lotus could do as it set the fastest lap of the race – over a second faster than the nearest car. Raikkonen's final stint was 18 laps, Alonso's 23 and Maldonado's 25. Alonso was vulnerable to attack from Raikkonen in the final laps, but he ran out of laps. Perhaps if he'd stopped one lap earlier he would have passed Alonso for second at the end.

Starts are a vital part of race strategy and we saw the experience of Raikkonen triumph over the nervousness of Grosjean at the start. Although the younger man was ahead on the grid, Raikkonen was ahead in the opening lap and Grosjean fell behind Rosberg, whose pace was much slower and so held him up. The Frenchman lost eight seconds in the first nine laps. Worse still, Mercedes pitted Rosberg first as a defensive move and he stayed ahead in the second stint, so Grosjean had to pass him on track.

The first win for Lotus this year is surely not far away.

Monaco Grand Prix
Monte Carlo, 27 May 2012, 78 laps

History will show that Mark Webber was the winner of this race ahead of Nico Rosberg with Fernando Alonso third. But, of course, it wasn't as simple as that. Rosberg tried a strategy gamble to get the lead by pitting first on lap 27, but it didn't work out as Webber reacted to it. Sebastian Vettel surprised everyone with his strategy and from ninth on the grid came within five seconds of a winning position. Fernando Alonso made a gain of two places to score a podium and he was happy with that. But with the benefit of hindsight, Alonso could have won. However, he was not prepared to take the necessary gamble. Such is racing and the finely balanced world of race strategy.

In many ways the most important observation to make about this race is that for the fourth time in six races, the car leading on the first lap has gone on to win. Although some have described the 2012 season as a 'lottery' due to the unpredictable behaviour of the Pirelli tyres from track to track and from day to day, this pattern shows that getting the basics right both in qualifying and in the start is still the foundation of a winning result. It also shows how much better the Pirelli tyres perform when they are able to run in clear air, rather than in the wake of another car.

On a circuit like Monaco where overtaking is hard, good race strategy is the only way to make up places as we will see by studying the strategies of Ferrari and Red Bull on Sunday. As last year, the tyres lasted longer than expected and the race turned out to be quite different from that predicted by strategists, who forecast two stops for the top six cars. Vettel's performance in the opening stint forced many to rethink.

Pre-race strategy proved wrong

Pre-race strategy plans were that the leading cars would stop twice around laps 26 and 52, starting the race on supersoft tyres, then taking new softs at each of the pit stops. But this prediction was based on limited running on the supersoft tyres in practice due to poor weather. In the event they lasted much longer than expected.

Several things happened in the race which disrupted the predicted strategies and moved everyone to a one-stop plan: first there was a forecast of rain around 28 laps into the race, which forced most teams to leave their cars out as they would not want to have to stop again for rain tyres having made an initial pit stop. Second, Sebastian Vettel ran a long first stint on soft tyres, which showed that the softs were still very fast even after over 40 laps of running.

Once everyone saw this, there was no question of the leaders making a second stop, as this would give the win to Vettel. So they lapped very slowly in the second stint, preserving the tyres to the finish. Rosberg ended up doing 51 laps on his set of soft tyres.

Understanding the need to run in clear air, Fernando Alonso dropped back from Lewis Hamilton in the opening stint in order to preserve the tyres. He was also practising a technique on the supersoft tyres that gave him better tyre life on a stint: the supersofts don't like wheelspin out of slow corners (longitudinal slide). Alonso was straightening the wheels before applying the throttle, taking a little less out of his tyres at every corner than some of the others. This paid dividends at the end of the opening stint.

Ferrari's failure to gamble proves correct

Alonso had started well, survived a tangle with Romain Grosjean in the run to turn 1 and almost passed Lewis Hamilton. He tucked in behind him in fourth place on the first lap. But then dropped back to around three or four seconds behind the McLaren, focusing on preserving the supersoft tyres.

However, by the time Hamilton pitted on lap 29, Alonso had moved back up close to him. As soon as Hamilton went in, Alonso pushed hard and took advantage of the problems Hamilton was having with warming up the soft tyres, to jump him for third place when he made his own stop a lap later.

With hindsight, Alonso could have won the race by staying out another lap or two on the supersofts, as they were faster than the new soft tyres, which Webber and Rosberg were struggling with. Webber did 1m 24.518s on lap 30, which was three seconds slower than Alonso's last lap on supersofts. What probably stopped Ferrari from taking that gamble and going for gold was Rosberg's sector times on his first flying lap on new softs on lap 29, which was 1m 19.181s. Seeing this and thinking quickly, Ferrari would reason that Rosberg was straight on the pace on new tyres and therefore Hamilton would likely be the same, so it was time to bring Alonso in. But Rosberg, Webber and Hamilton all then struggled on the soft on laps 30 and 31 and the window of opportunity was there to jump them after all.

The team reasoned that had the gamble not paid off Alonso would have slipped to fifth place. On balance they made the right decision – consistency is the name of the game in 2012, the 15 points Alonso gained on Sunday took him to the lead of the championship.

Vettel's charge

By this point another driver was bringing himself into contention: Sebastian Vettel. The world champion started the race in ninth place after a poor qualifying session. However, his race day strategy was good enough to earn him fourth place for a number of reasons. Firstly, by not running in Q3, he had given himself a choice of starting tyre and went for the softs, planning a long first stint.

The prediction of rain around 28 laps into the race also played into Vettel's hands. The front-runners were slow on the worn supersofts by the time they pitted and the gap back to him was not as large as it would have been if they were two-stopping. By lap 31 he was leading and his pace on worn soft tyres was far better than that of the leaders on new softs. There is also a strong feeling that Webber held up the pack during this phase to bring Vettel into play. Whether it was discussed that he would hold them up until Vettel was in a position to jump all of them is not clear, but Webber did refer on the radio after the race to being grateful to the team for letting him win.

The quirk of the Pirelli tyres is that they operate in a very narrow temperature range and if you can't get the tyres into that range they don't perform. For lap after lap Vettel pulled away from Webber: by lap 37 the gap was 16 seconds. If Vettel could get the gap up to 21 seconds, he would be able to pit and rejoin ahead of Webber and go on to win the race. But this was the high point of Vettel's charge. On lap 38 Webber began reducing the gap. Now Vettel and the Red Bull strategists were focused on when to bring him in and who he would slot back in front of.

Vettel stayed out longer, still getting good performance from the soft tyres. It was clear that Hamilton was the one they could beat and, as he fell back from Alonso and was 21.4 seconds behind Vettel on lap 45, they picked that moment to bring Vettel in. He rejoined ahead of Hamilton in fourth place. Hamilton complained to the team about not warning him of Vettel's threat. He was now down to fifth, having started the race in third. No wonder he was frustrated that Alonso and Vettel had beaten him through superior strategy and tyre management.

Di Resta also had a very strong result by starting on the soft tyres and pitting for the supersofts on lap 35. He did extremely well to keep them alive for 43 laps and went from 14th on the grid to seventh at the finish.

Canadian Grand Prix
Montreal, 10 June 2012, 70 laps

The Canadian Grand Prix was always set to have a close finish because of the nature of the track, the options for race strategy and the effectiveness of the DRS rear wing for overtaking. And the data shows that the performances of the McLarens, Red Bulls and Ferraris on race day were remarkably close, with perhaps only a tenth or two of a second in it. The difference was tyre management and, more importantly, strategy.

Post-race, Red Bull and Ferrari have been accused of making strategy errors that cost them the race, but is it true? The race had three leaders, any one of whom could have won: pole sitter Sebastian Vettel finished fourth, Fernando Alonso led with seven laps to go and finished fifth, while Lewis Hamilton was the only driver to make a two-stop strategy really work … and he won.

Gambling at the front of the grid
The danger with doing a one-stop in Montreal is that, although you are in front of a two-stopper when he comes out from his second stop, he's on fresh tyres and with the DRS wing he will find it easy to pass you. However, with a 71 per cent chance of a safety car, which would swing the race to the one-stoppers, it can be worth a gamble for midfield runners looking to make up places.

To gamble from the front row of the grid, however, is a different matter. Practice on Friday had shown the teams that tyre degradation was not a problem and that it would be possible to do one-stop effectively, even if it would mean a fair amount of nursing the tyres. However, McLaren were convinced that they needed to do two stops, so it would be an attacking race for Lewis Hamilton. They believed that a two-stop would be around ten seconds faster than a one-stop.

McLaren only really had one car running on Friday, as Jenson Button lost most of the day to an oil leak and a double gearbox change. Meanwhile, Ferrari didn't really do any long running, the longest was a 12-lap stint by Massa, but this was punctuated by slow laps. And this may well have contributed to what happened on Sunday.

The track temperature on race day was 15 degrees hotter than Friday and going into the race even teams who had plenty of data on the long-run performance of the tyres could not be sure that one stop would turn out better. The only way to find out would be to try it and to monitor the heat degradation, because when it comes in with these Pirelli tyres it is very sudden and the lap times drop off straight away. The rear tyres were the limitation, and the soft tyres looked like the preferred race tyre.

The leaders got away in grid order with Vettel leading Hamilton and Alonso. But at the first round of stops, where they all switched from used supersofts to new softs, the order changed: Vettel pitted first on lap 16, Hamilton on lap 17 and Alonso on lap 19. Hamilton jumped Vettel in the stops and Alonso jumped both of them. But it took Alonso's Ferrari time to warm the tyres up and Hamilton attacked and re-passed him for the lead.

So for the second stint the order was: Hamilton, Alonso, Vettel. At this point all three had the option to stop again. Only Hamilton knew for sure that he would be doing that and so, with clear air ahead of him, he kept pushing. He opened out a gap of four seconds on Alonso and maintained it. For Alonso and Vettel the problem was not knowing how hard to push, as they didn't want to find themselves one stopping and have the tyres go off at the end, but equally they didn't want to do too little and find at the end that the tyres still had plenty to offer.

Hamilton noticed that the other two were not staying with him and asked his team if they were certain that Alonso and Vettel were not one-stopping. The team reassured him. This confirmed to Red Bull and Ferrari that Hamilton was stopping again and they will have recalculated their race model based on this information. Predictions would have them ahead of him after his second stop; what they couldn't predict was the tyre degradation on this warm day.

Decision time for Red Bull and Ferrari

In the laps leading up to Hamilton's stop, Alonso's pace was consistent: in the high 1m 17s and low 1m 18s, Vettel's was a few tenths slower and he sat three seconds behind Alonso. When Hamilton pitted, on lap 50, Ferrari and Red Bull had a decision to make. Should they react and pit too? In Vettel's case he would not have got ahead of Hamilton by doing that, but he may have caught Alonso.

Ferrari's decision was more finely balanced. As he came down the back straight, Alonso had a lead of 14.8 seconds over Hamilton, about the time it takes to make a four-second pit stop. With Ferrari's strong pit-stop performance there was every reason to believe that Alonso would be at least side by side with Hamilton as he exited the pits, but more likely just ahead. However, they knew from the first stops that Hamilton might be able to pass them again as they struggled to warm the tyres. They were concerned about Vettel too. So they did not pit Alonso on lap 51.

But they had perhaps also taken their eyes off the other cars coming through from behind, especially Grosjean. At this stage Alonso could have pitted and rejoined ahead of Grosjean, consolidating his position. However, they had some time to reflect, because even if they were to pit and come out behind Grosjean, the Ferrari on fresh tyres and with DRS would have no problem passing the Lotus on worn tyres.

The longer they and Red Bull left it, the more other cars came into the picture, like Perez, who's signature strategy seems to be to get to the flag quickly on one stop. So even a delayed pit stop in the laps after Hamilton's would still have given both Alonso and Vettel a podium, but they didn't do that either.

This is one of those situations where it is easy to say with hindsight that they made a mistake. Ferrari argues that they thought they would get similar tyre performance to Lotus and Sauber and make a one-stop work. However, what puzzles rival strategists is that by the decisive moment, around lap 51-52, Felipe Massa's tyres were 40 laps old and already showing signs of going off. Perhaps Ferrari estimated that Alonso would have better wear, but they were looking to get 51 laps out of Alonso's tyres, ten more than Massa had done to that point. So it's hard to see where their confidence to stick with one stop came from.

Even as late as lap 60, when Grosjean was just ten seconds behind Alonso, the models showed that Ferrari could have pitted Alonso, who would have rejoined five seconds behind the Frenchman. On fresh tyres Alonso would have been able to pass him in the remaining ten laps, as Vettel did with Alonso when Red Bull realized their mistake and belatedly brought Vettel in with seven laps to go.

Lotus's potential is still just that

Grosjean's result shows that the Lotus has the potential at times to do one stop less than some of its rivals and still be competitive. Its weakness lies in single lap qualifying pace: if Grosjean or Raikkonen could start in the front five, ahead of Rosberg for example, then they could really make their tyre advantage pay.

Perez's excellent podium again highlights his ability to keep the pace up while also protecting the tyres. It must be a combination of many details in his driving that he has brought with him into F1, because Kobayashi in the other car can rarely stretch the tyres out in the same way.

Perhaps more worryingly, this was the second race that could be done by cruising around on a one-stop strategy and, although the climax was exciting due to Hamilton's strategy, the majority of the race was quite dull and processional. These cars and tyres work best in two- or three-stop races, where the drivers are able to have periods when they can push more.

European Grand Prix
Valencia, 24 June 2012, 57 laps

Formula 1 finally got its first two-time winner of the season in the eighth round, after a fascinating race in which Fernando Alonso came from 11th on the grid to win. His victory owned a lot to an excellent start, where he made up three places, to some fine pit-work from the Ferrari mechanics (Alonso's first stop was two seconds faster than Raikkonen and allowed him to jump the Lotus) and to race strategy. He also rode his luck when the safety car was deployed on lap 28, one of the race's defining moments.

He had several slices of luck in fact: Sebastian Vettel was running away with the race when his Red Bull car stopped with an alternator failure and a similar problem sidelined the second fastest car, the Lotus of Romain Grosjean. And another pit stop problem for McLaren moved Lewis Hamilton out of Alonso's way at the crucial second stop, under the safety car.

Alonso's unlikely victory

It had looked a very unlikely win after qualifying, where Ferrari made a tactical error in not sending the car out early enough in Q2 and then not using a second set of soft tyres to ensure that he made it into the top ten shootout. They were trying to ensure that they had two sets of new soft tyres for the Q3 session, but misjudged the competitiveness of the field and missed the cut.

However, although his starting track position was poor, ironically this qualifying error helped on race day as Alonso had one new set of medium tyres and two new sets of softs to play with. It meant that he could use new tyres for all three stints in the race and, as everyone's tyres were fading at the end of stints, ultimately this was the thing that kept his nose ahead. By making a great start and taking all his opportunities to overtake and gain positions, Alonso gave himself the chance to win the race.

Before the start, the feeling was that one stop was slower than two by 16 seconds, which is almost an entire pit stop, but that the one-stopper would be ahead after the final stops and that track position could prove significant. A set of new medium tyres was expected to last 25 laps and the softs 20 laps. Most teams looked at the tyre degradation figures from Friday practice and concluded that it would not be possible to do the race competitively on one stop.

What the teams are looking for is the point in the wear cycle where the degradation becomes so bad that the tyre performance drops off a cliff. What makes this so tricky is that it varies from circuit to circuit. At some venues, normally the hotter tracks, it is when the tyre is 70 per cent worn; at others it's later in the tyre's life. You don't know until you get there.

Some teams felt that one stop might be possible: Force India's Paul di Resta and both Mercedes drivers considered it and started the race with that as the plan. But only Di Resta saw it through. Arguably he would have been better not to: had he opted to cover the late second stops of the Mercedes drivers and fitted a set of soft tyres as they did, he could have finished ahead of his teammate Hulkenberg.

A strange race tactically speaking
In the past at Valencia, overtaking has always been very hard and therefore track position in the race was everything. But things have changed with this generation of Pirelli tyres and the DRS wing. A perfect example of this was the way that Michael Schumacher, Mark Webber and Nico Rosberg's races evolved in the final 20 laps.

Webber and Schumacher qualified outside the top ten: Webber had a technical problem and qualified 19th, while Schumacher was 12th. Both men started on the medium compound tyres, which made a one-stop strategy a possibility. Mercedes planned to do this with Schumacher, but once again the predictions based on the tyre performance in Friday practice turned out to be wrong on race day. The rear tyres were overheating on some cars within the first five or six laps, so one stop became a major challenge.

Rosberg was also planning on one stopping, but his pace was very slow and by the time Sebastian Vettel made his first stop, Rosberg was already 32 seconds behind him. But the safety car helped bring him back into the pack and he too made a late switch on to soft tyres and ended up sixth. Di Resta was two seconds behind Hulkenberg and 27 seconds ahead of Rosberg after that late stop and should have covered it by pitting himself. He would have stayed ahead of Rosberg and, looking at the relative pace on new tyres, would easily have overhauled Hulkenberg for fifth place in the closing stages.

From lap 46 onwards Schumacher and Webber were a second a lap faster than the leaders and so could make progress through the field towards the podium, which Schumacher eventually got.

The safety car factor

The front-runners all made their second stops when the safety car was deployed on lap 28, meaning that they had 29 laps to go to the finish, of which five were at low speed behind the safety car. Webber and Schumacher had been helped as the safety car closed the field up and they were able to pit ten laps later and on new softs to cut through the points' positions towards the podium. Nico Hulkenberg, for example, was 16 seconds ahead of Schumacher on lap 42, but was passed by the Mercedes driver on lap 56.

The safety car always changes the game from a strategy point of view. In Valencia it did a number of things. First it put all the front-runners on a lopsided strategy, whereby the middle stint had been shorter than planned as they intended to go to around lap 32 and the safety car obliged them to stop on lap 28. This committed them to a long final stint on medium tyres. This provided an opportunity for Mercedes and Webber. It also provided an opportunity for Di Resta, but Force India didn't take it.

Second it led to a shake up of the order at the front as another problem pit stop for Hamilton dropped him behind Alonso and into a pack of cars. Had that stop gone smoothly, Hamilton would have been ahead of Alonso in the final stint, would have avoided the collision with Maldonado and would have fought Alonso for the win, arguably having to settle for a podium as his tyre wear was clearly not as good as the Ferrari's.

British Grand Prix
Silverstone, 8 July 2012, 52 laps

The British Grand Prix saw a tense strategic battle between Red Bull and Ferrari for the win. They went different ways on race strategy and ultimately Red Bull prevailed, Webber passing Alonso five laps from the end. The challenge of McLaren was blunted again, Lewis Hamilton losing ground on his championship rivals while Lotus again scored strongly with both cars as Grosjean did a unique strategy on Sunday.

Heavy rain during practice and qualifying days had left the teams with very little information about how the tyres would perform on race day. There was only one hour's practice on Saturday morning and this showed that on a cold track surface the soft compound tyres were graining badly (the top surface of the rubber rolling up). Ferrari, in particular, were wary about it on race day.

The weather was very erratic all weekend and, against expectations, it stayed dry for the race. Many teams including Mercedes and McLaren had planned for a wet race. Although the track temperature was shown as above 24 degrees, the ground was still too cold to get the soft tyres working well and the hard compounds turned out to be the better race tyres. The key to doing well in the race, then, was to manage the soft tyres.

Could Alonso have won the race with different strategy?
Ferrari and Alonso were wise to start with the hard tyres, as they proved the best tyres to race on. They started out wanting to minimize the time spent on the soft tyres and as soon as the tyre covers came off on the grid it was clear what the pattern of the race would be: Alonso would run two stints on hard tyres and a short final stint on softs, while Webber would

do the opposite, an opening stint on softs and then two longer stints on hards.

Alonso's race would be dictated by keeping the soft tyre stint to a minimum at the end, while Webber's would be all about staying in touch with Alonso in the opening stint and then coming on strong at the end.

Ferrari had another weapon at their disposal: they sent Massa out on softs for the first stint, so they would have data on tyre performance. This turned out to be less helpful than they thought. Massa's first stint was 13 laps during which time the team came to believe that the soft tyres were not as bad as expected. This would prove crucial later in the race, as it meant that Alonso committed to a 15-lap final stint on softs. Had he pitted a couple of laps later on each of his first two stops, he probably would not have lost the lead at the end. Without that data they would have been more inclined to stay off the soft tyres and would have done a strategy that might have brought Alonso the win.

Alonso built a lead of five seconds over Webber and when the Australian stopped on lap 14, Alonso went just one lap longer. His pace on the hard tyres was still good, he set a couple of quick laps before his stop on lap 15, certainly comparable with Webber's first two or three laps on new hard tyres in the second stint. So there was margin to play with. The gap between them was maintained at five seconds throughout the middle stint. Webber pitted again on lap 33, which left him 19 laps to go to the finish on another set of hard tyres.

Alonso stayed out four more laps, pitting on lap 37 with a lead of four seconds to protect in the final stint. Although Webber had a couple of faster laps than Alonso before the Ferrari pitted, Alonso again was able to find speed from the used hard tyres prior to his stop and another lap would have been possible. With two or three more laps in the opening stint and another lap in the second, this would have put him back out on track after a stop on lap 41 with a small margin over Webber, but just 10 or 11 laps to do on soft tyres to the finish. On this basis he would probably have been able to hold on to the lead to the end. Alternatively, he could have done what Hamilton did and run a short middle stint on softs of no more than ten laps, reacted to Webber's stop on lap 33 and finished on the same hard tyres as the Red Bull driver.

Of course, hindsight is a wonderful thing, especially the day after the Grand

Prix when one can look at all the what-ifs. Ferrari and Alonso have done brilliantly to lead the championship at this stage and Silverstone was their strongest points haul of the season, with a fine fourth place for Massa. They move into second place in the constructors' championship.

They have made a few strategic mistakes this season that have cost Alonso points, but on the whole they've been consistent in taking their opportunities. However, there's no getting away from the fact that, although their hunch at the start was correct that the hards were the better race tyres, there was definitely a win to be had on Sunday with a slightly more imaginative approach to strategy on the soft tyres.

Doing things differently: Hamilton and Grosjean
There were two other interesting strategies on Sunday from McLaren's Lewis Hamilton and Lotus's Romain Grosjean, which also shed light on what might have been for Alonso.

Like Ferrari, both teams decided early on that the hards would be the faster race tyres. Hamilton, like Alonso, started on them, while Grosjean was involved in a first-lap incident with Vettel and had to pit on lap 2. He went to the hard tyres and then did the whole race on them, with only one further stop, so essentially he did a one-stop strategy. He did a 24-lap stint and a 26-lap stint and remained competitive. He was 22nd and last on lap 3, but came through to finish sixth behind his teammate Raikkonen, who had raced with Vettel and Massa. On lap 50, his tyres were 24 laps old and he set the second fastest lap of the race.

It was another stunning performance by Grosjean and an illustration of the pace and durability of the hard Pirelli tyres, as well as the Lotus' ability to find great race pace. With better qualifying performance, they would have a car capable of winning races.

Hamilton went for a hard/soft/hard strategy and did a long first stint, which appeared to have got him into a position to race Grosjean for sixth. He got the soft tyres out of the way with a short middle stint, but didn't have the pace in the final stint and faded. McLaren are having problems balancing front and rear tyre temperatures and it's costing them badly.

German Grand Prix
Hockenheim, 22 July 2012, 67 laps

The top three cars separated by less than three seconds with a handful of laps to go – it's the ideal scenario for F1 racing and just what we had in Germany. All three leaders had followed the same strategy of soft/medium/medium tyres, but this was a weekend that showed a lot about how far many teams have come in getting on top of the Pirelli tyres, described by some as a "lottery" early in the season.

The tyre selection for Hockenheim was the same as in Melbourne and four other events this season. In many ways the racetrack and its demands on the tyres were comparable with Melbourne – it was the way the teams reacted to those demands that showed who had progressed and who was still struggling to balance tyre temperatures, which is affecting their strategies and how much impression they can make on the race.

Earlier in the season some teams experienced a difference in temperature from front to rear tyres of as much as 20 degrees. This played havoc with balance. Ferrari, Red Bull and Lotus lead the way in terms of progress made on balancing temperatures, Sauber have been pretty good all along; while McLaren have lost out recently but are now getting closer and Mercedes still seem to have significant problems.

In Germany there wasn't much to choose between the performance of the soft and medium tyres. It came down to preference, although some teams that go well on the softs found that they would be around two seconds faster over a stint, particularly in the early laps.

The pre-race wisdom was that the soft tyres would be similar on pace to the mediums in race conditions, even though they had been 0.7 seconds slower in qualifying trim. The softs were expected to be good for up to 21 laps and the mediums 24 laps. This tended to push teams towards thinking about a soft/medium/medium strategy, which is what the podium finishers used, but it did give scope for soft/soft/medium and we saw that this was actually a little faster. With such a tight battle at the front, had one of them taken a gamble we might have had a different result.

The battle among the front three

Alonso's engineer Andrea Stella has said that the only time they were worried on Sunday was after the first stop when the medium tyres were taking time to come in. Alonso had pitted on lap 18 and Vettel didn't stop for another two laps. Alonso did a 23-lap middle stint while Vettel did only 21 laps. Arguably, looking at what Raikkonen did on soft tyres in the middle stint, there might have been an opportunity there for Red Bull. Having watched Alonso go to the medium tyres, by switching to softs Vettel might have got ahead of the Ferrari, but in all probability Alonso would have reacted by doing a soft tyre stint at the end, while Vettel would have been forced to use mediums and this probably would have evened things out. It's a fine margin, but it would have been interesting to see Red Bull try it.

Red Bull and Ferrari did not do a lot of race preparation work on the tyres in the brief time the track was dry at Hockenheim. So they went for the mediums as the preferred race tyres, also Ferrari put Massa on to them on lap 1 after he was forced to pit for a nose change, so they were gathering data on them as the first stint unfolded. The softs degraded at 0.1 seconds per lap on Sunday, while the mediums degraded at 0.08 seconds per lap, so there was very little in it. It was more about relative pace.

Strategy-wise the main move amongst the top three was an undercut by Button on Vettel for second place at the final stop. This was helped by the fastest pit stop carried out by an F1 team in 2.31 seconds as Button pitted a lap earlier than the German and then put in a fast out-lap to be in front when Vettel came out.

Raikkonen and Lotus on form: if only they could qualify well

There was another strong showing by the Lotus team with Kimi Raikkonen classified fourth but promoted to third after Vettel's penalty for going off-track. Once again they showed that if they could get to the front they have the race pace to win. In Hockenheim they pitted Raikkonen early, on lap 11, and stayed on the softs. In doing so he jumped Webber, Hulkenberg and Maldonado. Then by using Lotus's gentle action on the tyres, he did a 27-lap middle stint, which included overtaking Michael Schumacher and gave him the platform for his fourth-place finish.

Raikkonen was the highest placed finisher to do soft/soft/medium, which

Lotus are convinced was the fastest strategy last weekend. It didn't work for everyone: Schumacher tried it, but the Mercedes' continued roughness on rear tyres meant that he ended up having to make a third stop, which cost him fifth place. He was also hamstrung by having only one new set of medium tyres for the race.

Kobayashi stuns with a reverse strategy

We have seen a number of drivers in the Pirelli era come through the field in a quick car using a reverse strategy to everyone else, but it's usually because they have saved new sets of tyres from being eliminated early in qualifying. On Sunday Kamui Kobayashi came through from 12th to fourth (after Vettel's penalty) on a medium/medium/soft strategy – but as qualifying had been wet everyone had new tyres to use, so he didn't have that advantage. So how did he do it?

The Sauber is extremely fast on full tanks so he had a strong opening stint and, as he had started on mediums, he was able to go to lap 22 before his first stop. At that point he was up to fourth. He came out from the pits in ninth place, but in a position to attack with two short stints of 21 and 24 laps. He passed Webber and Perez in the middle stint and Hulkenberg in the final stint and then inherited a place from Schumacher when he made his third stop.

He even looked like he might mount an attack on Raikkonen on his final stint on softs, but his pace dropped off at the end. Nevertheless it was a great return to form for the Japanese driver and an illustration that if you have a quick car you can make a different strategy work. Also it was impressive how easily he was able to overtake.

However, like Lotus, Sauber have to deal with the fact that they do not qualify well.

Hungarian Grand Prix
Budapest, 29 July 2012, 70 laps

The Hungarian Grand Prix was far from being a thriller in terms of on-track action with hardly any overtaking after the first laps. But it was a very interesting tactical race that leaves a lot of questions to answer: such as could Lotus have won the race if they'd done things differently? Why did Button and the Red Bulls make three stops? And how close did Hamilton come to not winning?

On Sunday morning most of the strategists were saying it would be a wet race. The forecast had not changed for five days and rain was set to fall between 1 and 2 p.m. local time. But as the day went on the bad weather moved away from Budapest and it was hot and sunny with the chance of rain receding. In the end a giant storm came in around 7 p.m. local time, which didn't affect the race but succeeded in delaying teams' flights out of the airport.

Rain during practice on Friday afternoon had reduced the amount of data teams had on long-run performance, so once again it was a bit of a stab in the dark as to how to approach race strategy and tyre choice. Three stops looked to be faster than two over race distance, but the problem was that a three-stopper would be behind the two-stoppers after his last stop and would have to overtake.

The feeling was that Hamilton would drive away from the rest, using his apparent pace advantage of around 0.4 of a second per lap. The soft tyres were considered to be up to half a second per lap faster than the mediums based on Friday practice, but after ten laps the lap times on the mediums were expected to be stronger than the softs. But could all the teams make it through 70 laps competitively on just three sets of tyres?

Once again reality turned out to be slightly different from expectations.

The challenge for victory by Grosjean and Raikkonen
The opening ten laps told the story: Lewis Hamilton had dominated qualifying, but he wasn't able to pull a gap on Grosjean's Lotus. It was going to be a close fight.

Further back Raikkonen had let himself down in qualifying by not matching Grosjean's pace and started fifth on the grid, which became sixth when Alonso passed him on the first lap. He lost around four seconds sitting behind the Ferrari in that opening stint. This didn't cost him the race win necessarily, but it meant that he wasn't able to jump Vettel at the first stop, which he would have done otherwise. This would have set him up for a clearer track in his middle stint and then it would have been interesting to see how close he and Hamilton were after the final stop.

Grosjean, in contrast, looked comfortable in second place. Lotus was of the view that the soft tyres were faster and they would do two stops with a soft/soft/medium strategy. They stuck to their plan. Other teams were worried about getting through 70 laps on two stops and so favoured a soft/medium/medium strategy. This was a race tailor-made for Lotus with its easy action on the tyres.

Lotus had two players in the game: Grosjean lost his chance of a win by taking too much out of the tyres at the start of the middle stint. This meant that at the end of the stint he didn't have the pace to stay out longer and try to jump Hamilton at the second stops. By this stage Vettel had pitted on lap 38 and, with a margin of just three seconds to play with on tyres that were spent, Lotus had no choice but to cover Vettel by stopping Grosjean.

Contrast this with Raikkonen's execution of the strategy. He ran a 20-lap first stint and easily jumped Alonso at the first stop. This brought him out fifth, around 4.5 seconds behind Vettel, (where he would have been had he not lost a place to Alonso at the start). Facing a long middle stint on soft tyres (it was 25 laps in the end) he made no effort to close the gap, instead nursing his tyres for around eight to ten laps then slowly reeling Vettel in before the German's second stop on lap 38. At this point, in clear air he let rip – 1m 25.7s on lap 41, 1m 25.9s on lap 42. As Vettel and Grosjean got their medium tyres up to temperature, Raikkonen took almost two seconds a lap out of them. He would easily jump them at his second stop.

The strategy worked perfectly, the question then was whether he could get Hamilton too. His burst of speed had taken the edge off the tyres – he did a 1m 26.6s on lap 43. Meanwhile, on lap 44 Hamilton on new mediums did a 1m 26.3s. He was just too quick. Lotus brought Raikkonen in for fresh tyres to consolidate the gains over Vettel and Grosjean and then see what he could do to Hamilton in the final stint. He tried to pass, but couldn't and had to settle for second place.

Had Grosjean matched Raikkonen's technique of nursing the tyres for six or seven laps at the start of the second stint, sitting out of his dirty air, and then attacked Hamilton at the end of the stint, he could have jumped him and won the race. Such is experience. I'm sure he'll look at Raikkonen's performance and learn from it.

Not a day to stop three times

Pre-race predictions about three-stopping proved prophetic: it was faster on paper but required overtaking and, despite the DRS system, overtaking at the Hungaroring proved elusive. Last season's race was rain-affected so we never really saw how little difference DRS would make on a track that has always been almost impossible to pass on.

Button did three stops, his tyre life not as good as Hamilton's in the opening stint, his rear tyres going off more quickly. But what wrecked it was after his second stop, which was 19 laps into a stint on new mediums, he came out behind Bruno Senna who had similar age medium tyres to the ones Button had taken off. He kept Button behind him until his stop on lap 42. However, during this time, Button remained around six seconds behind Hamilton, the same margin as before Button's second stop. He had not had the opportunity to use the pace of the new medium tyres and this allowed Vettel to jump him at his second stop. Alonso then jumped him when Button made his third stop on lap 45.

He was the first front-runner to pit at the first stop on lap 15, which was still within the two-stop window. He reported that the second set of tyres was still fine when he made the early second stop. There wasn't a possibility to undercut Grosjean at that stop, as he was almost six seconds ahead of Button. It was just the wrong call to go for three stops, but clearly they felt that they couldn't do the race in two, despite Hamilton doing just that in his McLaren.

Meanwhile, Webber stopped three times because his differential had problems and this led to higher tyre wear, while Vettel switched to three stops near the end after losing time in the opening stint when he lost third place to Button, who was not on the same pace as Hamilton and Grosjean. Vettel went for a new set of softs for a final sprint to see if he could claim a podium, but he had to delay the stop in order to get enough of a gap over Alonso and this left him with not enough laps to catch Grosjean for third place.

Belgian Grand Prix
Spa Francorchamps, 2 September 2012, 44 laps

Jenson Button's victory in the Belgian Grand Prix makes him the leading points scorer of the last three races, the reversal of a trend that began in May and saw the British driver and his McLaren team lose their way.

Button was suffering from a lack of performance due to mismatched temperatures between the front and rear tyres and the team have been experimenting with various ways of solving that, including heating the tyres from the inside using heat soak from the brakes. They've now found a solution, partly involving aerodynamics to increase rear-end grip and aerodynamic balance, but also mechanical set-up and the result has been 51 points in three races. His performance in Belgium showed that he not only got the tyres working well in qualifying to take pole position, but also was able to comfortably do the race with only one tyre stop. His second stint, on the hard compound Pirelli tyres, was almost 106 miles, the longest that McLaren has done on a single set of tyres in 2012.

In Belgium the McLaren had the largest performance advantage seen so far this season. The pace and the strategy provided a wake-up call for the rest of the field. Button is still 63 points behind Fernando Alonso in the championship, but on this form he will be a contender at the end of the season. So how did he manage to do only one stop and what were the strategic keys to the race? And what about the others: why couldn't Lotus compete for the win and could Schumacher have finished fourth if he had done the same strategy as Hulkenberg?

Heavy rain hinders practice, again

The build-up to this race was dominated by heavy rain on Friday, which meant that the teams learned nothing about long-run tyre performance. They were shooting in the dark on Sunday, the only data coming from a handful of dry laps on Saturday morning when they were also preparing for qualifying. It left little time for drivers to establish how to get the tyres to work.

Also part of the strategy in Spa was deciding whether to go for a low downforce set-up, with less wing to help straight-line speed in sectors 1 and 3, or whether to go for more downforce to help with sector 2. Most went for more downforce, with Button and Alonso among the exceptions. Gearing was also important and several drivers found themselves with a less than ideal combination of gearing and downforce, with the result that they were hitting the rev limiter on the Kemmel Straight and losing speed. All of this led to a mixed-up grid with two Saubers and a Williams at the front, Red

Bull struggling for pace with Vettel in tenth place and Hamilton down in seventh.

Pirelli brought harder tyres to this race, being a little more conservative than they have been so far and this opened up the possibility of making only one stop. The same will be true in Monza.

The feeling pre-race was that a one-stop strategy would be around five seconds faster than two, but would leave the driver vulnerable at the end of the race to cars on fresher tyres. McLaren were certainly thinking of one stop for Button starting from pole, circumstances permitting, while most of the others were planning two stops, especially as the track temperature started rising before the start.

The start line accident changed the strategy in two ways. Firstly, by eliminating four competitive cars, it changed expectations of what many drivers might get from the race. Secondly, it brought out a safety car. This slowed the field down and meant that the first four laps of the race, which are normally the hardest on the tyres as the cars are at their heaviest, were relatively easy. This encouraged a number of drivers and teams to change plans and try to do one stop. Among them were Williams and Mercedes, which was surprising because they have been among the hardest cars on the tyres in race conditions this season.

It didn't work out for them or Williams, thanks to a late puncture, which robbed Senna of eighth place. It did, however, work for Red Bull's Sebastian Vettel. He was helped by qualifying outside the top ten so he was able to start the race on a new set of medium tyres, whereas his front-running rivals were all on used mediums at the start. This small detail was important to the outcome for Vettel, who was able to get to lap 21 on his first set of tyres, which meant he needed to do 23 laps on a new set of hards in the second stint.

Button enjoys a margin

Jenson Button was able to make the most of the largest performance margin over other cars we have seen this season so far. The McLaren's underlying pace was around half a second faster than its nearest rival at Spa and Button was able to exploit that fully both in qualifying and in the race.

He could do one stop relatively easily, helped by the crash, which eliminated rivals, also by the safety car and by the freedom to run at the front in clear air. Being able to control the pace, not have to defend from other cars meant he could focus exclusively on managing the tyres and this meant Button had complete control all afternoon.

The challenge from Lotus did not materialize as not only did the Lotus not have the expected race pace, but also they seemed to struggle to get temperature into the tyres. This was evident at the restart where Hulkenberg jumped Raikkonen. Lotus was on a two-stop strategy and without the pace to exploit that fully, there was no challenge from Raikkonen.

Button even had sufficient margin in the final 15 laps to make a precautionary second stop and still win the race, but he had the pace and liked the balance of the car on the tyres he had. He was still lapping in the 1m 54s in the last few laps, a similar pace to the Lotus on tyres that were eight laps newer.

Vettel managed the race skilfully too, using the one-stop plan and the pace of the Red Bull on hard tyres to jump the two-stoppers and move up from tenth on the grid to second at the flag. It's debatable whether that would have worked if the four front-running cars had not been eliminated at the start, but Red Bull adapted well to the changing circumstances and Vettel drove a very positive race, making several important overtakes to ensure his progress.

Schumacher loses a strong result

Michael Schumacher also drove well on Sunday, making some excellent passes and defending robustly, as is his style. But the question remains, could he have finished ahead of Hulkenberg in fourth place if he had done a similar two-stop strategy, rather than change tactics after the safety car and switch to a one-stopper?

The German ace got past Hulkenberg on lap 13. When Hulkenberg pitted, Schumacher was on new medium tyres and ran a 19-lap first stint, which left him 25 laps to do on a set of hards. It was a big ask, but by staying out past lap 13 or 14, he was committed to stopping just once.

Schumacher was ahead after Hulkenberg's second stop on lap 27. But he only had four seconds advantage and 17 laps to go to the finish on the same set of tyres, ahead of a similar pace car on fresh tyres. It was never going to work. The Mercedes was relatively fast on full tanks, but as we have seen often this year, the competitiveness didn't continue as the car got lighter and the tyre wear increased. Schumacher was forced to make an unscheduled stop for tyres on lap 35 and lost three positions.

Had he pitted on a similar pattern to Hulkenberg and stayed on a planned two-stop, he would have fought him for the fourth position, but possibly would have lost out due to the Mercedes pace fading on lighter tanks. Nevertheless, the failed one-stop bid cost him places to Massa and Webber and he ended up seventh.

Italian Grand Prix
Monza, 9 September 2012, 53 laps

The Italian Grand Prix was one of the most exciting races of the 2012 season so far, which is unusual for Monza. The track has a high-speed character and opportunities for overtaking, but doesn't always provide excitement. However, this year's race was brought alive by the strategy decisions made by some of the teams and the bold gamble to try to do the race with only one pit stop. It was marginal in terms of tyre life and some of the tyres that came off the cars at the end had no more than a lap of life left in them.

Meanwhile, Sauber, which has a far smaller strategy department than the F1 front-runners with far less sophisticated tools at its disposal, managed to play a blinder and sent its driver from 12th on the grid to second at the flag thanks to a brilliantly planned and executed strategy and to an outstanding performance by Sergio Perez.

Extensive mileage in practice
Unlike recent Grands Prix, the teams were able to do extensive mileage on Friday in practice and learned a lot about the tyres. Before the race, simulations showed one stop to be faster than two by ten seconds. However, one notable limiting factor was the wear on the inside shoulder of the right front tyres. On some cars they seemed to be wearing down to the nylon, so managing that was crucial.

Despite this, most teams set out with the intention of stopping only once.

The choice by Pirelli of medium and hard tyres was pretty conservative by recent standards, something of a shift in approach. This may have been influenced by some lobbying earlier in the season by teams who were struggling to get the tyres to last and by some problems encountered last season at Spa and Monza, which Pirelli did not want to repeat.

The two cars with the best tyre wear this season are the Lotus and the Sauber. Here they had another chance to use this to their advantage as the others would be very marginal on tyre wear at the end of the first stint and in the last laps of the race. Lotus did not have the pace to exploit this in Monza, but Sauber did.

Perez turns the tables

Sauber used a similar strategy in Monza to the one which had brought Perez a podium in Montreal from outside the top ten on the grid: they took a new set of the harder tyres at the start, ran a long first stint and then stopped once.

In Monza, with Perez in 12th place on the grid, Sauber knew that many cars aiming to do one stop would be struggling to get to a first stop that would leave them a manageable number of laps to do on the hard tyres at the end. This would make them vulnerable at the end of the first stint and in the final laps of the race. Perez used the hard tyres at the start and had very good pace on them. He also helped his cause by passing Senna and Rosberg in the opening laps. He picked off Di Resta on lap 6, Kobayashi a lap later and then waited in eighth place behind Raikkonen.

Once the cars in front – who were pushing to make it beyond lap 20 for a stop – started to struggle, he was able to capitalise and pick up places. Raikkonen had to stop on lap 17 as his tyres were going off, but Lotus knew that they could get to the finish without problems on the hard tyres. Massa stopped, then Vettel and Alonso together, then Button and finally Hamilton. Perez was now leading on lap 24. He was aiming for lap 28 to make his stop, but was told that the wear was good so the new stop time was "Target plus 4" – lap 32. Sauber changed that, however, as it became clear that the tyres had gone, so he pitted on lap 30 for a new set of medium tyres, rejoining behind Raikkonen, who was 13 laps into a 36-lap stint.

Perez's pace on the mediums was astonishing: once past Raikkonen, he was able to run a second per lap faster than the leader Hamilton. This continued into the phase Sauber had anticipated, where ten laps from the end the

Ferraris, which had stopped on laps 19 and 20, were two seconds slower than Perez. He passed them easily to take second place.

He was not able to catch Hamilton, however. The McLaren driver had been taking it fairly easy in the second half of the race, as illustrated by the fact that from lap 39 onwards he was running on the same pace as Raikkonen, whose Lotus didn't have much pace on worn tyres. Raikkonen, incidentally, did a very good job to manage the car with its ultra-low downforce set-up for a fifth-place finish.

Why Mercedes stopped twice

It was clear before the race started that one front-running team was planning to do two stops. The Mercedes drivers had both saved a set of new medium tyres from qualifying, which would only be worth doing if you planned to stop twice, as the rules state that you must use one set of each compound in the race and they were starting on the medium tyres from qualifying.

Sometimes the call between one stop and two is marginal, but here with one stop being ten seconds faster than two, it was quite a lot to give up unless you had to. Once again Mercedes were concerned about tyre wear.

Also they had a painful experience in Spa, which they did not want to repeat, whereby they attempted to one-stop, but found that they couldn't and lost track positions after the forced second stop. To do that at Monza would mean losing any chance of points, so they had to do two stops. The Mercedes was fairly competitive in Monza, certainly with Schumacher, and he was in the hunt for fourth place, but had to settle for sixth with the track positions he lost by stopping twice. That said, he was catching Massa and Raikkonen at the end and another lap or two he would have passed them both for fourth place, something he might have achieved had he made his second stop a lap earlier.

Singapore Grand Prix
Marina Bay, 23 September 2012, (2-hour limit reached)

The Singapore Grand Prix can definitely be classed as a "what might have been" race, as the intervention of two safety cars meant that we were denied an exciting and unpredictable finish. Also the retirements of Lewis Hamilton and Pastor Maldonado spoiled what would have been intense competition at the front.

None of this will have bothered Sebastian Vettel, who took his second win of the season, nor Fernando Alonso, who extended his championship lead over all his rivals bar Vettel. Despite the anti-climactic ending, the strategy decisions and factors that shaped the race are very interesting and worth a deeper analysis.

Softs v. supersofts

One of the key factors in the weekend was that the gap in performance between the Pirelli soft and supersoft tyres was greater than expected. In qualifying it was as much as 1.6 seconds on some cars. In the race, many teams found that the soft tyres were not working to the optimum – they were designed to be more resistant to high temperatures, but didn't perform on the slippery surface.

Degradation was always going to be the limiting factor in Singapore, especially with the rear tyres, so the opening stint was crucial. Everyone expected high degradation in the opening stint. Teams that were unable to get to around lap 13 or 14 on the set of used supersofts from qualifying were going to have to stop three times. And as the pit lane in Singapore is the slowest of the year, at 29 seconds, there was a premium to being able to extend the tyre life and do it in two stops.

So most of the top teams went out at the start aiming to do two stops, but waiting to see how bad the tyre degradation would be in reality. Among the rival teams' strategists there was a suspicion that Red Bull would put Mark Webber on a three-stop strategy and use it to gather information on the supersoft tyres in order to help Sebastian Vettel's race effort. Webber's tyres were two laps older than Vettel's, so the team could monitor the degradation. However, there were also signs that Webber had an over-steering problem and this led to higher rear tyre degradation, so he was obliged to do a three-stop in any case.

Second safety car spoils the show

There is always a safety car at Singapore, and this year we had two. The first, on lap 33 for Narain Karthikeyan, fell in the window for the second stops and lasted six laps. Most of the front-runners took advantage of it to make a stop, although Fernando Alonso and Pastor Maldonado were slightly caught out by it as they had stopped five laps earlier.

But the second one, on lap 40 for Michael Schumacher hitting Jean-Eric Vergne, really changed the game. It meant that the cars were able to spend another three laps at reduced speed, making a race total of nine laps behind the safety car. Add in the fact that because of the safety car delays the race ran to two hours and only 59 of the 61 laps were covered. This meant an 18 per cent reduction in the number of racing laps – a real boost for drivers who were gambling.

This saved quite a few cars – which would otherwise have run into serious trouble in the closing stages of the race – from making a third stop. We would have seen the cars with higher wear coming under pressure from those with better wear as we saw in Valencia, for example, and it would have made for a very exciting finish.

Sebastian Vettel and Fernando Alonso certainly fall into this category. Vettel stopped on lap 10 with clear signs of tyre degradation as did Alonso a lap later. Red Bull were on a three-stop plan with Webber and may have been obliged to do the same with Vettel without the nine laps of safety car; it certainly helped them to make it to the end in two stops and it's likely that Alonso would have had the same problem. Ferrari had some issues with overheating the rear tyres in Singapore, so the safety cars were a blessing.

In contrast Jenson Button had been conserving tyres in the opening stint and managed to get to lap 14 before the first stop. He was preparing the ground for the end of the second stint and the end of the race, when he would be able to attack Vettel on tyres that were four laps newer. The McLaren seemed to be working very well in Singapore and even Hamilton would probably have made the finish in two stops, despite pushing hard in the opening stint and a front tyre issue that forced him to make his first stop on lap 12, slightly earlier than planned. The first safety car took Button's advantage away and the second one meant that Vettel had no tyre issues at the end.

Force India – success and disappointment
For the second year in a row in Singapore, Force India's Paul di Resta got a very strong result, in this case a career-best fourth place. Di Resta is

another driver who was able to make it safely with two stops; he pitted on lap 12 and then took advantage of the first safety car to stop a second time, losing only one track position to Alonso, who had already stopped. He followed him to the flag. He had stayed with the Ferrari for most of the race, but in the final stint the Ferrari was a little faster on the new soft tyres.

Without the second safety car Di Resta too might have struggled on tyres that were 28 laps old. Luckily for him there were no fast three-stopping cars coming up behind. Di Resta benefitted from the Mercedes of Rosberg holding up cars behind him in the run up to the second stop, creating a gap for him to drop back into.

Teammate Hulkenberg was one of those who tried a three-stopper and lost out due to the second safety car. Hulkenberg had qualified 11th and started on the soft tyres. His strategy was to run a long first stint, but he lost time behind Raikkonen and Schumacher in the second stint, just before the safety car. The second safety car meant he couldn't take advantage of track position and he stopped when it came out, then tried to do two ten-lap sprints on new supersoft tyres, but it didn't work out and he lost further track positions with a third stop on lap 50.

Japanese Grand Prix
Suzuka, 7 October 2012, 53 laps

The Japanese Grand Prix this year was a fairly straightforward race, largely due to the lack of competition at the front after Fernando Alonso was eliminated at the start and Mark Webber and Romain Grosjean were thrown down the order following their collision. Nevertheless strategy played a central part in Felipe Massa's breakthrough result and led to some of the other talking points of the race, like the Perez v. Hamilton battle and Schumacher's challenge for points from the back of the grid.

The thinking on tyres

Before the race, the thinking was that two stops was the way to go. The main concern was the blistering of the Pirelli tyres, which does not initially affect the pace, but does upset the balance due to vibration. The inside shoulder of the front tyres was a particular worry. Pirelli had brought hard and soft tyres to Suzuka and the softs had proved to be a second a lap faster in qualifying conditions and around 0.4 seconds per lap faster in race conditions.

The hard tyres were slower, but did not blister as much as the softs and were also more durable. To make it to 53 laps starting with a set of soft tyres that had already done three laps in qualifying, meant getting to around lap 14/15 before the first stop and then running two stints of up to 20 laps each.

Simulations showed that two stops would be faster than three stops by ten seconds, but teams were prepared to switch to three if the tyre degradation proved too much. It didn't. Our strategy calculator had predicted that stops for new hard tyres on laps 14 and 34 were likely and so it proved, although in some cases the first stop was delayed by a couple of laps due to the safety car deployed for the start-line accidents.

In the end, because of those two accidents, which eliminated Alonso and Rosberg and put Grosjean and Webber down the order, the race was a foregone conclusion for Vettel and strategies were conservative and the stint lengths were pretty even. Also the lap 1 safety car helped drivers extend the first stint by a couple of laps, which made a difference.

Massa: playing it long pays dividends

Felipe Massa had a very strong drive in the second Ferrari: starting tenth he finished in second place, his first podium for two years. It was built on great strategy and a fantastic start, which saw him rise to fourth on the opening lap, thanks to avoiding the chaos of the Webber/Grosjean collision and the Alonso/Raikkonen incident.

Because he had failed to reach the final part of qualifying, Massa had a set of new soft tyres to start the race with and two new sets of hards available, and his strategy was based on making maximum use of these. Thanks to his strong start he found himself racing Button and Kobayashi for second place and his new soft tyres gave him a tactical advantage in the opening stint as he could run a couple of laps longer than both of them.

The McLaren was a little harder on its tyres in Japan so Button was in on lap 13, Kobayashi a lap later. When he stopped, Button's pace was similar to Massa's and he believes that the team stopped him too early. He's right. When he came out of the pits he was behind Ricciardo in the Toro Rosso, who had been between 0.8 and 1.2 seconds per lap slower than him prior to the stop. Another lap or two at that pace and he would have cleared him, but clearly McLaren played it safe because his tyres were close to the "cliff".

Pitting three laps later meant that Button was 16 seconds behind Massa when he came out of the pits and that went out to 19 seconds in three laps, enough for Massa to pit and clear both him and Kobayashi, who was also stuck behind Ricciardo. Massa was also quick on the hard tyres and posted his best result for two years, which shows that he hasn't lost his speed. Perhaps his problem of the last two seasons has been more psychological.

Other strategies worth noting

Sergio Perez tried to do the same thing as Massa to get ahead of Kimi Raikkonen. Although behind him on the track, the Sauber was faster than the Lotus in the first stint and the team strategists tried to run two laps longer than Raikkonen, who stopped on lap 13. Raikkonen was vulnerable because he had had to substitute an older set of tyres for the start, having damaged his qualifying tyres in a spin. But the plan failed because Perez ran out of tyre life. This meant that when he came out from his stop on lap 15 he was not only still behind Raikkonen, but also behind Hamilton. The psychology of being behind the man he's replacing at McLaren next season was interesting and Perez appeared keen to prove a point, but he lost control of his car when battling with Hamilton and was eliminated.

Mark Webber recovered well from his first lap incident with Grosjean. He finished in ninth place, eight seconds behind the fifth placed car. The Australian pitted on lap 1 for new tyres and then had the misfortune of seeing the race restarted when he had still not caught up to the pack behind the safety car. He was still 20 seconds behind the last car at the restart.

Effectively, Webber did a one-stop strategy from there, using another new set of hard tyres at his stop on lap 26 and driving to the flag. This showed that the revised Red Bull is not only very fast, but also good at looking after its tyres thanks to updates on the rear suspension and rear aerodynamics, which improve traction and reduce wheelspin.

Michael Schumacher also had to come through the field from 23rd on the grid after a penalty. He started on new hard tyres and his strategy made use of the fact that he had two new sets of soft tyres available, so he stopped for them on laps 17 and 36. He gained 12 places, but spent much of the first half of the race behind Paul di Resta. When he finally got ahead, the underlying car pace wasn't there as it was for Webber, so he missed out on points by finishing 11th.

Korean Grand Prix
Yeongam, 14 October 2012, 55 laps

After the unpredictability of the first half of the season, the Korean Grand Prix fell into the pattern we have begun to see recently – and will probably see in the next two races – of most runners doing a two-stop strategy with drivers largely choosing to race on the harder prime compound tyres in the second and third stints.

But there were a few counter strategies and some other unusual aspects to Sunday's race, not least the strange late race messages from Red Bull Racing urging the winner Sebastian Vettel to slow down due to concerns over his front tyres. We saw a surge through the field by the two Toro Rosso drivers and a lack of movement from other midfield runners, despite the early elimination of Jenson Button, Nico Rosberg and Kamui Kobayashi. And we saw Pastor Maldonado attempt a one-stop strategy that did not pay off because the car wasn't fast enough.

Before the start all the strategists were expecting two stops, with a faint possibility that someone might try one stop as the tyre life was all right, but the performance looked like it would be far less competitive. Nevertheless Pastor Maldonado and Williams tried it, with Maldonado ending up 14th, having started the race in 15th place. In contrast, Jean-Eric Vergne, who started the race in 16th place, ended up eighth by doing the first two stints on the prime (soft) tyres and then a final sprint on the supersofts (the expected life of the supersoft tyres was 17 laps and the softs was 24 laps).

The race at the front – fairly static

As predicted, the race in Korea followed a similar pattern to the race in Japan a week earlier with the leading teams making two stops, around laps 14 and 34, for new prime tyres. The difference was that the tyre choices in Korea were supersofts and softs, whereas in Japan it had been softs and hards.

There were concerns about graining of the tyres and also with wear on the outer shoulder of the front tyres in Yeongam and several teams experienced it, with Red Bull the most extreme example: Sebastian Vettel was ordered to be careful in the final laps as his tyres were close to the limit. This was a curious episode, which has yet to be fully explained. Pirelli were not aware of any issues on the tyres and, although they were getting marginal, there was apparently still some rubber on them when they were inspected at the end of the race.

Little changed at the front, with Vettel and Webber swapping places at the start and Alonso finishing third as Hamilton struggled with a broken rear anti-roll bar and thus forced to stop three times. The main movers among the front-runners were Massa, who moved up from sixth to fourth, and Hulkenberg, from eighth to sixth. Massa was racing Raikkonen and Hulkenberg was racing Grosjean. In both cases the Lotus driver lost out despite starting ahead of his opponent.

Massa kept up his impeccable record of starts by jumping Raikkonen on the opening lap. Raikkonen stayed with him, but they pitted together on lap 14, so there was no opportunity for the undercut. Both came out behind Perez who was running longer. Massa got past him on lap 17; Raikkonen didn't and lost a couple of seconds, which gave Massa some breathing space. Then, on lap 21, Massa passed Hamilton for fourth place, but again Raikkonen couldn't get past. He blamed the new Coanda exhausts for cutting the power. Either way, he spent five laps behind the McLaren before it pitted on lap 26. Raikkonen was now ten seconds behind Massa and the race was over between them. There was nothing for Lotus to do with strategy to get back the position.

Meanwhile, Hulkenberg also jumped his opponent Grosjean at the start – possibly as a result of Grosjean being on high alert over causing some kind of accident again. It helped Hulkenberg and they ran seventh and eighth in the opening stint; they pitted together on lap 13, so again there was no chance for the undercut. The Lotus looked like the faster car, but Hulkenberg defended doggedly. Lotus tried the undercut on lap 31 by bringing Grosjean in first when he was just 0.6 of a second behind Hulkenberg. Force India covered the stop on the next lap, but Grosjean had got ahead again.

It stayed this way until lap 40 when they came up behind Hamilton and

Hulkenberg managed to pass both cars to regain his sixth position. With no more stops to make and Hulkenberg having track position, he was able to hold on to the finish, as Grosjean lost time, first in traffic and then in the last five laps with tyre degradation.

The midfield battle – tough to make moves
In the last couple of seasons we have seen quite a number of moves with drivers breaking into the top ten, having started outside: Sergio Perez's podiums in Canada and Monza spring to mind. What was noticeable in Korea was that for the most part this was not possible for drivers like Perez, Di Resta and Maldonado – despite the early elimination of Rosberg, Button and Kobayashi, who started 9th, 11th and 13th respectively. Most finished more or less where they started, with Schumacher ending up three places back from where he qualified.

But the exception was the performance of the two Toro Rosso drivers. Before the race it seemed likely that deciding on a downforce level was a crucial part of race strategy, as the track has a split character with the final sector all about high downforce, but the long straights a good option for overtaking if you have a low downforce set-up.

Toro Rosso opted for the second option: they qualified 16th with Vergne and 21st (after a penalty) with Ricciardo. In the race they split the strategies with Vergne starting on soft tyres, running a long second stint on softs and ending with 17 laps on the supersofts, while Ricciardo managed to come through on essentially the same strategy as the top six cars. They came through to finish eighth and ninth and Ricciardo might have done more had he not suffered a problem with braking.

It was Toro Rosso's strongest race of the year.

Indian Grand Prix
Buddh International Circuit, 28 October 2012, 60 laps

The Indian Grand Prix was an interesting race by recent standards in that for once the teams' strategies were not influenced by worries about the tyres wearing out. Instead, they could focus on pure pace, the drivers able to push to the maximum throughout the Grand Prix. However, as a result there was little opportunity for drivers starting outside the top ten to make the kind of progress into the points which we have seen this year from Sergio Perez and, more recently, the Toro Rosso drivers in Korea.

There were two reasons for this: to a certain extent the teams have got wise to the 2012 Pirelli tyres and know how to get more out of them now than six months ago, when we saw seven different winners in the first seven races. But the main reason was that the tyre choice from Pirelli for the weekend, soft and hard compounds, was too conservative. After the race the Pirelli motorsport director Paul Hembery conceded that using the supersoft tyres would have made the race more like the others we have seen this year with two pit stops, which would have encouraged a variety of strategy options. This choice underlines a trend we have seen in the closing stages of the season of Pirelli being more conservative as the championship reaches its climax.

On Sunday almost everyone went for a single-stop strategy, as the tyres suffered little degradation or wear. The proof of this is that the four fastest laps in the race were all set on the final lap, so there was plenty left in the tyres at the end.

Crucial to start well
The weather was benign and stable all weekend in Delhi, so the teams were able to do extensive running on Friday and Saturday morning and had a complete picture of the way the tyres would behave in the race. Before the start, strategists were planning to make one stop around lap 25, as one stop was showing as between five and 15 seconds faster than two stops. Race pace looked evenly matched between the Red Bulls, McLarens, Ferraris and Lotus cars from practice.

Looking at the grid, it was clear that the McLarens, who were on the second row, had to try to pass pole sitter Sebastian Vettel and his teammate Mark Webber on the opening lap as they would both be vulnerable down the long back straight. Once they got into the faster corners of sectors 2 and 3 the Red Bulls would be gone.

Likewise for Fernando Alonso starting fifth on the grid, he had to get past the McLarens at the start to be able to push the Red Bulls and hope they made a mistake or hit problems. The strategy worked out pretty much as intended for him, with a second-place finish, but not for the McLarens, who came in fourth and fifth, one place lower than they started.

For the midfield runners, the chance to effect any major position changes through strategy were limited. In order to make progress through the field they had to rely on mistakes to take advantage of any chance to overtake. Luckily, these were quite likely on the dusty track.

The race: overtaking at a premium

In the opening stint Vettel was able to push very hard and open a gap, which gave him control of the race, but he found it tougher on the hard tyres as the Ferrari and the McLarens were slightly faster on them. Ferrari was consistently fast on both tyres, while the McLaren was slower on the softs but stronger on the hard tyres. In Vettel's second stint his pace backed off by between 0.7 and 1 second per lap, which was also partly due to running the engine lean and managing the gap to Alonso, once he had passed Webber.

Four drivers started the race on the hard tyres: Grosjean in 11th, Ricciardo starting 15th, Kobayashi starting 17th and Schumacher starting 14th. All of them gained two or three places except for Schumacher, who retired. In most cases this was not enough to get into the points, but Grosjean managed to get two points for ninth place, despite losing one place at the start to Maldonado.

The key to the final points positions for the cars running behind Rosberg in the opening stint was dealing with the Mercedes' lack of pace. Rosberg pulled back everyone behind him, opening up the possibility for a ninth or tenth place finish for anyone who had a workable alternative strategy. But only Grosjean managed to get past him as he ran a longer first stint, stopping last of all the runners on lap 36 and taking the soft tyres.

His plan in running longer on the hard tyres was to let the others who had stopped earlier age their hard tyres, so that the time delta when he came out of his stop on new softs would be greater and he could come through the field in the final 24 laps. It got him past Rosberg, but was thwarted as he was unable to maintain a gap in front of Hulkenberg before the stop and came out behind him. The German driver managed to hold him off on a new set of hard tyres.

It was a shame that Lotus could not fully exploit its pace on Sunday. In Friday practice it was as fast as the leading cars, but Grosjean's poor grid slot and Raikkonen being stuck behind Massa meant that they didn't get the result the car's pace deserved. Raikkonen managed to undercut Massa on strategy, by pitting a lap earlier, but lost the place back again due to having too short a top gear on the straight.

It was odd that Massa had problems with fuel load, however. He wasn't able to run a full race test on Friday and they may have got their calculations wrong as a result. He was 35 seconds behind Alonso at the end, so, working backwards, Ferrari would have started him on less fuel than his teammate as he was over 0.5 seconds a lap slower. Without seeing the difference in fuel consumption on a race simulation run, due to spending longer on the straight at full throttle (without DRS), they ended up critical on fuel.

Abu Dhabi Grand Prix
Yas Marina Circuit, 4 November 2012, 55 laps

Safety cars are a rare occurrence in Abu Dhabi, but Fernando Alonso has reason to curse them – they have now twice come along to upset his race strategy and dealt a blow to his hopes of winning a championship for Ferrari.

In 2010 a safety car at the start of the race allowed Petrov to pit for new tyres, enabling him to run to the end of the race, blocking Alonso and wrecking his strategy. This weekend the Abu Dhabi curse struck again. Red Bull presented Ferrari with an open goal by making a fuel load mistake in qualifying that demoted Sebastian Vettel to the back of the grid. But Vettel's recovery was greatly helped by two safety car periods that brought the strategy initiative back to the German driver allowing him to make up ground and end the race on the podium. With the goal gaping, Alonso failed to take the chance, making up only three points, rather than the 10 or 15 available.

Was Sebastian Vettel "lucky"?
Once again a conservative choice of soft and medium Pirelli tyres meant that the teams had the ability to do the race with only one stop, with the drivers able to push to the limit without fear of degradation or excessive wear. But Vettel's strategy on Sunday didn't just revolve around tyre choice or pit-stop timing. Red Bull opted to take Vettel's car out of parc ferme and to make changes to the set-up, which would allow him to overtake

more easily – wings were altered and a longer seventh gear was added, which would mean greater straight-line speed for DRS overtaking (improving his top speed by 5mph to 200mph). With two DRS zones on the circuit and a very fast car on a charge through the field, Yas Marina Circuit was no longer the overtaking desert it was for Alonso in 2010.

Vettel's strategy was to start on the medium tyres, run a longer first stint than the others and make up some places when they stopped, then switch to the faster soft tyres for the final stint and try to pick up a few more places in the closing laps. But it didn't turn out remotely like that. Instead, he was forced into an early stop for a front wing change and this put him a half-stop sequence out from the rest of the field. It turned out to be a blessing.

By lap 9, when the first safety car was deployed, he was already up to 12th. At this stage he was 23 seconds behind the leader. However, having damaged his front wing in early exchanges and then damaged it further behind Ricciardo, he was forced to pit behind the safety car. This dropped him to 21st place. Having started on the harder tyres, he took the softer tyres at the first stop, which turned out to be the faster race tyres on Sunday.

Crucially, in that same safety car period, Grosjean also pitted and, like Vettel, went from medium to soft. The Frenchman's plan from there was to try to get to the finish without stopping again. This would provide the barrier to the rest of the field, holding back Webber, Perez and Maldonado after their stops. As the gap widened between Grosjean and the car in front (Button) this created an opportunity for Vettel to push hard on his new soft tyres and then slot into the gap after a second stop. It meant that a minimum fourth place was up for grabs.

Although they considered not stopping Vettel again, because he managed to get into second place, ahead of Alonso and Button when they pitted, the radio messages early in the second stint indicated that they wanted him to push on the tyres, so clearly the intention was to stop again. This was the less risky option in championship terms, with a guaranteed fourth place in the offing.

Had Red Bull been in the mood to gamble, however, rival engineers believe that Vettel would have been able to do 42 laps on the softs and make it to the finish. This would almost certainly have led to a thrilling duel for second place in the closing stages between the two world title contenders, Alonso and Vettel. Alonso was very fast at the end of the race as he tried to catch Raikkonen, but Vettel's straight-line speed, even on worn tyres, meant he would have been able to put up quite a fight.

When the one-stop pit window opened on lap 25, Vettel was in tenth place and 22 seconds behind the leader, essentially where he was before the front wing incident. But, by putting himself out of synch with the other cars, this helped him at a crucial stage of the race. Between laps 24 and 31 he went from tenth to second and then by pitting again on lap 37 he ensured that he held on to all but two of those places. Only Alonso and Button got back ahead of him due to his second stop.

But the real stroke of luck was the second safety car. Vettel was very fortunate that just as he came out on fresh soft tyres the safety car came out and cut Button's lead over him, from 15 seconds with 17 laps to go, to nothing. That set Vettel up for the podium. Button gave him plenty of room when he made the passing move, not wanting to affect the championship. Had Vettel tried that move at the start of the season, he might have ended up off the track.

Raikkonen finally gets his win

Kimi Raikkonen finally got his comeback victory in the Lotus. It had been clear from the long runs in Friday practice that once again the Lotus was quick enough to challenge for the win. Qualifying had been the stumbling block all season, but here Ferrari tripped up and then with Vettel's penalty, Raikkonen found himself fourth on the grid.

His win was built on a stunning start, which moved him up to second place, and then when Lewis Hamilton stopped, Raikkonen was able to do something he'd dreamed of all season: run in clear air at the front, as all of the seven winners in the first seven races had been able to do. Raikkonen then showed what the Lotus has had to offer all season, twice building leads of ten seconds, only to have them cut by the safety cars.

United States Grand Prix
Circuit of the Americas, Austin, 18 November 2012, 56 laps

Before the race started, teams were certain that this would be a one-stop race. The Pirelli tyre choice of medium and hard was quite conservative and there were no signs of the extreme degradation that had been such a feature of the first half of the season. Degradation was 0.02 seconds per lap for the mediums and 0.01 seconds per lap for the hards. Pirelli had been influenced by the high temperatures in Texas in the same week last year, especially as average temperatures this year have been about 5 degrees warmer overall – everyone expected it to be hotter, than it was, in other words.

The effect of all this was that the tyres would take time to warm-up in the cool ambient conditions, but drivers were able to push to the limits for all 56 laps without needing to nurse the tyres. This had a knock-on effect on strategy for qualifying as drivers found themselves doing a five-lap run in order to get the tyres to their perfect condition for a quick lap.

However, Austin proved to be unique on the current F1 calendar, the circuit proving to be by far the most difficult on which to align tyre temperatures. Even with all the knowledge the teams had developed over the season, they were all scratching their heads about getting the tyre temperatures balanced front to rear.

On the first day of practice the grip level had been very low, due to the recently laid tarmac having a sheen of bitumen on the surface. This began to be ripped away, revealing the grippy stones underneath, but only on the racing line. As the weekend wore on and more rubber went down the grip level came up, giving a 10 per cent improvement from Friday to Sunday.

The biggest concern was what this would mean at the start of the actual race, with the dirty side of the grid estimated to be one second slower reaching turn 1 than the clean side. There were estimates of two positions lost at the start for cars on the dirty side. As a result, Ferrari opted to deliberately penalise Felipe Massa, due to start sixth on the grid, by giving him a five-place gearbox penalty, which dropped him to 11th and allowed teammate Alonso, who had underperformed in qualifying, to start in seventh on the clean side of the track. It was a strategic decision and it worked very effectively, as Alonso made up three places at the start, giving him the platform for a podium finish, despite the poor qualifying pace of the Ferrari.

All the front-running teams identified backmarkers as a potential problem in the S-bends before the long straight – lose time through there and you would be vulnerable to a DRS overtake on the straight.

The duel for the win

Lewis Hamilton and Sebastian Vettel fought a great duel for the victory in Austin and there were fine differences between the two cars' performance on the tyres. The Red Bull was able to bring the tyres in more quickly and, as a consequence, Vettel did six laps on his tyres of which only two were pace down laps. However, Hamilton did seven, with three hard laps.

Although they lost the battle for pole position, on race day the McLaren had a slight pace advantage over the Red Bull. Both cars were strong on the medium tyres, Hamilton able to bridge a 2.5 second gap once he got clear of Mark Webber to close up to Vettel. But then his slightly older tyres reached the point where the performance dropped off. He lost almost two seconds in the three laps before his stop on lap 20. When he exited the pits he was behind Raikkonen and spent four laps unable to pass.

Vettel pitted a lap later, to cover Hamilton, and re-emerged in the lead. However, it soon became clear that the pattern we have seen recently of the McLaren being stronger on the harder prime tyres was being borne out again. Hamilton was primed to strike as they reached half-distance. Although the McLaren had a pace advantage, Hamilton was not able to get close enough to Vettel at turn 11 to challenge using the DRS on the straight. But on lap 42 he took advantage of Vettel encountering the back-marker HRT of Narain Karthikeyan in the S-bends to close up and make his move on the straight.

Because of Red Bull's tactic of setting the car up for downforce rather than straight-line speed, the McLaren had a 7mph speed advantage over the Red Bull for this race and with the extra 6mph from the DRS effect, Hamilton was able to pass. Although Vettel came back at him, the straight-line speed deficit meant that he couldn't get close enough.

Button makes a counter strategy work

Jenson Button was forced to start the race from 12th place on the grid after a throttle failure in qualifying. This gave him the right to choose what tyres to start on and to use new tyres. Many team strategists felt that starting on the hards would not be competitive, but Button was able to use the pace advantage of the McLaren to good effect. The strategy was to run a longer first stint and use the more sustained performance of the hard tyres to gain track position when the cars ahead made their stops after lap 20.

He lost around six seconds sitting in a train behind Di Resta, Perez and Senna in the run up to their stops, but once clear of them he had very good pace on the hard tyres and managed to get faster every lap until his stop on lap 35. McLaren were monitoring the gap to Grosjean in the Lotus and when they saw on lap 34 that Grosjean was faster than Button they pitted him, despite the fact that Button's pace was still improving. This brought him out close to the Frenchman, but he fell behind. He was able to exploit the extra grip on the softer tyres to make overtakes under braking, such as the pass on Grosjean, and was quick once he passed the two Lotuses, but he was never going to catch Massa for fourth.

Interestingly, Fernando Alonso seemed to struggle getting the hard tyres warmed up and Ferrari technical director Pat Fry admitted after the race that the car had not had the pace of its rivals on those tyres. As this same tyre combination is set for use again in São Paolo, this is a concern for Ferrari if the race is held in the dry. At the moment the forecast predicts a 60 per cent chance of rain on Saturday and Sunday. However, Felipe Massa seemed to have fewer problems on the hard tyres so there will be something to be learned from his data.

Brazilian Grand Prix
Interlagos, 26 November 2012, 71 laps

The Brazilian Grand Prix was a roller coaster of a race, with positions and fortunes changing from lap to lap as intermittent rain caused chaos. Sebastian Vettel managed to survive a first lap collision, a broken radio and a slow pit stop to fight back from 17th place on lap 1 to sixth at the end to secure the points he needed to win the world championship for the third time. Fernando Alonso, meanwhile, went from seventh on the grid to second at the flag, but did not have the pace in the Ferrari to challenge Jenson Button for the win, which would have given him the points to clinch the title.

With conditions so hard to predict and so changeable, this was a day when the strategists were reacting to events and working on instinct. For some, with nothing to lose, it was worth taking a gamble on a tyre choice. For the two title contenders it was all about being certain they were there at the chequered flag to win as many points as possible.

Temperature proves to be the key factor

Rain had been forecast for race day all week. However, in the hours before the race the chance of rain was receding from 80 to 40 per cent and the teams had to face up to the possibility of a dry race and very different conditions from practice and qualifying. But the key factor was always going to be the temperature. Stifling on Friday it was cool on race day, but a rise in the temperature, which was a distinct possibility, would mean more thermal degradation on the tyres and therefore more pit stops.

There were three cars out of position: Maldonado in 16th after his penalty for missing a weight check, Grosjean in 18th after hitting De la Rosa in qualifying and arguably Rosberg, who had overqualified in the Mercedes in 9th place and was set to fall back in the race.

Indications were that teams would go for a two-stop strategy with the first stop around laps 20 to 25 with a middle stint on a new set of hard tyres. They would then review performance before deciding whether to switch to used mediums or another set of new hards for the last stint. However, the track conditions before the rain began were different from Friday practice where the track temperature was almost 50 degrees, compared to less than half that on race day. So even without rain, teams were set for a reactive strategy.

Once again Pirelli's tyre choice had been conservative, the Italian firm opting for the hard and medium tyres because of several high-energy corners. The hard tyres were well out of their optimum working range in the heat during Friday practice and there were signs of blistering. But on race day, with lower temperatures, the hard tyres were better suited.

Of the leading cars going into the race, only Di Resta had a new set of mediums left, while Ferrari only had one new set of hard tyres, compared to the two new sets of Red Bull and McLaren. The Ferrari also had a deficit of around 0.3 to 0.4 seconds in pure car pace to deal with. The team had split its long run tests on Friday, with Massa running the mediums and Alonso the hard tyres, so they had plenty of data on which to base their strategy. It was clear that they favoured the medium tyres on race day as they and Lotus were the ones to move onto them in the dry.

Button and Hulkenberg take a chance

The conditions in the early part of the race were difficult, but the teams were ready to react as far as strategy decisions were concerned. The key strategy call was to stay out when rain started to fall in the early stages with the dry tyres on which the race had been started, but few teams were able to do that, as they could not generate enough temperature in the tyres. Button and Hulkenberg were the exceptions.

There was a brief moment when it looked like they were on the wrong tyres. But then drivers who went onto the intermediate tyres too early suffered from graining and it swung back their way. When the drivers who had switched to intermediates were forced to pit again for the hards it left Button and Hulkenberg over 40 seconds clear of the field, having made no stops compared to the two made by the others.

It is worth noting that Force India has something of a track record on tricky wet days like this of copying what Button does, as he has an uncanny knack of being on the right tyres at the right time, and there have been several occasions when Force India has matched his moves and got a strong result.

In this instance both Button and Hulkenberg were able to get sufficient temperature into the tyres to deal with the water on the track, although there was a thin dry line for most of the early stages of the race. This made overtaking difficult because off-line there was no grip and several cars went straight on instead of out-braking their rivals. It was only later that the track became fully wet.

The decisive moment of the race was the deployment of the safety car on lap 23 due to the debris on the track, which had led to a puncture for Nico Rosberg. This greatly helped Hamilton, Alonso, Vettel, Webber and others who had lost ground early on through pit stops and spins. It wiped out the lead that Button and Hulkenberg had established and brought Hamilton into their battle, which ultimately led to the collision between Hulkenberg and Hamilton.

When everyone moved back onto dry tyres, Ferrari and Lotus went for the medium tyres while most went for the hards. This was a hedge in case they needed to go to the finish on that set of tyres, with over 40 laps remaining. Lotus were prepared to go to the end on the mediums, given their better tyre usage, but Ferrari would have struggled as they suffered graining on the surface of the front tyres.

JA on F1 Podcasts

In 2012, in association with UBS, we introduced a new feature to the *JA on F1* website, which has proved very popular with F1 fans. Running for approximately 30 minutes, this is a monthly podcast containing audio interviews with leading figures in the F1 world. The podcasts are available for download on www.jamesallenf1.com

Number One: 1 March 2012

Ross Brawn (Mercedes): on the 2012 car, when he will stop racing, whether Schumacher has still got "it", race strategy this season and the "tragedy" of the FOTA split.

Zak Brown (CEO of F1 sponsorship specialists JMI): on the F1 business climate in 2012, the impact of the Euro crisis on F1, and why there are few new sponsors on the new cars.

Darren Heath (celebrated F1 photographer): on the art of taking the perfect high-speed shot.

Mark Webber (Red Bull driver): on why he had a tough year in 2011, and how he can beat teammate Vettel in 2012.

Number Two: 28 March 2012

Tony Fernandes (Caterham F1 team owner): on how Asian audiences view the sport and how they differ from European audiences.

Zak Brown (CEO of sports marketing agency JMI): on why Asia is important to F1.

Manish Pandey (writer and executive producer of multi-award winning film *Senna*): on his next project and why Bollywood is the best way to build a following for the sport in India.

Dave Forman (head chef of the Force India team): on giving curry to mechanics and the risks and rewards of feeding sushi to not just two, but seven, F1 drivers.

Shaikh Salman bin Isa Al Khalifa (CEO Bahrain International Circuit): on why this year's race goes ahead after the troubles in the region last year.

Number Three: 30 April 2012

Heikki Kovalainen (F1 driver): on not being able to deliver on the dream drive at McLaren.

Frank Dernie (veteran F1 engineer): on why drivers succeed and fail in F1 and on driver preparation and motivation.

Jamie Alguersuari (F1 driver and broadcaster): on learning the hard way.

Nick Harris (elite athlete trainer): on what it takes on the physical and mental side to iron out a driver's weak spots so he delivers 100 per cent every time.

Paul Hembery (Pirelli Motorsport Director): answering Schumacher's criticism of the tyres.

Number Four: 1 June 2012

Alan Permane (Lotus F1 Trackside Operations Director) on the tyre "lottery".

Zak Brown (CEO of F1 sponsorship specialists JMI): on business and sponsorship.

Ron Howard (film director): on his forthcoming Hunt/Lauda film *Rush*.

Jean Cristophe Babin (CEO Tag Heuer, sponsors of McLaren and Monaco GP): on what sponsorship brings to the sport.

Number Five: 1 July 2012

James Allison (Technical Director Lotus F1 team): on activities behind the scenes to adopt (or try to ban) rivals' innovations.

Sir David King (former Chief Scientific Advisor to HM Government): on how F1 can help move the world to a more sustainable future.

Mike Gascoyne (Chief Technical Officer of Caterham F1 team): on innovating within a tight budget.

Frank Dernie (veteran F1 engineer): on the days when F1 engineers had limited budgets, but freedom in design.

John Rhodes (architect at Populous – Silverstone design consultants) on future circuits, and how to improve the fan experience.

Number Six: 2 August 2012

Sir Frank Williams (Team Principal Williams F1): on the season so far, and an assessment of Maldonado.

Sir Jackie Stewart: analyses the performance so far of Vettel, Hamilton and Alonso.

Monisha Kaltenborn (CEO Sauber F1 team): the most powerful woman in F1 gives a frank assessment of Sauber's up and down season and tells us what it's like to handle the fragile male egos in F1 team principals' meetings.

Nicholas Tombazis (Ferrari Chief Designer): on how Ferrari has turned the season around.

Plus a lap of Silverstone, JA instructed by Felipe Massa.

Summer Special: 21 August 2012

Featuring: Ross Brawn, Mark Webber, Tony Fernandes, Manish Pandey, Heikki Kovalainen, Frank Dernie, Paul Hembery, Alan Permane, Ron Howard, Sir David King and Mike Gascoyne.

Number Seven: 13 September 2012

Sir Jackie Stewart (founder of the Mechanics Trust): on the work of the trust.

Patrick Head (Williams co-founder): also talks about the Mechanics Trust, driving standards and driver protection.

John Watson and Derek Warwick (former F1 drivers): on mechanics' contribution to the sport.

Stephen Hood (Creative Director of Codemasters): on the new F1 2012 game.

James Calado (GP2 driver) and Derek Walters (Racing Steps Foundation): on young driver prospects and hurdles to be overcome.

Jo Ramirez (former mechanic): on working with many of the great drivers.

Plus a lap of the new US GP circuit in Austin, Texas, as driven in the Codemasters F1 2012 game.

Number Eight: 28 September 2012

Tom Cary (*Daily Telegraph*): behind the scenes of Hamilton's move to Mercedes.

Mark Blundell (former McLaren driver): on how Hamilton's move to Mercedes may affect him.

Rachel Clarke (media expert): on how social media is affecting F1.

Manish Pandey (writer and executive producer of the film *Senna*): on his close friend Prof Sid Watkins, who died recently.

Graham Watson (Caterham Team Manager): on the logistics of moving F1 around the world.

Zak Brown (CEO of F1 sponsorship specialists JMI): on Singapore and F1.

Graeme Lowdon (Marussia Team President): on cost control and staying alive at the back of the grid.

Number Nine: 6 November 2012

Jean Todt (FIA President): Part 1 on higher entry fees, 2014 engines and costs; Part 2 on the need for more funds for the FIA and for "harmony".

Bruno Senna (Williams driver): on the team's Partner Day and his season to date.

Susie Wolff (Williams development driver): on women driving in F1 and her recent test drive.

Toto Wolff (Williams Executive Director): on buying into the F1 team.

Pastor Maldonado (Williams driver): on his 2012 season.

Number Ten: 4 December 2012

Sebastian Vettel (F1 World Champion 2012): on his third world title.

Mark Webber (Red Bull driver): on how he'll approach 2013.

Christian Horner (Team Principal Red Bull Racing): on how he'll keep his team motivated.

Plus a review of the 2012 season with: Sam Michael (Sporting Director Vodafone McLaren Mercedes), Paul Hembery, Darren Heath, Zak Brown and Mark Hughes (leading freelance F1 writer).

Index